TESTAMENTS

OF HONOUR

PERSONAL HISTORIES
OF CANADA'S WAR VETERANS

BLAKE HEATHCOTE

FOREWORD BY RICHARD GWYN

DOUBLEDAY CANADA

Doubleday Canada and colophon are trademarks.

NATIONAL LIBRARY OF CANADA CATALOGUING IN PUBLICATION DATA

Heathcote, Blake
Testaments of honour : personal histories of Canada's war veterans / Blake Heathcote.

Includes index.
ISBN 0-385-65846-X

1. World War, 1914–1918—Personal narratives, Canadian. 2. World War, 1939–1945—Personal narratives, Canadian. I. Title.

D811.A2H42 2002   940.4'8171   C2002-902063-8

Jacket images: Testaments of Honour Archives
Jacket and text design: CS Richardson
Printed and bound in Canada

While great care has been taken to ensure accuracy within these narratives, this book is primarily one of personal history and thus reflects the particular memories, opinions, and perspectives of the individuals involved.

Published in Canada by
Doubleday Canada, a division of
Random House of Canada Limited

Visit Random House of Canada Limited's website: www.randomhouse.ca

FRI   10   9   8   7   6   5   4   3   2   1

CONTENTS

*The man who feels no sentiment for the memory
of his forefathers; who has no natural regard for his ancestors of his
kindred; is himself of unworthy of kindred
regard or remembrance.*

DANIEL WEBSTER

*It's all well to dream of glorious war
in a snug armchair at home. But it is a very different
thing to see it firsthand.*

THACKERAY

FOREWORD

A HALF-CENTURY AFTER THE WAR was over they came to be called the Greatest Generation, an expression coined by television anchor Tom Brokaw. They were, as a generation, radically different from those who came later—one more innocent, more stoic, less worldly, whose members had gone out, most of them almost without thinking about it, certainly with little agonizing and with no posturing, to do their duty for their society, even if it meant the sacrifice of their lives.

It was this sense of duty and of obligation that was their principal hallmark. In Canada, this meant that out of a population of little more than eleven million, more than one million—nearly an incredible one in ten—served in uniform. More than 100,000 Canadians either were killed or suffered serious injuries or were captured. None of these wounds made the slightest difference to their resolve, or to the nation's. Together, those at the front and those serving at home transformed a small, largely agricultural society, one that was parochial and colonial in most of its attitudes into a major economic power, one capable of equipping, training and manning what became, by 1945, the world's third-largest navy, its fifth-largest air force, and an army large enough to fight simultaneously on two major fronts, in France and later Holland and Germany, and in Italy. By their effort, and by their blood, and no less by their experience overseas, they created a new Canada, one far more sophisticated and complex than the pre-war version and so able to strike off in entirely new directions, building a welfare state, taking in millions of immigrants and refugees and so decisively changing the kind of people that we were, expanding our cities until several of them grew into major metropolises, building new universities and creating cultural centres. Perhaps the most profound change effected by the war was that before we were quasi-isolationist and afterwards we became one of the most international-minded of nations.

Over that half-century, though, this connection between what we had become and those who made it possible was lost. It was never explicitly rejected, rather it was forgotten amid the onrush of new events, or just pushed to the edges of peoples' memories. Polls among high school and university students showed that few knew which countries had fought on which side in the Second World War and that many thought Canada had always been neutral in the quarrels of others in the same way that we now take part in so many United Nations peacekeeping missions.

The veterans themselves were in part to blame. They were the Silent Generation. They didn't often talk about their experiences both because it was almost impossible to describe what had happened Over There to those who had stayed home, and because people of that era simply didn't talk about themselves. The word "I" was seldom used; the preferred pronoun was "One." Confessionalism, most certainly in public, but often even within the family, was almost unknown.

So the old soldiers began to fade away, not just physically as they grew older, but psychically, slipping to the margins of their society, occasionally trotted out for the ever-smaller Remembrance Day parades.

It was their grandchildren who re-discovered them. In a magical reaching out across the generations, young people began encouraging their grandparents to share their stories of chasing U-boats across the Atlantic, or more often of trying frantically to dodge away from them, of the lethal madness of trying to land on the stony beaches of Dieppe, of the long hell of German prisoner-of-war camps and the special hell of Japanese camps, of slogging it northwards from Italy's "boot" and of sloshing through water-logged Holland, or of rationing and V-bonds. They wanted to touch their own roots before these had slipped away from them.

At last they turned toward their grandparents, not just with love, but now with admiration, respect, even awe, and thanks.

Blake Heathcote's *Testaments of Honour* is both a personal and a collective thank you to those who once went out to save this society and then to rebuild it. After his grandfather, an artist who served in the First and Second World Wars, died, Heathcote set out to digitally archive all his grandfather's scrapbooks and sketches. Scanning the material and reading the notes made him realize how close to extinction the priceless storehouse had come. So Heathcote set out in his car, with a digital camera and scanner to capture the recollections of as many veterans as he could find before they went the same way as had so many of their colleagues before them.

At long last, some members of the Silent Generation have found a voice. Often shyly at first, they have described what it really was like during the last time that this entire nation committed itself collectively to a single overarching cause. Despite the often unspeakable pain and loss, it was for many of them the best years of their lives. For Canada, it was our best years as a nation, when we grew up and learned we could do almost anything we wanted. This book is a thank you to those who did it from those who are now able to do so much because of what they did.

Richard Gwyn

INTRODUCTION

IN MANY WAYS, *Testaments of Honour* was born quite by chance.

I grew up surrounded by many artifacts from the two world wars, as most everyone on both sides of my family had seen service in one or both of these conflicts. My paternal grandfather (pictured opposite) was a veteran of both wars, and it was my childhood fascination with the memorabilia of war—English magazines from 1940, a fragment of razor-sharp shrapnel, an inexplicable wood propeller—that prompted some of our first conversations. He'd answer questions when asked, but it wasn't until late in his life that he spoke openly about his experiences. I think he assumed no one was particularly interested in what he had done or been through. I've come to believe that most veterans feel this way.

It never occured to me that in those quiet conversations, I was brushing up against history. For years I'd been hearing fragments of stories, talking to P o Ws, pilots, intelligence operatives, artists, nurses, doctors, yet I still looked to find the "real" military in movies, books, and television. How real could their experiences have been? So, fifteen years after my grandfather's death, I set out to make sense of what this history meant to me.

I started by digitally archiving my grandfather's scrapbooks from the wars (he was an artist), and the nature of that exercise forced me to carefully focus on each image and give it some context and meaning. This act of slowing down made it possible for me to see how little I knew or understood about the experiences of those who served in our wars, and in so doing, I discovered where to start looking.

Through word of mouth, I began developing a list of veterans with whom I wanted to talk, having no objective in mind other than to listen to their stories. Within minutes of starting my first interview, war took on a decidedly human face.

I knew more or less what D-Day was, but I wanted to find out how it had felt to be there. What was it like at Ortona? Or being the 21-year-old skipper of a Lancaster over Berlin? Or working relentless nursing shifts in Normandy? Or hunting a sub in a rollicking, sodden corvette? I wanted to know why these men and women had signed up, some of them still in high school. How had they dealt with the enormous responsibility that had been placed on their shoulders? What did they find when they came home from war? I wanted to understand what it meant to have been a part of it. I wanted to understand the "why."

I decided to record the conversations on video to capture a fuller sense of the person: the expression in the eyes, the small smile. The procedure was very straightforward. I'd set a digital video camera to one side, and then the veteran and I would simply have a conversation. After brief formalities, the vets would usually relax and open themselves to memory. Then the most astonishing thing would happen: as they spoke of friends and events from a half-century ago, I'd see these men and women have thirty or forty years literally fall away from their faces. They became young again. With the camera doing the recording, all I had to do was luxuriate in these incredible lives.

Over the past few years, I've interviewed over 150 veterans and contacted hundreds more. The testaments featured in this volume capture only a few moments from a few individuals' stories, culled from hours of interview transcripts and videos. The photographs included in *Testaments of Honour,* in nearly every case generously shared from the private collections of the men and women who tell their stories here, offer us another window to the world they knew. Together the stories and photographs tell a small part of our history. There are so many extraordinary stories that haven't been presented here and thousands that I haven't yet heard (but with luck will). They include stories from individuals who have, to date, chosen not to talk of their lives. My hope is that *Testaments of Honour* will persuade them to come forward, and give voice to their experiences.

Testaments of Honour is a product of memory, flaws and all. We edit what we cannot, do not, or wish not to remember. But this is what makes the contributions to *Testaments of Honour* both unique and invaluable. These stories are history, our history, as seen through the kaleidoscope of a half-century of getting on with life.

———

Through talking with veterans, I've learned that those who've been participants of front-line combat speak of it—when they do speak of it—not to entertain with the thrills of a "near-miss," but rather as an on-going attempt to give shape to an emotional abstraction. Veterans talk to try and understand.

There is an enormity to what the veterans endured. Paradoxically this went hand-in-glove with the lack of personal expectation with which they undertook the responsibility laid before them. Their generation may have not been particularly well informed about the world and its machinations, but they felt strongly about their responsibilities. They did not want to shame their parents, or their communities, churches and synagogues. They took responsibility for their actions and blamed no one for their predicaments. Having grown up in the Depression years, they weren't encumbered with the sense of entitlement that I believe has hobbled so many later generations.

Our veterans' "growing up" years disappeared during that period of 1939 to 1945. Duty superceded self-interest. And it's important to recall that most of these people did their jobs all too aware of the lousy odds stacked against them. For those who were fortunate enough to make it back home after the war, how much had changed in the years they'd been away? For most, it meant starting all over again from where they'd been six years before.

It's astonishing how resilient those Canadians were, and are. Most, if not all, veterans came home manifestly changed. Many came home damaged, even if they weren't aware of the damage at the time. How so many came back from where they'd been and what they'd seen and done and became part of the world again is something of a miracle. Fastening bolts or shuffling paperwork must have seemed unbearably trivial after the kind of life they'd been living where more often than not, tomorrow was a lifetime away. Many had lost their sense of how to communicate with friends and family, and withdrew into themselves. Sometimes it took fifty years for them to come out again.

They also came away with experiences that fundamentally changed them for the better. After being in the service, they gained a great sense of self-respect by having been handed "a job to do" and having to see that job through, whatever the scale or whatever the cost, whether it was washing the hangar windows or stepping off a landing craft into enemy machine gunfire.

Canadian veterans understand that life is a gift. They know this because they were given the chance to marry, to raise families, and build careers, when many of those who stood next to them in battle had these possibilities denied them. Our vets know what their lives cost and that being Canadian means to have been given the boon of selfless determination. Their lives have been shaped by the knowledge that their generation left their families and homes behind to put their community and country first.

This is a debt we owe our Canadian veterans. As you read these stories, look up from your own life and remember those who made it possible.

Blake Heathcote

Alex MacInnis

———

BIRTH PLACE: PORT HAWKESBURY, NOVA SCOTIA
RESIDENCE: SYDNEY, NOVA SCOTIA
REGIMENT: CAPE BRETON HIGHLANDERS, WEST NOVA
SCOTIA REGIMENT, ROYAL HAMILTON LIGHT INFANTRY
THEATRE OF WAR: NW EUROPE, ITALY

I was born in Port Hawkesbury, Cape Breton Island, September 7th, 1919. I had four brothers and a sister, and I was the second oldest of the lot. I had an older brother who was with the North Nova Scotia Highlanders, and my sister was with the CWAC [Canadian Women's Army Corps]. All of us signed up.

Times weren't the best in those years right after the Depression. We wanted to get off our father's back. He was a section man, and he wasn't making much money. He was hard-working, God-fearing. He'd left home at fourteen and worked in the United States for twenty-two years, around Gloucester and Boston, on the ice teams. Then he came home, married my mother and settled in Cape Breton.

We had a good life growing up. We always had food on the table. We had a little farm for cash crops and such. We always got along pretty good, even in the Depression. I always say that the Depression years for me, and for a lot of people where I come from, were probably the best time of our lives.

Everybody knew everybody—there were only about nine hundred people in our town. You knew their circumstances and most everything about them. Everybody lived about the same; you helped your neighbour. In those years, you wouldn't do a good turn until after dark. My father would bundle something up from the farm, and then take it to somebody—but not until dark. You didn't want to be seen to be helping someone.

At the end of the thirties, I was pretty well aware of what was going on overseas. There was all kinds of propaganda going around, and we all knew Hitler was a bad man. But we knew he wasn't coming our way because we were all going to do our darndest to stop him. The murdering that was going on with the innocent people, and this master race, and Hitler was doing away with a lot of the infirm people. And the Jews… we couldn't just stand around and let it happen.

Joining the army, it was also a job. A dollar-thirty a day, which was pretty good in those days. I was the first fellow in the town to join; I must have been the hungriest. I joined September 7th, 1939, on my birthday— three days before Canada declared war. I went to Baddeck to sign up with the Cape Breton Highlanders. But then the West Nova Scotia Regiment was short thirty men to go overseas, so there were thirty of us from Cape Breton who volunteered. So we left the Cape Breton Highlanders and joined the West Novas. We were in a hell of a hurry to get over there, and in twice as much of a hurry to get back! We didn't really know what we were getting into.

The West Novas—they were fishermen and farmers from down 'round Lunenburg and Bridgewater there—the finest people you ever met in your life. There wasn't one of them that you couldn't depend on. You could lay your life at their feet, that was it. I thought there was nothing like the Cape Breton Highlanders, but those guys…

They were just farmers, just got off an ox-cart or something. I could hardly understand 'em. They had this twang, eh? "We'll have mamalade in the mawnin'." Oh, geez, they were great.

———

When we landed in England in 1940 and saw those fellows coming back from Dunkirk, it was a horrible sight. We were in the Battle of Britain, ducking bombs even before we got into battle three years after. You got used to dodging shrapnel. You were scared to death every night. We were near Biggin Hill, which was a Canadian fighter base, and they were always hitting that. But we became acclimatized to it. It was no good going on leave to London, because you got to London and you were in a rat-hole all night.

When we were training, we had wooden bullets. Old Ross 303 rifles, but wooden bullets. And when we were doing defence on the coast of the English Channel, we had fence posts driven into the sand, like a sawhorse, with a pole across it and a gas cape over that. It looked like a gun from the air, but that's what it was: a pole and two fence posts. That was our defence. In 1940, when the men were coming back from France, we had no equipment. We had nothing. We dug more God-damned holes in Britain for land defences in Britain, it's a wonder it didn't sink.

After Dunkirk, the Canadians were the best equipped army, yet we still had nothing. But the British were tough. We got on with them just fine. The guys in the West Novas were just one big family after three years together. You didn't have to look at your back; you could trust your life with them.

———

We were in Scotland, training up on Ben Nevis with Norwegian trainers, and cold—my God! We pretty near froze to death. We were ordered from there down to Manchester to ship out. We didn't know until they gave us summer clothing out at sea that we were going to Sicily. Coming in, we lost three ships in the Bay of Biscay; we watched them going down, sunk by U-boats. It was a beautiful day in July, about two o'clock in the afternoon. I watched the torpedo just missing our boat and hitting the ship next to us. Next thing you knew, everything was flying up in the air. We knew things were serious then.

When we landed at Sicily, there was no resistance on the beach. Until two or three days later, we started running into a bit, but it wasn't that bad. It was just the terrain that was bad in Sicily. We didn't lose that many men in the first while.

It took us thirty-nine days to mop up the Germans in Sicily. I think we were through there sometime in August. We lost a few men, but it wasn't the worst.

The worst was Ortona.

We regrouped and crossed the straits of Messina into Italy on the 3rd or 4th of September. Italy capitulated on the 8th.

We met a lot of resistance there on the mainland, but didn't realize how bad it was going to get. We got kind of acclimatized to the pace we were moving at. We met some good soldiers—the 1st German Parachute Division.

They were real gentlemen; real soldiers. Seasoned veterans, not dirty, like the SS and the young ones—the Hitler Youth—that we ran into in Holland. When I went back to Italy in '98, I met up with one of them—Wilhelm Fritz, a real nice guy. He cried, I cried. We spent an afternoon together in Rome. He said to me, "You stick your head up, I shoot you. Thank God you missed me!" Those fellows were a little different than we were. We volunteered; they had to do it. But there was no nonsense about them.

It was all something of an adventure for us until we reached a place called the Moro River. That's where Smokey Smith got his VC. That was the prelude to Ortona. It was a deep ravine and the Germans were well dug in. When we went across the river, every second bullet was a tracer. You could see the flame shooting past as they tried to nail down our position. It seemed every city and town in Italy was built on hills. They'd be looking down on you, and you had to fight your way up to them. It was rough.

Alex MacInnis in England during training in 1940.

Then we hit Ortona. Ortona is a medieval town, and all the houses are stone. You could go from the first house on the street to the last one without going out onto the street, because there was just a stone partition between each house or apartment. That's where the term "mouse-holing" comes from.

You couldn't go on the street because the Germans had blown a lot of houses down, so the street was all piled with rubble, and they had pin-pointed the machine guns on the street, so you couldn't get on it.

When we got in the first house, we used a PIAT [Projector Infantry Anti-Tank] mortar to blow a hole in the wall. If you heard anything making a racket on the other side, then you'd throw a grenade in. Then you'd get through that one, and blow a hole in the next wall. So you mouse-holed your way down the street.

There were a lot of booby traps working our way through Ortona. They'd put a crooked picture on the wall, and you'd touch it to straighten it up, and BOOM! If you got in a place and there was a piano, you just had to touch one of the keys and it was goodbye. Even in Sicily, they'd leave a big ripe orange on the tree. All the others would be green, except for this one, and you couldn't resist it. You'd grab it and BOOM!

Canadian troops moving through the ruins of Regalbuto, Italy, in August 1943. House-to-house fighting occured in conditions like these throughout much of Italy.

We were ordered not to touch any stuff, of course, but it wore you down, always being on guard.

All of a sudden—I think it was the 28th of December—not a sound. They'd gone during the night. But geez, we lost a lot of men there. That was the roughest. There were some bad battles around Caen and that, but I never got in them. And Wilmot and the other Novas saw some bad battles at the Hitler line, and thank God I wasn't there. Italy was a bad country to fight in.

At the end of it, you were so tired and battle-weary that you were almost dead yourself. You were there, but... they were gone, thank God, and then you'd drop. You didn't have to look at the match you were lighting or the picture you were straightening up on the wall.

———

When I was going into Ortona on Christmas Day in 1943—that was the fourth Christmas I been away from home—I came across this little boy. He was something like eight or ten, and he'd just been killed. We had some guys dying there on the field, some dead and dying guys, and the little fellow looked so out of place. I don't know what he was doing there, I have no idea. And that little fellow has followed me for fifty-eight years. I'd see him a lot, and nobody knew about him but me. And it seemed to me that I adopted that little fellow. He's always with me, and he never grows any older. What struck me when I first saw him was that he was about the same age as the little brother that I'd left at home, the last brother left at home.

I cried, going by him. I couldn't stop; he was dead. The blood was just fresh on him. And he looked so out of place there, all alone. He had no idea how the war started or why. He had nothing to do with it. And yet he died... well, I don't know how he died, or why he was there or how he got there. And that little fellow has travelled with me for the past sixty years.

I still see him a lot. I never told my wife about him; never told any of my family about him until last year.

Things like that on your mind, they never go away. I walked by that little fellow sixty years ago, and you'd think it'd be gone. But it wasn't and it never will be. He never left me.

You get funny moments in war. There was a guy from a regiment, name of Drillo, he came from Fall River. This little Drillo fellow wrote to

Canadian Medics and personnel carrying an injured flyer in the hills of San Vito, Italy, 1943.

his mother, telling her everything was great, not to worry. The next day they were going into battle. This war correspondent was walking by, and he saw this soldier with this white thing in his hand. So the correspondent stopped and picked it up, and it was the letter that Drillo had written to his mother. The correspondent said he didn't know then and he doesn't know now why this fellow had it in his hand. He must have known he was dying, the wounds he had. Did he want to be close to his family? Or maybe he wanted somebody to mail the letter.

She would have had the story that he was dead before the letter arrived. Maybe he felt more at home with it in his hand, knowing he was dying.

After that battle, we weren't pulled out of the line, but we needed to be. We moved six or seven miles north of Ortona to a place called San Tomasso, and we held that line for the winter. It was called a static line. A static line sounds great, but it's not so great. It wasn't just sitting there:

we had to send out patrols to try and pick up one of their guys to find out what the hell they were doing. That was worse than the battle!

At that point, we were all seasoned soldiers. And you could be a good soldier, and through no fault of your own you could get shell shock—through no fault of your own. You'd be in the line, then they'd take you to the back of the line five or six miles to get a few hours' rest. When you got back, you'd hear the battles going on, and the people screaming. You'd be in it all over again. You never got away from it. That's the unfortunate thing about it. And I don't know how you can tell people what that's like, to never be able to get away from it.

I was hit on the 14th of March, 1944. We were moving up towards the Hitler line. It was raining this night, we'd been there for two or three weeks, maybe. I had dug a hole, and I had a bully beef can and a shoelace for a wick and some gasoline. I had a nice little light in there.

The Germans are shelling us all the time. This guy comes up—we'd got some reinforcements—he was a young fellow, and he started asking some questions.

"Anybody getting killed here? Anybody getting hit?"

I looked and saw this mule train coming over the hill with some Gurkha Indians. So I said to this young fellow, "I'll tell ya, buddy. If we don't get the geez outta here, we'll find out."

A German corporal killed during fighting in Ortona, December 21st, 1943.

And no sooner than the words were out of my mouth when, BOOM! I got it. I guess that every time after that when that poor fellow saw a mule, he must've got scared. But I knew the Germans would be watching for our supply lines.

The same shell that got me, a piece of it took the hell off this mule. The Gurkha bent down to check him, and he must have touched the wound, because the mule gave it to him. And when he got up, the mule

9

gave it to him a second time with both feet, and the Gurkha didn't get up again.

I got it right straight through the knee joint, and when this fellow came over to see me I was laughing. He said, "What's so funny, you crazy bugger?" I pointed to my knee and the stuff that was coming out of it, and said, "That's Halifax coming out, right there."

So I made it back to England, not Halifax, and was there in the hospital for seven months. It wasn't such a bad time, with nurses waiting on us. I remember four o'clock on the morning of the 6th of June, the place was jumping off the ground with the sound of the planes going over. Oh my geez, you couldn't see the sky. So we knew it was on.

The Hitler Youth were in strength in France at that time; baby-faced fellows. But you couldn't touch them, couldn't go near them. I ran into one of them when I was in hospital in England; he was in the bed next to me.

"Canadese. Canadese pretty good soldier. German, little better."

He told me that if he could make it out of the hospital that night, he was going right back to the German lines. That was what those SS buggers were like.

I got out around the 1st of September, and was over in France by the end of that month. I was reassigned to the Royal Hamilton Light Infantry. I tried to get back with my own outfit, but they said no, they needed reinforcements in France by that time. I was sent to France with the Royal Hamilton Light Infantry with Colonel Whitaker.

Most of the guys in the RHLI didn't go overseas until a couple of years after we'd been there. And when they sent you home, it was done on a point system. I was in Italy nine or ten months and every month there was counted as two. Not to mention that I was over there a couple of months before they were.

When they started repatriating people back to Canada, I was the oldest fellow in the RHLI. And those fellows were together for a long time. So I understand them being pissed off with me. Even the officers. After being with them for five months, I was getting my ticket home.

The RHLIs had been through some tough times; they'd been on the Dieppe raid, they'd seen a lot of hard action. I went up to the Scheldt with Colonel Whitaker. Oh, my God, the water and the dykes—the Germans flooded everything. We were always slogging through water.

You couldn't dig a trench, because you'd take a shovel of earth out and two shovels of water would come back in the hole.

These were the bad Germans we were up against—the Hitler Youth. Oh, geez, it was bad, eh? I was with them there through the beginning of January 1945. I got hit again, but that wasn't the cause of me coming home. My time was up. I didn't feel the best about it myself, either, 'cause here I'd just been with this bunch for a few months, and now I was being repatriated before any of them. Anyway, that's the way it was. But the captain got wind of me being sent back and he called me up.

"I hear you're going back to Canada. Is that right?"

"Yes sir."

"Well, I'm going to tell you something else, too. You're going in on the line in the morning."

I'd heard about this before. It's your last time out and that's the end of it for you. But they were short of men. So I went in in the morning. It was cold snowing, about six or seven inches of snow on the ground, and there was still a lot of shelling going on around, so I set myself down to digging a trench.

I hadn't got very deep when a sergeant came up to me.

"You MacInnis?"

"Yessir, I am."

"Well, get your stuff together. You're going back to Canada."

"I got no stuff. Let's go." And I left my shovel where it was, hopped out of my last trench, and I was gone.

I remember coming home Valentine's Day, 1945, in a blinding snowstorm. Getting into Pier 21 in Halifax. One lone fellow on the dock, with a balaclava pulled down over his face. Some guys gone six months had the whole town come out to greet them. We were gone six years, and there was nobody there to see us. Just this one kid with a balaclava wishing he was someplace else.

———

After I got back to Halifax and was discharged, then got back home with my wife—we hadn't seen one another for five years. We started a family and I had to have a job, so on you go.

But you have all this stuff bottled up inside of you, and you don't realize it. It's like a death: you must deal with it. If you don't deal with it this year, you're going to deal with it next year—or five or six years after. And that's our problem—we never dealt with it. We said, "This is it. It's over. The war is over. Get home, get to work, and that's it." But it was always in your system. It seemed to me that in the American army, after six or seven months, you'd get a furlough. And when you got back to the States, everybody had a psychiatrist. I used to laugh at that. But that was a mistake.

When I came home, my wife said that to me. "You're not the man I married."

How had the war changed me? I don't know. It was hard for me to tell my kids I loved them. It took that from me. I just couldn't; you didn't like people, I guess. You'd seen what happened to people and what people did. I always had a chip on my shoulder, that you couldn't trust people. If I had gone back to the battlefields that we were on, I think I could have been a hell of a lot better father and husband than I was. It's hard to say.

I know I was different after the war. I was only young when I was a boy; I had to grow up overnight. You grow up probably too fast.

I was drinking when I came back. I was drinking heavy when I came back. I tried to drink it all. For the first five or six years I was home, I never had a Christmas dinner at home. I'd be gone drinking. We might've thought it was okay at the time. After the war, you'd see a lot of fellows drunk. But a lot of those fellows, they couldn't sleep unless they were half drunk.

I was one of the lucky fellows that was able to stop. And why did I drink? I don't know. I never liked the taste of liquor. But I'll tell you one thing: I could have a sound sleep when I got a few of them into me. But you can't blame everything on the war.

I don't know why people would want to start a war. I don't know. They know it doesn't solve anything.

My family didn't know anything about the war unless somebody else told them. And that's the disservice we did to our kids. I was married before the war, and my wife died about eleven years ago. Last year I talked about a story that none of my kids knew; it was the first time I ever talked about it.

Where it sank into me was a couple of years ago when I went back to Holland. Their little kids, they never let them forget about the war. They teach them in school. I don't know how you can stress it to kids now, but there's a better way than war. If you ever get into the front lines, and spend any time there, you'll never be the same again. By us collectively going [to war], we made the world a better place to live.

When I went back to Sicily fifty-five years after I was there, I didn't want to go. It's hard to explain, but after I was there two or three days, I could actually feel this weight physically lifting off my shoulders. It was some kind of closure. I never talked about the war, never talked about it. My young fellow read this little piece of paper that they sent home, telling us about the trip. And he said to me, "I never knew you were hit twice." And he's a grown man, eh? We just never talked about it. And that's a big sin that we committed to the children we're leaving behind.

In the last year or two, I started going to schools to talk about it, just in the hopes that you can make people realize that you should never go to war. If you can avoid it at all, you should never go. You're never the same after. The things that you have…if we had told the kids before how horrible it was…I don't know why we didn't. In the name of God, try and avoid a war if there's any way of doing it. Because war changes your life.

Am I a happy fellow now? No. Maybe if my wife was here, I would be. But the Canadians, you know? It was the same in the war. You do your job, come home and shut your mouth, and that's it.

Andy Anderson

BIRTH PLACE: TORONTO, ONTARIO
RESIDENCE: MISSISSAUGA, ONTARIO
SQUADRON: ROYAL CANADIAN ENGINEERS, 1ST CANADIAN
PARACHUTE BATTALION
THEATRE OF WAR: NW EUROPE, GERMANY

I was born in Toronto in 1922 and I think in contemporary words, you could say that I was a military brat, the product of a mother and father who both saw service in the First World War. My father went overseas with the First Canadian Division as an engineer in the First War. He ended up with both the MM [Military Medal] and the DCM [Distinguished Conduct Medal]. He was wounded. My mother was a nursing sister. And, as it turned out, she nursed my father, from a field dressing station in France, when he was wounded at Vimy, where they met for the first time.

Being in the Engineers would not have been my first choice, but because of my father's connection, the Engineers was the obvious place to go.

Promotion came fairly rapidly, if you came out of the militia. A lot of the training had to do with trench warfare. I remember my first leave in Toronto, having to write exam papers there for a promotion. Sitting at the dining-room table, I was studying this trenching manual and my father said, "My God, where did that come from?"

"I've got to write an exam on this. This is what we're learning."

And he said, "But that's what we used back in 1915!"

We spent weeks learning how to make fire bays and sandbags and dugouts, all lifted right from Vimy Ridge. After three months, they gathered us in the drill hall and the CO said, "This is Major Somebody, who has just escaped from Dunkirk. He is an engineer and wants to have a few words with us."

He said, "Take your manuals and throw them in the garbage, because there's a new thing out called a slit-trench. This is the way the war is going to be fought, from one- and two-person slit trenches. These are the dimensions and this is how you dig them. I've already written to Ottawa, so toss all your 1915 manuals away." The Second World War had begun for us.

I was a sergeant by this time and half the members of my squadron were lumberjacks and miners from Northern Ontario: Timmins, North Bay, and Kirkland Lake. They were ten years or more older than me, but I never had a discipline problem with them. I also came to learn pretty quickly that there was no sense talking to them about a manual. Because they just knew how to do things: I just had to control what they did. The Engineers have an awful lot to do with explosives and I'd been on a couple of courses and was becoming quite familiar with explosives and became a leader in the squadron as a kind of an expert in explosives.

There's a lot of danger and hazards working with that stuff. So there I'd be, nineteen or twenty years old, thinking I knew it all, teaching these miners and lumberjacks.

"Now you take a 27 detonator, then take the fuse and gently form it through; then you take your crimping shears and you gently crimp the detonator to the fuse, being very careful..."

Then they'd break off in groups to try it on their own and I'd see these miners just shove the fuse in and crimp it in their teeth.

"Holy Jesus!"

"Don't worry, Sarge," they'd say. "We know what we're doin'. Just you relax and don't worry about nothin'." What could I say to that? Except maybe, "Oh my God..."

Not long after, we were sent to England and began more specific training with Bailey Bridges and the like, but things didn't really run smooth for me. I had no great passion to be an officer, but I was getting pretty tired of having to train new junior officers who were coming right out of university with no leadership skills whatsoever. So after a while, I came to think I didn't have much of a future with the Engineers.

I got it in my mind that maybe there might be a place for me in an infantry regiment.

I'd recently met some buddies of mine in London who had just landed from Canada and were in the new 1st Canadian Parachute Battalion. I was really taken with their uniform, their wings, maroon berets and beautiful jump boots. One of my friends said, "We're at full strength, but I think they're looking for some specialists. Why don't you get your application put in?"

I was accepted and given one day to get back to my camp and grab the rest of my kit. The men that I left with the Engineers were horrified and said, "You're nuts! We'll never see you again! Who the hell wants to take airborne training?" Everyone thought I was as crazy as a bedbug, but I was thrilled.

I ended up in Bulford and just had time to unpack my gear in a reception centre when my buddies came in. Sergeant Art Stammers said, "Welcome aboard! You're joining the battalion, not the training unit. You're going to be our explosives guy." Six of us left the next morning for the British parachute training school. This was in April before D-Day and it was no secret that training was accelerated pretty rapidly because something was coming up. Graduating with my wings, I got back to the battalion and within days got assigned to B Company, which is where I spent the rest of the war. Everybody who transferred into the battalion reverted in rank to private, but I went through the promotion system fairly quickly and got my own platoon.

We had the finest officers. They were young, physically fit, very bright, and they knew men. They brought a hell of a pile of skills with them. Our commander was Brigadier James Hill, who unquestionably was the finest British general officer rank to come out of the war. He had a passion for fitness and skills and was an absolute holy terror, in that everyone in the battalion had to be absolutely, totally skilled with all kinds of weapons, including German [weapons]. He stressed initiative and fitness. We had to do ten-mile runs every two weeks in full kit with weapons, with names taken at the gates coming in. If you couldn't measure up, there'd better be some damn good reason. Then there were fifty-mile forced marches, all timed.

Leading up to D-Day, the brigadier met with the officers. We didn't know what the objective was going to be, but he just kept repeating, "There's gonna be chaos and confusion and it'll never be otherwise. So bear that in mind. You're gonna require leadership and initiative." We were finally alerted and lifted from our camp into a secure staging area enclosed by barbed wire. That's where Normandy was first mentioned and we were shown photographs and sand-table models. We were there a week, with the drop scheduled for the 5th of June, but the weather turned against us, so it was shifted to the 6th. The guys were all keen as hell and our drop went in just after midnight on the 6th.

Our drop zone in Normandy was very close to a town called Ranville, which was the battalion's objective. The main mission was to move in behind the German defences and seize all the bridge crossings across the Dives River to prevent armour and reinforcements reaching the beach. It was a matter of blowing the bridges up, or, failing that, holding them and stopping any reinforcements from crossing.

In retrospect, the intelligence information provided to us was not complete. We had daylight photographs of the drop zones, which were

OPPOSITE: **Paratrooper of the 1st Canadian Parachute Battalion advancing in an open field at Bulford Barracks.**

no bloody good at night because we were in total darkness. The other problem was that there had never been an assault in darkness. The airlift was taking off from English airfields scattered all over the country and we had to link up and hit the drop zone at roughly the same time, five minutes after midnight, in radio silence. It's no secret that the Normandy airborne invasion was almost a total disaster. Not only from the perspective of the 6th Airborne division, but also the American 101st, who were dropped right in the middle of Sainte-Mère-Église by accident and scattered all over hell's half-acre.

Lieutenant Marcel Coté from Montreal, who was in charge of our heavy mortar platoon, dropped thirty miles from the drop zone into Octeville near a German Luftwaffe base. Two men were killed and the others captured. So Coté, who survived, spent the whole war in a prisoner-of-war camp, but there was nothing he could do. In my judgment, the airborne drop was almost a disaster because of the scattering of both the 6th Airborne and the American 101st. Having to find a drop zone the size of a football field in the dead of night and be accurate was extremely difficult. But because of the training and the emphasis of the brigadier on initiative, our fellows that dropped anywhere near the drop zone may have been lost for hours, but they gathered people together and eventually, with compasses and maps, figured out where the hell they were. Within two days, we got to all the bridges, seized them, and blew them up or contained them. But there were a lot of lives lost and an awful lot of equipment lost on the drop.

When I dropped, it was pitch black—not even any moonlight. That's quite unnerving to parachute down in, particularly when you're alone and looking for buddies. Gradually, over a period of a half-hour or an hour, your group maybe found an officer, or a half a dozen guys that you knew. Somebody puts a fighting group together, says, "I think the objective is that way," and away you go. For days, the companies and platoons grew in size as guys wandered in alone or sometimes in pairs from all over the place.

There were some nervous times, because you're trying to stay concealed, moving from hedgerow to hedgerow, and there were German troops around. Particularly unsettling if you're only in a group of about six or eight. There were times when some of our guys were marching down a lane and some Germans came down the other side of the lane and they looked at each other and nobody fired a shot. Fortunately, the Germans were just as confused as we were. Coming in like that was a great shock.

If there was any success, it was that we were able to take all the objectives that we had and hold them, even with just a handful of men. No German reinforcements made it to the beach areas in and around Caen.

After three or four days, the Germans did come through and we had some pitched battles along the river. But by that time, our division was pretty well consolidated and we were strong enough in weapons and equipment to repel the attacks. But it was a dicey time for a few days.

You just lived on "compo" rations or whatever you had in your pack. There was no question of looting anything or getting into houses or getting any food from the French. You lived in one slit trench after another for a couple of weeks. But we overcame the difficulties and we stayed there until about the 1st of September.

We were taken out of the line after two and a half months of constant fighting. The whole division was moved back to England and it was a great relief to get back into camp again. We began the effort to bring the battalion back to strength. We were given ten days' leave, then started serious training again. Almost fifty percent of the men were now new and had not been blooded. Fitness was an absolute necessity, so the punishing fitness regime became even worse. The ten-mile runs, the fifty-mile marches, and the weapons skills were going to be accelerated and the battalion was going to be first class. That carried on until December and on the 22nd, there was a call saying, "The military police have been called in, the gates are closed and you've got to withdraw all passes. Gather your troops together; some flap is on and nobody's leaving camp."

"What the hell is this?" I thought. By ten o'clock the next morning, Brigadier Hill called a meeting of all the officers.

"Sorry to have to confront you with this problem, there's a crisis in the Ardennes. Von Rundstedt has mounted an enormous attack and Montgomery has been given command of the entire front, including the American sector. Montgomery's first order is that he wants the 6th Airborne division into the Ardennes quick. So gear your troops up for an airdrop into the Ardennes to stop this von Rundstedt breakthrough. Montgomery has made it clear that unless they are stopped, von Rundstedt and the Germans can be in Paris by New Year and Ostend."

We geared up with full weapons, ammunition, grenades, explosives, and stood alert. Late on December 23rd a message came, saying there couldn't be an airdrop: "…since the Ardennes is fogged in and snowed in, the air force won't fly us, so we're going to have to go in by sea." So on Christmas Eve, our battalion took off for the continent by sea on tank landing craft with all our gear. But we had no winter gear at all. We didn't know what the hell we were getting into; there'd been no briefing, no big sand-table lecture or anything. All we knew was that there was a crisis.

We landed at Ostend, boarded trucks and made our way right up very close to the front line. Then we found ourselves in freezing temperatures and snow with just our jump-smocks and regular boots. It was a painful time in there, the Ardennes. We finally made it to Rochefort in Belgium, which became our last objective. We captured that town from the Germans and then we did a lot of patrolling from that time, as the Germans retreated. We were a pretty worn-out rag-tag group by that time, coming from the Ardennes, and we still didn't have any winter clothing.

We were very close to the Americans; when you stopped them, there was a password for the day. But it was important not to concentrate on the password alone. You had to halt and question them, because there was usually an officer who'd say, "Hi ya, guys! How are you? Where are you from? Oh, I know Canada. Montreal! I know Montreal very well." Invariably, these bastards were Germans. Then you'd get them out of their Jeeps, line them up with your weapons loaded and question them about soccer and cricket and the Germans would eventually trip up. It was a smart move to have these guys running all over the place in American uniforms, but it was a very tense time.

We came to a halt in Belgium and got orders that we were going to Holland to take over from an American regiment that had been decimated up around a place called Bergervoort on the Maas River. We were taken by truck up into Holland and took over positions from several American regiments. We were pretty worn out, but our quartermaster trucks finally arrived, with rubber boots, winter clothing, sweaters, warm underwear and gloves for the first time that winter.

The difference between the Dutch civilian population and the French and Belgian populations was a revelation to our soldiers; it was day and night. They were—and are—generous and welcoming to a fault, willing to share everything, supportive with everything, even information; you could put your life in their hands. They had been punished pretty badly by the Germans. We opened their bakeries, got the electricity going and generally helped get the cities and villages working again. So we have a special affection for the Dutch people.

As spring came, we were shipped back to England. About the 15th of March, we were taken to a secure compound to prepare for the next operation, when it was revealed to us that we were going to be part of a massive final assault across the Rhine River and deep into the heart of Germany. For a week, the battalion was given briefings that were more intense and accurate than I'd ever experienced. Photographs were a few hours old; there were accurate sand-table models. The brigadier, learning from the experience of Arnhem, insisted that our drop zone be within a few hundred yards of our objectives, because he didn't want us to have a long hike to find them. The drop was going to be at ten o'clock in the morning, so everybody cheered, saying, "Thank God we're going to be able to see." Once we found our drop zone, we could run to our objective through the woods and into this village in five or ten minutes. The downside was that we were exposed to enemy fire, because these fields were obvious drop zones and the Germans were going to know about them.

It was a bright sunny day, the 24th of March, 1945, ten o'clock in the morning. A whole brigade dropped in an area the size of two football fields, right on target. I had some holes in the canopy of my chute from enemy fire and I could see others that were being hit, as well as some aircraft on fire. It was pretty horrible, but it's only a few seconds until you land. On landing, it only took a few seconds to get out of my harness, gather my kit bag and take out what I needed, then run like hell across the zone. I gathered up guys that I knew and by the time I reached the form-up area on the edge of the forest, our objective was only about fifty yards away through heavy growth. I had most of my platoon, maybe missing eight or ten guys, which is not bad at all. Our objective was a farmhouse where the Germans were entrenched. The attack went in with mortars and machine guns and we took it in a matter of seconds, with no trouble at all and had the whole bloody place secure in a matter of minutes. The other companies had equal success. There was chaos and confusion on the drop for some, but for our battalion it was a textbook operation. When I saw the objective, it was like

Captured German soldiers awaiting transport to a holding area.

looking at the sand table and the photographs. I could see the doors and pieces of farm equipment sitting outside, just like in the photographs—there they were!

There was intense fighting that afternoon, but we secured the area. The next day, we began our 250-mile journey, mostly on foot, across Germany, from village to village. Our objective was to get to the Baltic and the city of Wismar. For several weeks, we kept moving day by day by day, digging in, capturing village after village, and going like hell. Two hundred and fifty miles from the Rhine to the Baltic on foot, fighting all the bloody way, the Germans retreating all the time. The last river we had to cross was the Elbe, which was the last German effort at defence, where they'd assembled whatever they had left to defend their position.

That's the last time we saw Montgomery, who always used to come and gear us up for another push. He always amused me, because I never heard the first person used as much as he used it. The assault went in the next day. The story is that Churchill had issued orders for the British Airborne division to take the city of Wismar, which was supposed to be assigned to the Russians. Churchill wanted it to secure Hamburg for any political dialogue that followed and was determined to get it. All we knew was that we had to take Wismar.

We had the support of tanks for the first time. The brigadier said that the Canadians had come the farthest and we had the spirit to lead the charge, so Brigadier Hill assigned our battalion to lead. I remember riding Churchill tanks with B Company and the battalion, going like a son of a gun, stopping to blow up a few roadblocks from time to time. Suddenly, there were German regiments, surrendering in the fields on either side of the road, just collapsed, fully-equipped, fully-armed, no white flags or anything showing, nobody coming out, and we didn't stop. I got a little worried, because they had field guns and tanks just lying there in the grass, exhausted.

When we got to Wismar, there was very little fighting, but we were told, "Be careful, you're going to meet the Russians here. This is what they look like, these are their armaments, and these are their vehicles. So don't shoot them. They've been told what you look like, so be careful."

I set up a roadblock on the main highway leading from the Russian zone into the city. The civilians were fleeing and they were scared to death of the Russians, who were massacring them. They'd been on the road for days, carrying what they could, some of them with children. When they found out that we were the Allies, they just said, "Thank God." Mixed in with them we were getting escaped P o Ws and we told those guys that they got priority.

There were others who were escaping from concentration camps, mixed in with the civilians. They had striped clothing and were emaciated to unbelievable proportions and sick as could be. We had to get medics up from the field ambulance stations with litters to take them in tow. It was a job of trying to sort these people out and prioritize them. Who do you look after? Certainly the P o Ws and the Jewish prisoners, Ukrainians and Poles that had escaped from terrible camps and hadn't eaten for days, were first. Then there was the civilian population and then the German prisoners.

All of a sudden, the Russians appeared. I got a radio call that said, "Andy, you better get down here, there's some Russians at the roadblock."

"What do they look like?"

"They don't look like anything I've ever seen. They're in funny outfits and they've got lots of guns."

I went down to the roadblock and here was this rabble of Russian peasants in civilian cars with German weapons, half of them drunk and out of control. They kept saying, "Women, we want women." It was a tense time, because they kept growing in numbers. There was no discipline among them at all, nothing. This rabble thought that they were going to have a free run at the city. The Russians weren't happy about being held at our roadblock. The odd Russian, fully armed and drunk, would make his way in and almost every day, we'd find a civilian woman murdered or raped and we had to deal with it. On one of my last days in Wismar, a corporal ran up to me and said there was a woman lying in the ditch with her throat cut from ear to ear. She was about twenty-one years old, with her throat cut and the civilians told us that it was definitely a Russian who killed her.

I got fed up and said to my adjutant, Dick Hilbourne, "We've got to do something serious about this and lay a formal complaint." And he agreed. So he wrote a complaint and delivered it that afternoon to the Russians. When he came back, he said, "They promised discipline. They're going to identify the culprit and look after it." I had no idea how they'd identify him.

The next day, I got a call from the roadblock and there was a Russian Jeep and two trucks with lumber on board. Sitting in the back of the Jeep, is a guy with his hands bound, not wearing a cap. The Russian officer in charge said, "They're expecting us at the City Hall in Wismar." I confirmed that, and then waved them through. A day later, someone said to me, "Did you hear what happened?"

"No idea. What? Is the Russian in custody?"

"No, they hanged him! They built a gallows and they hanged him right there at City Hall."

I'm pretty sure the Russians said, "We've got to set an example," so they lined their troops up, picked some poor peasant, said, "You," and marched him off and hanged him. Some of our guys at headquarters in the city remember it very clearly.

First Allied Force meeting the Russian Army, May 1945, Wismar, Germany.
Andy Anderson (left in the beret) with the group, who have just finished several
celebratory shots of vodka.

There we were in Wismar, on the 8th of May. We were still dealing
with the Russians, displaced persons, P o Ws. When it was announced
on the radio that the war was over, V-E Day, it was just another day
for us.

But that night, when things quieted down, it was the first time in a
couple of years that I could really think about going home. I'd had a
fatalistic attitude that I was never going to survive the whole bloody
thing. With so many buddies that had been killed, I thought it would be
pure luck if I made it through. I remember talking to some guys that
night and they shared the same view: they didn't want to get drunk or
throw things around in the street, they just seriously thought about

family for the first time and thought, "Yeah, I'm going to see Mother and Dad again and my brother or sister and get back to Canada."

———

It was my great fortune, more by luck than anything else, to end up with the finest regiment during the war that I could ever have hoped to join. That pride still remains with me to this day. Some of the closest friends I'll ever have in my life are those guys from my regiment, right across Canada. It's given me a great understanding of the value we have in this country and the individuals that we have, wherever they come from. I got into this as a kid from Toronto with only a high school education and no experience of seeing the world at all. I matured very fast and I don't regret it for a minute. When I go out to speak to groups at legions, I always emphasize that there were many fine regiments from across Canada, from every province, who saw concentrated action in the worst conditions all over the world, of which we had no previous knowledge at all. I don't like to leave the impression that we were a bunch of heroes, the be all and end all of the war; we weren't. We were highly trained, highly skilled and highly motivated, but we were just Canadians, Canadian soldiers. This was a period in our history when there was a call for volunteers to serve the country and all our servicemen volunteered. It had nothing to do with the king or the flag. We had a duty that had to be done and we did it.

Charles Scot-Brown

Birth Place: Temiskaming, PQ
Residence: Toronto, Ontario
Regiments: 48th Highlanders, canloan,
Gordon Highlanders, 1st British Para-Battalion
Theatre of War: NW Europe, Germany
Decorations: CD, MID (2)

MY FATHER WAS THE SIXTH AND I WAS THE SEVENTH GENERATION of soldiers. He was a professional soldier with the 1st Division 6th Eaton Armoured Corps, which was a motor machine gun brigade, through the First War, from start to finish. He was never wounded during the war but was buried alive a couple of times with heavy explosions and was fortunate enough to be awarded the Military Cross and Bar. I've heard his friends mention he got his MC at Passchendaele and his Bar at Vimy, but I don't know. It's not unusual for people to be awarded various things that they just don't talk about.

I started off in 1941 to go to RMC [Royal Military College], but then it closed for the duration of the war. I'd already enlisted but couldn't take my commission until I was nineteen. So the Canadian army was caught with a seventeen-year-old.

I loved the Military. I'd been a Wolf Cub, a Boy Scout, a Rover; I'd been in Cadets in high school, then into the 48th Highlanders Reserve. I just wanted to be in the army and I thought I had the wherewithal to command troops in the field. I was disappointed that I hadn't gone to RMC, and then we were told that some of us would go to Sandhurst [England] to take our commissions. I was thrilled. We graduated in the early fall of 1943 and found ourselves back in Canada. The Canadians hadn't had the casualties in Italy they'd expected, so there was a backlog of officers and we couldn't get back overseas. Really frustrating for someone who just wanted to see battle.

Then one day an announcement came in saying the British army was very short of officers and any officer who would like to volunteer to get battle experience could sign up for something called CANLOAN. Our aim was to get overseas and fight and so almost our entire group volunteered for this way to get overseas.

I arrived in England and was assigned to the Gordon Highlanders. We did specialized training to take a heavily fortified area. We didn't know when, but we knew something big was going to happen, just by the movement of troops. The first warning we got was when all leave was cancelled.

We went into a concentration area, which is where you got your men together. We were issued new battle dress called Anti-Vapour, which was really just battle dress that had been soaked in chlorine in case the Germans used chlorine or mustard gas. In theory the gases would stay in your battle dress and never reach the skin. We found out that if you popped them into water, the chlorine came out, so I don't know what would have happened if there had been a bad rain.

Our vehicles were waterproofed and we checked our equipment. As a lieutenant, my job was to make sure that all my men's kits were well looked after, that they had good, serviceable boots and that socks were properly darned.

You couldn't move without decent socks. I remember the men were doing their darning and one of the Jocks had his sock and his thread all over the place.

"Who taught you how to darn socks like that?"

"I've never been taught, sir."

So my old boy scout days came in handy. I pulled the sock over my fist and taught him how to darn back and forth and then do the crossways. I had the feeling that somebody was looking over my shoulder. I looked around and the whole platoon was there and someone said, "He's not all bad, he knows how to darn socks." And when we got new boots, I used an old Canadian logger trick. You put on two pair of heavy woollen socks, lace on your boots, get them soaking wet, then go out and walk them dry. The leather molds right to your feet. You've got two pairs of socks on, so you get no blisters like some of the other platoons did. I knew some things we Canadians take for granted and I guess that made them think, "Maybe this crazy Canadian does know something." It gave them some confidence in me.

I was a lieutenant, just turned twenty, never been blooded. I wasn't afraid, but I had a healthy degree of apprehension. I knew I'd been well trained and was taking in a very highly trained platoon of vets. A lot of my guys had been at the Battle of El Alamein. They'd been right across North Africa and had landed in Sicily. My platoon sergeant had a MM [Military Medal] and I had about three other MMs in the platoon. They called it the "Hero Platoon" in the Gordons.

After being jammed in the concentration area like sardines, we were moved down to the Thames Estuary and loaded onto the Mother Ship on the 4th of June. This was a small converted liner that ferried LCAs [Landing Craft Assault] to a few hundred yards off the Normandy beach. Each LCA held thirty people and only when we were on the ships on (what turned out to be) D-Day minus one, were we told that our objective was to land at Gold Beach, then take a heavily fortified RADAR station inland.

Charles Scot-Brown, a CANLOAN officer with the Gordon Highlanders, landed on D-Day in the British sector, shown here the morning of June 6th, 1944. CANLOAN officers suffered extremely high casualty rates and forty-one received the Military Cross.

The invasion was delayed for a day because of weather and we stayed put because we had all our maps and orders. Sitting around got me thinking. I talked to my platoon sergeant.

"Hutch, you know I love those Jocks, so if I screw up and do anything stupid, hit me on the head and don't let anything happen to them."

"Well, sir, if you feel that way, we got nothing to worry about."

Those men were just lovely people and fine soldiers; they weren't the least bit worried about it, which was very reassuring to me.

We landed at H-Hour plus five hours, about eleven o'clock in the morning. It looked like massive confusion, although people seemed to know what they were doing. The beach masters were out there and the beach troops were doing a good job. Boats were coming in and being off-loaded; there was all kinds of activity. There was some shelling, so the first thing we did was get the hell off the beach as fast as we could and get inland. There's an old saying: "The closer you are to the battle, the less you get shot at," and that was our aim.

Being in a battle is a very restrictive thing, because you only know what is going on a hundred yards to your right and a hundred yards to your left. It was like being a kid going into a candy store with fifty cents: you had enough money that you could get anything you wanted, but there was so much to look at, you got completely confused.

It took us about an hour and a half before we were on our start line and we crossed that at one-thirty, which was the time we were supposed to, and away we went. It took us about two and a half, three hours to reach the RADAR station, and about an hour and a half to take it. It was just starting to get dusk by the time we had everything secure and mopped up and all the dead bodies out.

My platoon was thirty-seven men and myself. I had three killed and eight wounded, which was very light. In any attack, you take certain key people and keep others back, in case anything disastrous happens. Then you have a nucleus to re-form around. On this particular assault, I left Hutch back at A echelon and took another sergeant, who was killed rushing the enemy. He was trying to get underneath the machine gun fire to get grenades in the pillbox slots around the RADAR station. He just ran a little too far and was exposed a little too long. He pushed a little too hard.

When I saw *Saving Private Ryan*, there was a scene where the captain played by Tom Hanks was very upset when he lost his sergeant at the RADAR station. That was just how it looked and felt to me. I kept thinking, "Did I do something wrong? What could I have done to save him? Why did he do that? Should I have gone instead of him?"

All those thoughts flashed through my mind in a second.

It was just Hutch's luck that he'd stayed behind. War is nothing but knowing what you're doing, and luck.

Casualties come fast and furious in the infantry. I think our style of training was different from the Americans. They ran sort of a sausage machine —they cranked everybody in and cranked them out. We had the regimental system, with regimental pride, and we had a very positive attitude towards the war. The Americans had a tendency to figure they were going to get killed. Our attitude was, no matter how bad it is, somebody always comes back off that battlefield. And that person is going to be me. Wounding and death just isn't in your mind. It's not going to happen to you.

Just before he was killed in the bombing of Bristol, my father said, "You know, Charles, somebody, somewhere, flips a page every day and if your name is on that page, you are gone." Dad was killed in the bombing of Bristol in 1942. In those days the trains went right into the station. He was arriving on the train at Bristol to visit my grandparents and the Germans bombed the station. That's the only way the Germans could have killed that tough old codger. If he'd been one-on-one in a battle, they'd never have killed my dad.

I had that fatalistic attitude and wasn't the least bit worried that I was going to make it home. When I was a kid, the First World War guys used to jokingly say, "The thing about war is you never worry about the bullet with your name on it; it's the two hundred and fifty thousand with 'To Whom It May Concern' that will scare you."

I was wounded midnight the 10th of July. We were doing an attack on two commercial smoke stacks, which the Germans were using as observation points for their gunners. We'd been trying for about three weeks when command decided to get the Divisional Engineers to just blow the suckers up. I did the patrols for three days before they went in. Unbeknownst to us, the Germans had withdrawn the Wehrmacht Division who were in the area and put in 21st Panzers, which was like walking through a wheat field and coming slap-bang into a brick wall.

The whole thing was a disaster and they never did blow up the tower. Our battalion had about 750 men at the Start Line, and when we formed up the day after the attack there were nine officer casualties and 234 men, and we were down to something like 400 in all ranks. Across the Start Line, we probably went across at about 750. A bad day, a bad night.

But I missed much of this, because I stepped on an S mine, a shrapnel mine. A shrapnel mine had three little prongs sticking up and if you pushed those down by stepping on them, these things shot up into the air and then exploded. They'd blow a hundred and fifty to two hundred pieces of shrapnel—nuts, bolts, whatever they threw into the suckers. You never know where it's going to go. I heard a sort of a pop when I stepped on it and thought, "Oh, oh—."

In battle, your ears become very sensitive to anything that's different. After hearing this pop, I dove down into a ditch. I didn't think I was hit at first. My batman walked into it and was very, very badly wounded. In battle, you can't stop. So I went over and picked him up to put him where the stretcher-bearers could catch him. Then I fell flat on my face and it dawned on me that I'd been wounded, too. So a day or two later I was back to England.

———

I was out about a month. That was the beginning of using penicillin and we were young and healthy; we healed quickly. Also, if you got any shrapnel or bullets in muscles, they wouldn't take it out. They'd do more damage trying to remove it, so they'd just leave the stuff there. I still have twenty-three fragments in my shoulder.

Doreen and I had gone to high school together, and I'd kind of proposed back at Borden before I signed up with CANLOAN. When I was wounded in Normandy, I'd been at the Canadian General Hospital in Colchester for about three days. The nurse came in and said, "There's a young lady here to see you."

I said, "What?"

In those days the officers' wards were just like a barrack with the beds all lined up, and all the guys were saying, "Bring in Charles's talent and let's have a look at her."

Doreen was a very attractive gal. She walked in and I said, "What in the hell are you doing here?"

She said, "If you're over here, I'm going to be over here to make sure that no English woman steps on my trapline," or words to that effect. So when I was able to get myself up on crutches, the padre married us.

I was having trouble getting back into the reinforcement stream and back to the Gordons. They were my blooded regiment and they were my love. At the London District Assembly Centre there was a sign saying any officers wishing to volunteer for a parachute course, see the adjutant. That afternoon I was on a train to a parachute course and from there I was posted to 1st Parachute Battalion in the 1st Airborne Division in early September.

It was only a week or two after I joined them that we parachuted into Arnhem with Operation Market Garden. This is hindsight, which is always 20–20, but the planning people chose DZs [drop zones] west of Oosterbeek, about twenty-three clicks from Arnhem, where we actually had to go. It was a beautiful, sunny day, the 24th of September, people were going to church and coming out to our DZs, and then suddenly everything came to life. We were only supposed to be there about four or five days and ended being there almost nine and a half. It just wasn't a good scene.

The basic planning of any battle plan is that your start line must be secure. The closer your DZ or LZ [landing zone] is to the objective, the more effective it is. We had this long distance to travel to get to our objective and it took us a hell of a long time. Plus, unbeknownst to us, we landed right on top of an area that the Germans were using to re-tank and re-equip their Panzers. These were guys who'd seen a lot of battle and weren't going to be taken prisoner; they'd fight their way out. We didn't know that until long after, but there were Germans everywhere. But our aim was to get down to the key bridge at Arnhem.

We were to hold the north end of the town in case the Germans counter-attacked, but ended up just scratching and digging and hiding. We were trying not to get captured and trying to move offensively. On top of all this chaos, our wireless equipment didn't work.

It was about the fifth day. We were on the outskirts of Oosterbeek, moving along the backs of the houses on the main road. You never move along the streets in a village or town; that's your killing zone, that's where you get dead. We were going up the back yards and over the fences and all this stuff you did when you were kids playing cowboys and Indians. And believe me, we were playing cowboys and Indians in that place.

This Dutch farmer stopped me and asked, "How are things going?"

"I wish to hell I knew," I said. "My radio is no good, so I threw it away to carry more ammunition."

"Would you like to speak to your headquarters?"

Puzzled, I said, "I'd love to."

"Then why don't you come into my house and use the telephone."

"Do you mean to say the telephones are working with all this chaos?"

"Oh, yes."

The next thing I knew I was talking to command.

"Where in the hell are you, Charles?"

I put my hand over the phone.

"What's the address here?" The farmer gave me the address, which I relayed.

"Are all the telephones working?"

I asked the farmer, and he said, "Yes."

"Yes, they're all working," I reported.

"Okay, everywhere you go, give us a call."

By this time I was down to about five men left in my platoon and I picked up about six engineers. We picked up any kind of weapons and ammunition we could and finally made it to the bridge. By that time there was chaos and things were not good. Thirty-eight sections were lost through lack of proper communication and everybody got scattered. But we knew where we had to go and what we had to do. We knew how to fight in the field, but all we were doing was holding the bridge.

We were only supposed to hold it for three days, but we held it for nine. We were being shelled and mortared and had a lot of casualties. Looking back, I can't figure out how those of us who got out did get out. We did everything we could, but the people who were supposed to get to us didn't, and that's all you can say.

I had a phobia. I was never going to be captured. We were told we could give up if we wanted. It would be with honour and not a disgrace if we were taken prisoner. However, if we wanted to try to escape, the only way out was to swim the river. So I was down to my gotchees in nothing flat. I took my camouflage jacket and made a bit of a Mae West. My batman had been wounded in the left shoulder, so he hung onto my back with his right arm and the two of us went into the water.

We floated downstream for what seemed like forever and were picked up by the Poles about nine kilometres away. It was scary. I was very tired and the water was colder than you can imagine because it was almost the end of September. When I finally got my feet on the ground, I could hear this funny language, and I stuck my head in the water and I shook it and I figured, "Gee, that's not German," so I yelled out, "Englishman, Englishman." I didn't want to say Canadian, because I was with a British unit.

They shouted back, "Polskie, Polskie," which was the first time in my life I ever wanted to kiss a Pole. They were great guys and fabulous soldiers. They looked after my soldier who was wounded, and gave us a good belt of rum, which we needed. In those days, they didn't have big words like hypothermia. You were just cold and wet and if you had a good belt of rum and a cup of coffee or tea, you just got on with it.

I used their phone and within twenty-four hours got myself back with the Gordons who were stationed only about twenty kilometres away. After running through the back fields of Oosterbeek and Arnhem, now our objective was to get across the canal to clear all the Germans and we did six canal crossings in about nine days.

The Gordons crossed in assault boats, which were nothing more than a wooden frame with canvas stretched over and a board in the bottom. We were getting ready to cross one of the canals and a shell landed in an area where these boats were laid out. All of a sudden there was a heavy explosion and my hand went up in front of my face and my gloves flew off. At first I thought it was my hand being blown off in front of me, then I looked and saw it was still there. I had a deep cut, but didn't think anything of it. I covered it with a shell dressing and made it across the canal, but two of my Jocks were killed and six were wounded on that trip.

The next day my hand was starting to swell, so I went back to CCS [casualty clearing station] and they pumped me full of penicillin for about four or five days, sewed it up, and I went back into the line.

Not long after, a message came that Doreen had been killed. She shared a flat in St. John's Wood with a girlfriend who'd gone out for dinner one night. Doreen had decided not to go with her, but to stay home and write me a letter instead. That night the house was hit by a V-2.

I was shaken, but there was always so much going on that you didn't

Charles Scot-Brown (extreme left) with members of the 1st British Para-Battalion in September 1944.

have much time to think or to feel. As soon as I got back from Doreen's funeral, my CO sent for me.

"Charles, I want you to take out a fighting patrol and see if you can grab a couple of Germans for us."

I took a patrol out that night and we brought back two Germans. I figured that wasn't too bad: two for one. I was angry; I kept asking myself, "Why her? Why her?" But it was her time, it wasn't mine. I guess that's the only way you can look at it.

———

Several weeks later, we were on the German side. The Germans used a lot of Nebelwerfers in there—Moaning Minnies. The first thing you do in that kind of attack is to hit the ground and try to get to someplace where the blast can't get right at you. The old saying in the infantry was, "Down, crawl, observe and re-fire." I guess I was getting old and tired by that time—I was twenty-one—and was a bit slow hitting the ground. My Balmoral flew off and all of a sudden my whole face was covered with blood.

The Nebelwerfer rockets were a big long spherical shell about four or five feet in length, maybe a bit longer. When they exploded, they peeled like a banana. They were very heavy on the blast, but fortunately didn't have any shrapnel. If they'd shrapnelled, they would have been a very nasty piece of work. As soon as you heard their whine, you hit the ground. And once you'd heard the first one, you knew the other five shells would be landing pretty much in the same spot. If it wasn't in your area, you didn't worry.

This one was in our area, I guess. I had a habit, which I still have when I play golf. I stuck my head up and as the blast came it blew my Balmoral off and sort of peeled my scalp back. My batman pulled the flap of my scalp back down and wrapped a shell dressing around it. I went back to the RAP [regimental aid post] and our MO [medical officer], George Brown, stitched me up and off I went to the CCS. The next day the RAP and battalion headquarters had a direct hit from an 88, and George was killed. George was a fabulous character. He'd been with us all the way through; such a wonderful guy. That was a real shock for us.

But I found in battle, you never really did become that close to anyone. Lots of acquaintances, but in the infantry, as officers you have very, very few close friends because your brother officers are changing every thirty days. You intentionally never become close friends. But the whole battalion really felt it when we lost George.

———

In early April 1945, we were on our way up through Hannover and stopped in a little place called Belsen, which was the first time we had ever seen a concentration camp. Up until that time we knew nothing about them. We'd heard rumours, but no concrete information.

We were shocked; in fact, we couldn't really believe it. It was that horrible. Fifteen to twenty thousand mobile skeletons, and thousands more not moving at all. The smell was horrifying. Our doctors immediately called up every field ambulance to come to the area. Your instinct, when you see someone like that, is to feed them. We were warned not to give them anything, not water, tea, candy or even a cigarette. In no uncertain terms we were told that if we fed them, we would kill them, because they were in such a weakened condition.

Field ambulances arrived and they started them on intravenous to bring as many of them back as possible. What happened after that, I don't know, because we had to move through. Right behind us were the Polish Armoured Division and when they reached Belsen, they were livid. I think that's the only time they stopped and it was because a lot of the females in Belsen were Polish girls. It was not a good time to be caught wearing a field grey German uniform after those guys saw what was going on there.

The people in charge of the concentration camps weren't the front line fighting soldiers. They were the Gestapo, the police, and the SS.

The German regulars were similar to us. The guys we fought, the guys in the front line, were well trained. They knew their business, were expert at sighting weapons, and boy, they didn't make many mistakes. The one thing they forgot was that we would not take the line of least resistance in a battle.

Sometimes we would flank, sometimes we'd go right through a forest or a swamp, because we figured the harder you worked, the fewer casualties there would be. If you took the easy way, that's where your enemy's fire was probably going to be. So you'd go where he couldn't hit you and you could get close enough to knock him off before he nailed you.

We used to say that the further back from the line you get, the braver you get. And in the front line you don't take any chances, you do everything you're supposed to. But the further back you got, the greater and tougher and meaner the soldiers got, whether they were on our side or the Germans. You'd go back to a leave centre area and the first thing your frontline soldiers wanted was to get a bath and get clean. But these guys that were driving trucks from the supply depot would be walking around and you'd swear to God they were the toughest guys in the world. Unkempt, sometimes with battle dress jackets open, their caps on the back of their head.

A Canadian officer looks at concentration camps victims after liberation, Germany, 1945.

Whereas you seldom saw a Canadian or British combat soldier who wasn't shaven. The fighting soldier's greatest thrill was a bath and being able to sit down in peace and quiet with a nice hot meal. The simple things were what you wanted.

The person that's been in a war doesn't want to re-hash it. You've cleared it out of your mind. I think all of us wanted to get back home and get on with the peace. "Just let it go," was the general attitude.

———

The young people today know nothing about their own country. They can tell you who the rock stars are, but they can't tell you who developed this country, who explored this country, who fought for this country. We have to get the young people to learn about their country and walk proud. They take Canada, a wealthy country, for granted. They don't realize the cost in manpower, in work, in desire, in keenness, in inventiveness, in cunningness and stealth that it took to develop this country.

The Dutch do it. Their children are taught how their town, their village, their house, and their country was liberated. These are the things that should be taught in the schools. How can you walk down the street unless you know what happened on that street to make that street what it is today?

I think in smaller communities there's more awareness of what happened in their towns. They know their great-grandfathers went to World War I and their grandfathers went to World War II. But when you get into the large cities, people seem to know absolutely nothing about it and this is where you've got to do it, in the cities, because this is where the new Canadians are.

We've got to make young people realize what it cost to provide the privileges that they take for granted and what it cost the people who gave it to them.

George Borgal

BIRTH PLACE: PLEASANT HARBOUR, NOVA SCOTIA
RESIDENCE: HALIFAX, NOVA SCOTIA
SHIPS: HMCS *BRAS D'OR*, HMCS *SAGUENAY*, HMCS
KOOTENAY, HMCS *CAPE BRETON*
THEATRE OF WAR: ATLANTIC, ARCTIC, NW EUROPE
DECORATIONS: CD

MY NAME IS GEORGE GORDON BORGAL. I WAS BORN IN PLEASANT Harbour, Halifax County, on the 4th of January, 1921. My dad was an inshore fisherman during the summer, and also worked in the Tangiers gold mines and in the woods, cutting wood and pulp in the winter.

Dad was a nice guy. Very little to say, very quiet; Mom ruled the house. She was a very nice person as well, but kept us in line. I had two brothers—one older and one younger—plus a younger sister. My older brother and I competed a lot in school. As a matter of fact, at one time we had one teacher in the school. It was a country school, with one teacher for primary to grade twelve, and she kept us in line by giving us work to do. Usually it took a school year to do a grade, although we did grade five and six in one year. So my brother and I would compete by racing to finish our assignments first.

After grade seven, our family moved into Halifax. It was entirely different. One teacher we had then was English and spoke with a strong accent. This we weren't used to, and I used to miss a lot of the stuff she was saying. I found it very difficult, but ended up going back to the country when my grandmother got sick for a time, then back to Halifax.

You were taught by watching your father and uncles and so forth: repairing boats and engines. My brothers and I would watch them during the winter, taking apart an engine that wasn't working, and see them getting it ready for spring, doing the maintenance on it. They had an old engine that wasn't used, so we used to take it apart and put it back together. In those days, you didn't have any toys; you made your own toys and fun. It was all part of learning.

I ended up going to Joseph Howe School here in Halifax, which was fifty percent black and fifty percent white at that time. We had our little squabbles, but nothing like you see today. One of my best friends was black. We used to play hockey and that sort of thing. His father was on the railroad, and they were doing better than a lot of us.

The school was an old wooden thing. I remember our other teacher without the accent asked us to write a story about what we'd done in the summer, and I wasn't a writer, but I thought about how I used to take apart and rebuild engines, so I wrote about that.

When it came time for her to put marks to the papers, she called out the names, and went from A right through to Z. But when she went through the Bs, my name wasn't called. Then at the end, she said, "Now this one." And she came down to my desk, and said, "What book did you copy this out of?"

So I told her what me and my brother used to do. She listened to this, very quiet, then said, "My advice to you is, when you grow up, become an engineer." I didn't, but living in the country like that, you made your own toys.

During the Depression, times were pretty lean, but we didn't suffer any; we got three squares a day. I left school about grade ten, just to help out with the family. A friend of mine had a job delivering groceries, and when he gave up that job, I got his old bike—paid him so much a week—and took over his old job delivering. The fellow I worked for would take telephone orders, like, "Send me over a bag of potatoes." And he'd say, "Fine," then send me over to another store to buy a bag of potatoes and I'd deliver it to the people who'd called.

I used to get home about two A.M. Sunday morning after Saturday's deliveries. My pay was six dollars a week. I left that job after awhile and took over my friend's job delivering—he'd got another job—and that store provided the bicycle, and I got seven dollars a week. The hours were a little better, but not much.

That was 1939. Both me and my friend had joined the naval reserve in 1938. No particular reason. We could get work in the summer for two weeks with them. I was too young at first, so they made me a boy bugler and my pay with them was fifty cents a day. That's the first year. We had a card to go to the canteen and buy stuff. They had a dog as a pet there at the base, and he liked ice cream. We spent a lot of money going to the canteen and buying him his ice cream. When it came time for me to pay my canteen bill, I had a bigger bill than I had money coming to me. The CO gave me a good speech, gave me some good advice. Told me I should save ten percent of my salary for old age; and I should give ten percent to my church; and so forth. When I figured out all my contributions out of my fifty cents, there wasn't much left!

While I was in training, I was supposed to learn to blow this bugle that they gave me. It was a pretty cruddy thing, all green and such. I had to clean it up and then try and play it up in the dormitory. The other fellows there didn't like that much. So there was a dobie house—that's a little spot where you go to wash your clothes—it was down on number five jetty. I'd go down there and try to get some sound out of it, but I didn't know what I was doing. The guys on the ship over on the dock used to yell at me because they didn't much like what I was doing.

It ended up that I finished that training without ever learning to blow the bugle. But they gave me a badge that I put on the sleeve of my uniform saying I was a bugler. The following year I was old enough to become an ordinary seaman, so I went in for gunnery training.

To a point, I was aware of what was going on over in Europe, but I didn't pay that much attention to it. During my first year as a seaman, in 1939, I became what they called a seaman gunner, part of the guns crew on a destroyer. It was a very sharp noise firing it, but they didn't give us earplugs, so we used to use cotton batting. They told us to keep our mouths open and the concussion would somehow balance out. But that didn't really work, and I now have only thirty-five percent hearing in each ear.

My family had no objection to my joining up, although they had no military background themselves. In those days, with so little work around, if you could get in the navy on a regular basis, it was good. Being on the reserves, if they needed somebody they could transfer you up and make you permanent, which is what happened to me in May 1940.

On September 3rd, 1939, I was home—it was Sunday afternoon—and I heard on the radio that Great Britain had declared war. About a half-hour later, the phone rang and it was the chief at the naval reserve base. And he said, "You report in tomorrow morning, fully booted and spurred."

So I reported in on Labour Day. I reported on Monday morning, and was told to take my hammock up to the dormitory and find myself a spot. The next morning, Tuesday, I started my first job, which was as a sentry on the convoy room. That's where the merchant ship skippers used to get together and the navy guys would explain to them what the routine was on a convoy. It used to be quite amusing for the old merchant captains to come along and see this young fellow standing guard with a rifle and an eighteen-inch bayonet. One of them said, joking, "You point that thing at me, and I'll stick it up your so-and-so." So I took my rifle and pointed it at him, as if to say, "Try me." But they all just laughed.

Finally, after asking over and over, I got myself on a ship. It was the *Bras d'Or*. She was a minesweeper. The *Bras d'Or* was a converted lightship about the size of a fishing trawler. A lot of trawlers were converted to mine sweeping, because sweeping fish and sweeping mines are quite similar. It had gear out on either side with cutters that ran under the surface of the water and would cut the mines loose. It had a crew of about thirty-five.

Being raised in a fishing village, you learn to handle and steer boats. So being on a boat was pretty natural to me. We got along fine as a crew. If you got into a fight onboard, the coxswain would get a pair of boxing gloves for each, then you'd go up on the quarterdeck, with the crew around the two who were fighting, and they'd do three two-minute rounds. Or first blood. Then it was stopped. At the end, they had to shake hands or they weren't men. Get the drift? Then they'd be friends after that. You were like a family on a ship; you helped one another. If you wanted a hand, you got help.

At the beginning of the war, anything that floated was bought for the navy. The *Bras d'Or* was an old thing; they got it out of some old shipyard, and it was unseaworthy. The captain had no faith in her whatsoever; none of us did.

One day, I was on the wheel, as a special job, entering and leaving the harbour, and the cook missed ship. When I got relieved on the wheel, the captain said, "You do the cooking."

"I don't know anything about cooking."

"Well, what in the devil's wrong with you? Haven't you ever seen your mother cooking?"

"Yessir."

"Well, go do what she does."

I went down, got a whole bunch of eggs, boiled them up, and that was breakfast. Then I went into the icebox and saw this big chunk of meat. I'd seen my mother put such a thing in the oven, so I put it in a pan, put a little water in it, put it in the oven. Got some potatoes and carrots, tossed them in. And we had a roast for dinner; I cut it up for them, and everyone was pretty pleased. I got cleaned up, and we eventually came back into port. There was the cook, waiting for us. The gang on the boat, just skylarking, were shouting to him, "Get outta here. George is a better cook than you! Away you go!" It wasn't so at all, of course. And I discovered afterwards that I'd used up four days worth of meat rations in that one meal.

Our runs were usually only for a day, and we'd be back in harbour at night. And we'd take turns going out at night to do patrols as well.

This went on 'til about May 1940, when I got word that I would be accepted in the permanent force. The captain told me that he'd recommend that I leave then and transfer to a destroyer, and I agreed. It's what I wanted to do. So I transferred to the destroyer *Saguenay* and went off to a gunnery course. She had a sister ship, the *Skeena*; these were ships built specially for the Canadian navy, with reinforced bows to handle small ice.

On my first trip overseas on the *Saguenay*, we came across two lifeboats from a Norwegian merchant ship that had been torpedoed, so we took them on board. They'd been out three days, but were in pretty good shape. One guy told me, "We weren't too concerned. We had our sail up; we'd have made it in a week or so."

We took them in to Greenock, Scotland, and then I was in the war.

As part of the gunnery crew, we didn't have any headgear or protection. We were given hoods for flash protection, but we never wore them. When an action alarm sounded, you went to your gun, to where you were supposed to be.

You weren't allowed to shower at sea because there wasn't enough water. But we used to have what we called a birdbath. You fill a sink with water, and more or less sponge yourself down all over. In a way, you were cleaning your bird: that's where the name came from!

This one day, I was having a birdbath and an alarm went. Wherever you went on the ship, you had your lifejacket and gear with you. Problem was, I was covered with soap. I grabbed my kit and away I went to the gun. We were travelling at high speed, and the salt water was spraying back over me. Boy, was it itchy getting it all over you.

From that point on, we were on convoy duty. An escort group would bring the merchantmen across, and we'd come out to meet them, then bring them into harbour in Scotland. This was what we were doing, out of Greenock, then Londonderry later on, and Scapa Flow. Normally about every three convoys, you'd get three or four days in port. Depending on what they required of you.

The routine was just something that you did; it was what it was. No different than if you'd been a carpenter. We didn't think about it much.

OPPOSITE: HMCS *Saguenay* picking up survivors from torpedoed Norwegian merchant ships, October 1940.

We were torpedoed on December 1st, 1940. We were about four, five hundred miles sou'west of Ireland. We'd left the convoy because one of the merchant ships was straggling behind, and we went back to hurry her up. We always were a little bit suspicious of certain ships travelling in the convoy that came from "neutral" countries, maybe being a little in favour of the Germans. I'm not saying it was true in this case, but it could happen.

It was just before four in the morning. When we approached this merchant ship, a submarine fired three torpedoes at us. One went ahead, one went under the bridge, and the other one hit behind the bow. I was standing on a bench on this open bridge at the time, leaning against the

Burial at sea on HMCS *Saguenay*, December 1940, following a torpedo attack.

metal, when we were hit. The explosion lifted the bow up and I went flying. In those days, you didn't have protective gear to wear. All I had on was a greatcoat and an oilskin over that to keep me warm. I landed on top of a couple of officers over by the ASDIC [Allied Submarine Detection Investigation Committee] hut. My left leg was numb when I got up, and I felt the ship start to roll, back and forth, and I thought she was going to go.

I threw off my binoculars, unbuttoned my coat to blow up my Mae West, and let my coat slide off my shoulders to get at it. But when I did that, I couldn't get my arms out of the sleeves. I was handcuffed in that position. Wow, that was a feeling, I'll tell you.

The gunnery officer got himself to his feet and he helped me out of it. I went to the side of the bridge and saw that she had settled up a bit. You were always told that the best lifeboat is the ship you're on.

We'd been doing our four-on, four-off shifts. You didn't get much rest when you were on convoy duty. The fellow who was supposed to relieve me hadn't shown, so I asked another guy who was being relieved to go below decks to find this so-and-so and tell him to get up here.

He later told me that he had gone down through the canvas blackout dodger when the torpedo hit. And of course, the flash from the torpedo goes through the passageways. He had a beard, and his beard just disappeared. His face and lips were pretty badly burnt. If I'd had been relieved on time, I would have been down there with him and been burnt as well, or worse.

Our mast was broken and a fire broke out and our bow was gone. Even with all the damage, the captain maintained twelve knots. The submarine surfaced and started coming towards us; B gun, forward of the bridge, opened fire on the sub. I remember looking through my binoculars and seeing the shell hit just before the conning tower. The next shot went over the sub, then it crash-dived and took off.

I heard after the war that it was an Italian sub, not German, and that they'd fired their last three torpedoes at us. If they'd had another, they would have fired it at us and we would have been done.

The convoy had seen the fire and sent a ship back. Flames drove us off the bridge to a secondary steering position. The captain had turned the ship around, so now we were travelling astern to the wind. The XO [executive officer] came along and told me to relieve the X gun aft, on the quarterdeck.

The HMS *Highlander* arrived, and we were to leave only a skeleton crew on the *Saguenay*. Everyone else was being transferred over by whaler. I wanted to stay with the *Saguenay*. Some of the men were married and I figured they should get off first. But they were moving people by watch, so I eventually had to go over to the *Highlander*.

When I arrived, they were serving tots. The guy serving said to me, "Are you a grog?"

"No, I'm a U.A."

Which meant under age. The guy behind me punched me in the back and said, "You could've taken the tot and passed it along!"

They got the fire out on the *Saguenay*, and she was cruising back to Greenock stern first. There were twenty-one men killed in that attack. One of the men who was killed was my friend from back in Nova Scotia who'd helped me get that job delivering groceries a few years before: Harvey Hare.

The tug came out and met us. But the captain took her in all the way. The *Saguenay* went in to Furness to be refitted, and the *Highlander* took us into Liverpool.

When we were offloaded onto the jetty, the army fellows came up and marched us off to a train, like prisoners of war, escorted the whole way. Some of us didn't even have proper clothing; some were in sock feet. They were keeping an eye on us and keeping us together. All for security. They couldn't be certain who we were or what we knew.

They put us on the train and locked us in and off we went to the south of England. The train stopped briefly in Crewe, right opposite a pub. Some of the guys were saying, "What we wouldn't do for a beer."

Somebody found one window open, so we gave this one guy all the money we had and squeezed him out the window.

"You go get us some and pass it back to us through the window." He was in his sock feet, too. But off he goes.

A few minutes went by, and the train starts to pull out. This guy comes running out, still in his sock feet, carrying all this beer, dropping bottles as he ran. He never did catch up with us till the next day at HMS *Drake* in Devonport.

After that, you get what's known as "survivor's leave." We didn't know where to go; Scotland was all we knew, so that's where we went, a couple of guys and me. Glasgow. One of the guys was a MacIntosh and wanted to look up his relatives, so we decided to help him. We were staying at the Sally Ann, and weren't making much headway finding his people, so for one reason or another—maybe he'd got a name or something—we ended up staying in a place called Motherwell, just outside of Glasgow.

We didn't know where to start looking there, so we went to the police station to see if they could do anything for us. We didn't make much headway there either, but the chief of police made friends with us. He was awfully good to us. It turned out he'd just lost his son in the air force and he sort of latched on to us.

He was very good to us. We'd go to the station, shoot pool, have a cup of tea. No sooner would you step off the bus than a police car would pull up and take you to the station. He took us to Edinburgh, Holyrood House—all these places—by car. We'd get back into town just as a restaurant was closing, and he'd talk them into keeping it open for us. The staff would be held back, just for us. The police chief would say to the owner, "I don't suppose you'd have any scotch, would you?" Scotch was taboo then, it was all being exported.

"I think I might be able to find a bottle," the owner would say. And a bottle would appear and everyone would sit down with us and have a drink.

Whenever we'd come into port after that, I'd make a special trip out to Motherwell to see him. I'd bring silk stockings to his housekeeper, tobacco to her husband, and chocolates to him. Whenever I had the chance. He's passed on now. But after the war, his one ambition was to come to Canada and hitchhike across the country. But he didn't make it.

———

After we finished that survivor's leave, they added Christmas leave to it and we got back to Devonport between Christmas and New Year's in 1940. We worked on work gangs for several months while our ship was being worked on. Our job was filling in bomb craters with pick and shovel. There were sixty of us under a Scots chief. We laid gas pipes, we built roads. It was all fine; just something else to do. That's the way it was: you kept busy and you were happy.

During this time waiting for the *Saguenay* to be repaired, I picked up a newspaper from Halifax. I was glancing over it and there on the front page, eight lines down, was the headline, "*Bras d'Or* lost with all hands." She was sunk up the St. Lawrence while escorting a ship down to

George Borgal (left) and his best friend and future best man, Murray MacDonald, with police chief George Lamont's housekeeper, Billy Dermit, and her husband, Joe Dermit, in Motherwell, Scotland, outside Glasgow.

Sydney. She just disappeared. Nobody knew what happened to her. She was unseaworthy, she was old, she was something that should never have been put in the position she was in. But that didn't make it any easier to read about. I think she'd gone missing the next trip after I'd left her.

———

I took a gunnery course during that five-month break, and by May, the ship was recommissioned and we went back. We did our trials, and headed back north.

When the *Bismarck* sank the *Hood* (May 24th, 1941), we were sent out with the home fleet to chase her. At speed, we could do upwards of thirty-five, thirty-seven knots. But we didn't have the capacity for distance at high speed. We weren't involved in any action with the *Bismarck*, but we went over the area where the *Hood* had been sunk, through the oil that was lying there on the water. I remember we were doing about twenty-six knots then, and the spray coming back and hitting us with this residue from the ship.

After that, we went back on convoy duty. We were on the Iceland route, to Newfoundland. I remember it was on January 4th, 1942, my birthday, four in the morning, we sailed from Reykjavik. The water was flat calm, like oil. Completely still. I was always told by the fishermen in a fishing village that, "if you see the water like that, then look out: something's coming."

That night the storm hit. We spent a week in a hurricane. The convoy dispersed. There was a Norwegian whaling factory ship who stood by us. The wind was 135 knots. The seas were seventy-five feet. We were pounded. The cooks couldn't cook after a while; salt water got into our fresh water supply. As best I can remember, for two or three days we didn't have water.

The four magazine cordite cases had their racks broken, and they were tumbling around down loose in the magazine. We'd go into the sea bow down, then we'd come up and the wind would catch us and wrench us around and slam us back down into the sea. When the bow would go down, you'd look aft and see the stern up in the air, vibrating, like a diving board. We'd taken on about one to two feet of water in the wardroom, the officers' quarters, and the captain's quarters.

One time she hit so hard, she stove in her bottom and we took on water there, too. We rigged a pump to pump her out, but then that clogged, so we had to do a bucket brigade to keep the water moving out. The stanchions were three, four inches around, and they were all bent. We lashed down as many of the cordite cases as possible.

It was even too rough to be comfortable in a hammock. (Hammocks were wonderfully comfortable.) To me, for that length of time, it was even worse than being torpedoed. It took the captain's launch, snapped it in half, so it was just two pieces of wood hanging off the keel, and hit the whaler aft taking both whaler and davits. It split the whaler on the other side of the ship down the middle.

We finally got into Newfoundland, and went alongside of our sister ship, the *Skeena*. We pulled up to the jetty, and were all dying to get to this water pipe they had there on the jetty. We wanted to rinse out our mouths with fresh water and to get a drink of it into us. But we were told not to drink anything but small amounts until our bodies got used to it. The *Skeena*'s crew came onboard and helped us clean up.

I remember seeing our captain coming down off the bridge; he hadn't slept for most of that week. He looked a wreck, his clothes all sodden and stretched, his face pale and drawn. He disappeared into the *Skeena*'s captain's quarters and we didn't see him for more than twenty-four hours while he got a much-deserved rest.

As soon as we were able, we slipped St. John's and came back to Halifax. It took about three months for a refit, and then we went back on convoy duty, escorting one of the *Lady* boats, *Lady Rodney*, I think, to St. John's and then to rejoin our Escort Group. En route, a convoy passed ahead of us when we gained ASDIC contact on a possible submarine. In the morning watch, with the convoy proceeding to the St. Lawrence, a straggler, the *Azra*, cut thirty-five feet off our stern which included propellers and depth charges on the quaterdeck. The depth charges were armed for use if the submarine was detected, and exploded as the stern sank and as the freighter was backing off. Her bottom was blown out and she sank slowly bow first in about three hours. She lost her first mate who had gone below to check damage and became trapped. *Saguenay* also lost an engineering officer who was taking passage and who was in one of the officer's cabins when the collision occurred. We picked up *Azra*'s survivors using one of our whalers. The seas were running right up on *Saguenay*'s decks, so we had to pump out fuel to keep the ship up. We were towed back to St. John's and I went to Sydney on a minesweeper with sixty of the survivors.

The *Saguenay* was then taken to Cornwallis and used as a training ship, which ended my career on her. We used to call that ship "The Lady that refused to sink."

I finished my leave, and when I came back, they told me I was drafted to a corvette. I told them I had to get my kit, and this guy behind the desk said, "Don't you know where your kit is?!"

"I can tell you if you come out from behind that desk," I told him. "The last time I saw it was off the coast of Cape Race."

I was a leading seaman at that time and didn't really want the duty on a corvette. Through the master-at-arms who I knew from *Saguenay* when it was torpedoed, I got word to the commander and I managed to get my draft changed. I went back over to England to join the crew of the *Kootenay*. She'd been drafted from the Far East, where she was before the war, and still had deck fittings that simply weren't going to work in convoy duty up north. But there were too many of my rank onboard anyway, so I couldn't stay on that ship. When I was asked where I'd like to go next, I said, "New construction." I'd seen my fair share of old, refitted ships.

I went back to Quebec to wait for my new ship, a frigate that was being completed, the *Cape Breton*. These ships were designed primarily to remedy what were considered defects in the corvette design. The basic corvette hull was widened and lengthened, and was given twin screws. This resulted in a faster ship with twice the range, and much more seaworthy. A far better ship to sail on, and far more comfortable than a corvette.

Just before it was commissioned, there was a fire in the boiler room. The local fire department was called, but they wouldn't let the fire truck in at the gate because it didn't have a pass. The captain went up to the gate and jumped on the fire truck.

"Open the gate," he shouted to the guard. Then to the driver of the truck, he said, "Take her through. If the gate's not open, you take it with you."

And the gate was opened.

It wasn't a big fire; only delayed us a couple of weeks. We headed out. We went to Boston, got RADAR installed, and that's where I met my wife-to-be for the second time. Her family used to live in Halifax, but they'd moved a few years before. We kept in touch, and later on, after the war, we got married.

Back on convoys, we were doing runs up north to Murmansk. In 1944, during the invasion, we worked the Channel running U-boat patrols. There were some sub attacks and German patrol boats harassing the shore, but none of this involved us. Come June 6th we had been at sea since May 20th, cruising off the southwest coast of France. I was relaxing in our mess deck with a few shipmates, when suddenly the shrill whistle of the Bos'un's pipe was heard over the ship's PA system.

It was the captain, Lieutenant Commander M.C. McLaren. Without preamble, he said the following:

"This is the day and this is the hour. As I speak to you now, thousands of brave lads are preparing to storm the beaches of Normandy. Spare a few moments now for the brave boys, as today, for many of them, will mark the dawning of eternity. Indeed, we may well be among them before the sun sets on this momentous day in world history. However, we will place our trust in He who holds us all in the palm of His hand."

———

A few days later, we were on patrol in the Channel. We came across a landing craft returning from France and the engine had broken down. They'd managed to unload the soldiers from it and put an engineer on to try and get it going. But he couldn't. A storm was coming on and as it started blowing the landing craft started to break up. We happened to come along just in time and pulled alongside and pulled the crew off of it. We tried to tow it back, but it was taking on water. Finally it turned over, so we sank it with gunfire.

We got to know the guys from the landing craft a little bit on our way back to harbour, and they were thankful and all. We unloaded them and that was that.

In 1998, we had a reunion and it was advertised in England. One of the guys from the landing craft caught wind of this and said, "I wonder if that's the *Cape Breton* that rescued us?" So in due course, a letter was sent over and one of our fellows picked it up. Two of these fellows eventually came over to Canada for the reunion to thank the crew for saving their lives. I wasn't able to make it to that one, but I heard about all this.

One of these guys was so thankful that he invited us to his fiftieth wedding anniversary. And if we'd like to come, he said he'd send us the tickets. I thought, "Gee, that's a little much." But he was serious. So my wife and I and two other couples went over and spent two weeks there, and we couldn't pay for a single thing. Everywhere we went, he'd prearranged it that everything was taken care of. Because we'd saved his life fifty-five years before.

———

After the invasion was over, we went back to Halifax for a refit; I went off to Cornwallis for another gunnery course, and that's where I found myself when the war in Europe ended.

I was slated to head out to the Pacific, and even shipped out to the west coast. But I wasn't happy out there. The war in the Far East ended, and I wanted to get back east. So I managed to get myself drafted for an assignment back east in Halifax training seamen. And I started life with my new wife, already pregnant with our first child.

———

You grew up fast during the war. I was a boy when I went in, and was in the whole war. It didn't take too much bouncing around for you to mature. Getting bombed every night in England changes you. You got used to it, but it changed you. In terms of getting along with people, I never had much problem. Crews worked together. If you were a trouble-maker, you'd be the loser, and the rest of the crew would be sure about that.

I think it would be good for people to know what really happened, the good and the bad. And I think it's real important that the women who were left behind, looking after families, get recognized for what they did, too. I know of one case in the States where this woman had a pension; she was young, and her husband had passed away. She met another fellow, but if she'd married him, she'd have lost the pension. And if that hadn't worked out, she would have been without the pension. A lot of them were left with nothing.

Here's what I felt should have happened. Service people, serving over-seas in the front line, should get double pay. If they are killed in the line of duty, their wife carries on receiving the money he was earning. Also, their children would have their university paid for by the government. And that all profits made by companies selling materials towards the war efforts, that their profits should go towards paying for the war after it's finished.

I only wish that our government would take a stronger position in providing our armed forces with the proper up-to-date equipment. Not leave it as it is today. And not to leave it as we found it when we went to war in 1939.

You can fight bad weather with training and good equipment, if your ship is strong. But if it isn't...

John Stroud

BIRTH PLACE: CLARKSON, ONTARIO
RESIDENCE: TORONTO, ONTARIO
REGIMENT: TORONTO SCOTTISH REGIMENT,
ROYAL RIFLES OF CANADA
THEATRE OF WAR: HONG KONG

WHEN WAR BROKE OUT IN 1939, I WAS STILL IN SCHOOL. I ENLISTED in June 1940 because my friends were all joining up. I was overwhelmed with these guys looking so good in their uniforms, shaming us that we hadn't joined yet. I didn't know what I was getting myself into, but I didn't much care.

I enlisted with the Toronto Scottish and we were posted to Stanley Barracks at the CNE for a month or so, then to Valcartier north of Quebec City for training. The training was no nonsense with the Toronto Scottish. Route marches, trench fighting. I became a Vickers machine gunner. But I was getting restless in Quebec, so I volunteered for duty with the Royal Rifles. We got sent east to Newfoundland, and spent several months doing guard duty at Bay de Verde. Non-stop foghorns, non-stop fog; I decided I hadn't joined to sit beside the ocean listening to this noise twenty-four hours a day, so I volunteered for a section that was going into action. With all my spare time in Quebec and Newfoundland, I had never stopped taking courses. So with my machine gunner's ranking, first aid, and motor transport training, I had no trouble getting the okay to move. We found ourselves on a train going west; no idea where. One day we were issued shorts; the rumour was that we were going to Africa. We arrived in Vancouver, were put on a ship, and still thought we were going to Africa by the roundabout route, because a lot of ships were being torpedoed out of Halifax at that time.

On the ship on the way over, a sergeant found out about my machine gun training and invited me to join the Headquarters Company. He said they were getting Bren gun carriers, motorcycles, Vickers machine guns—all the stuff I wanted to do. And I wouldn't have to march! My company's CO offered me sergeant's stripes if I stayed, but I didn't care about rank: I just wanted to do what I wanted to do. So I went with the company to make sure I could get into the fight.

Until we arrived in Pearl Harbor in the summer of 1941, we didn't know we were going to Hong Kong. We landed there [in Hong Kong] November 17th, and it didn't take long for things to start to happen. British Intelligence was on the ball. We were moved out of our Hong Kong barracks two days before the Japanese bombed Pearl Harbor.

On December 8th, we were in our pillboxes when the Japanese came over at eight o'clock in the morning. Our equipment had been shipped separately on a tramp steamer, and everything had been abandoned on the docks in Manila when war broke out, so we had nothing much to fight back with. We heard the drones of aircraft engines and figured the British were sending in new planes. Somebody looked out the window and said, "Jesus Christ, what's that 'egg' on the side of the plane?" They were Japanese fighters, of course.

I opened up with a Bren gun that was in place, and the bloody pilot turned around and came at me, and machined gunned us. We heard the bombs dropping on our barracks and on the docks and oil refineries on the Kowloon side, across Gin Drinker's Bay. That's when we knew we were in for it. These Japanese had been fighting for two or three years in China, and were battle-hardened soldiers. And to make things worse, their code of honour was, "You shall not be taken prisoner of war, nor shall you take prisoners."

I was part of a "Hit" group: wherever there was trouble, we went. We were busy for the next seventeen days. On one patrol, we heard a rustle in the bushes—I had a Tommy gun and a few grenades—and one of the guys called out, "Who goes there?" The answer was in English: "Hi Joe!" We moved up and it was the Japanese, sneaking up on us. I opened up with my Tommy gun, got bayoneted in my foot, but we drove them back. The doctors had a look at me and said I'd better stay in the first aid station for a few days.

I didn't want to hang around there with so much happening, so I left. Two days later the Japanese overran the station: they killed all the orderlies, the patients, and the doctors. Then we started hearing about what was happening to the civilians in Kowloon: rape, murder, and looting.

Everything came on very sudden, and we weren't reinforced. The Japanese swept down from the Kowloon side, killing a lot of Brits. We sent a group of Canadians to reinforce their retreat, and were able to get back across the bay by the ferry service—the Star Line, still operating today—to Stanley Barracks in Hong Kong. One of the guys had killed a Japanese officer and found a perfect map of the island in his pocket: every pillbox, every defence. They knew everything about our positions. But we were young bucks: we felt, "the more, the merrier." We just wanted to get at them.

The British artillery stationed in Stanley Barracks opened up on the first Japanese landing and drove them back. But then the Japanese hit the island from about six different positions, and it was impossible to repel

Canadian prisoners of war at Shamshuipo camp in Hong Kong, 1943.

them. They finally made a landing at Lye Mun. A group of about a hundred guys from B Company were surrounded. The Japanese told them to come out with their hands up, and as each Canadian did, the Japanese bayoneted them. Killed them all. No prisoners. We found this out after Hong Kong had fallen and we were forced into a work party. We came across groups of Canadian and British soldiers, their hands tied behind their backs with barbed wire, tongues cut out, eyes gouged out, and bayoneted to death. By then we knew what to expect.

Christmas Eve. We'd had no water and no food for three days. We moved into Stanley Fort, where the British had substantial supplies, and gorged ourselves for the last time. Christmas Day we were told we had to make our last stand: the Japanese had us surrounded. I did not shake in my boots. I had joined the army to fight, and I was getting my fill of it. The Japanese had been shelling and mortaring us heavily all day, and we had lost quite a few men. By dark, we were out of ammunition. Word came

down that the governor of Hong Kong had surrendered, and we were ordered to lay down our arms.

I buried my Tommy gun, and so did some of the other guys. We weren't going to let the enemy get their hands on them. The Japanese marched us to our first P o W camp, at North Point. The camp was located beside a dump swarming with flies and mosquitoes. If that wasn't bad enough, the huts had holes in the roof from shelling, and the Japanese had kept their donkeys in them, so there was dung everywhere. I'd only been there a week when I got malaria, and a week later, dysentery. Other guys were afflicted as well.

There was a big road that ran past the camp. If a civilian was caught walking down it, the guards would call them over, then hit them over the head with a crowbar or a bat. We had to dump their bodies down in the bay. At night, there were screams in the streets from refugee girls dragged into the Japanese guardhouse and gang-raped, right across from our huts. You could hear the screams all night. Then they'd bayonet them and dump their bodies in the bay as well.

This was just the beginning of our lives as P o Ws. We were getting an idea of what we might be in for. But honestly, the only thing on our mind was food, because we were slowly starving to death.

We worked at the airport, widening the runway. The Japanese hadn't a clue how to make the cement for the tarmac, so they had us do it. We mixed it with too much sand, but it looked beautiful. More importantly to our captors, we completed it on schedule. A high-ranking general came in for the inaugural landing. All the Japanese—the engineers, the officers, the NCOs—came out to admire it. The plane came in, hit that sandy concrete and flipped over.

All hell broke loose. The general cursed everyone up and down, the officers beat the NCOs, and the NCOs beat the engineers. But they didn't touch us; didn't know we had anything to do with it. It's one of the fondest memories I have of being a P o W.

Working on the airstrip, we came in contact with a guard we called "the Kamloops Kid." This was a guy who had been born in Kamloops,

British Columbia, and his father had served with the New Westminster Regiment in Flanders in World War I and had been awarded the Military Medal.

The Kamloops Kid visited Japan prior to World War II to improve his Japanese, and the war broke out while he was there. He volunteered for the Japanese Imperial army as an interpreter, and when Hong Kong fell, asked to be transferred there. He was sadistic to Canadians in particular. He said, "At school in Kamloops, you Canadians, you called me 'The Little Pig'."

What the hell did that have to do with us? But he hunted down Canadians, especially anybody who might be from Kamloops; God help them if he found any. He was twenty-two, a tall, good-looking guy. He used to strut around the camp, a big long sword at his side, looking for trouble. He'd backhand you across the face as a matter of course, but as far as I know, I was the only one he used his sword on.

A couple of us were tossing a baseball around in the yard. The Kamloops Kid called to have it thrown to him, so I tossed it. He threw it back, and I did the same. He threw it back a little harder, and so I sent it back and put a little curve on it. It hit him in the face, and he went nuts and came after me with his sword. He jabbed me in the head, and because I'm a bleeder, I bled like a stuck pig. He thought he'd cut my eye out, and went away satisfied. But I'd only been caught above the ear.

He said, "That'll teach you, you smart bastard," as he walked away. He always called me "Smart Bastard."

"I don't care what you do to me," I said under my breath. "You're Number One on the hit list when the war is over."

There was an escape tunnel at North Point that ran right down to the bay. We didn't use the tunnel to try and escape, but we'd heard there was a cache of cigarettes and puddings hidden at the far end of it. We'd also heard there was a dead Chinaman who'd been killed in there that we'd have to crawl over to get to the stuff. Even if we'd tried to escape, we were on an island with no boat, and we couldn't very easily blend into a crowd. If we could have made it over to Kowloon and into the hills, there were the Chinese guerrillas who would have helped us. They'd helped several Chinese and British soldiers who'd made it.

We were going blind from the sun and lack of food. We worked twelve-hour days and malnutrition was setting in. In November, almost a year after we'd surrendered, we were moved to Shamshuipo, which had been our original barracks when we'd come to Hong Kong. Shamshuipo is where the sickness started really getting to us. I had a recurrence of malaria and developed dry beri beri from malnutrition. I had symptoms of "electric feet," which feels like needles being stuck in your legs. When the dysentery and malaria came back, my health really went down and I tested positive for diphtheria. They had no antibiotics for it; it comes out in your neck, which swells up, and you choke to death from it.

In the "Dip" Ward at Shamshuipo, I thought, "I'm a goner now." Fortunately, the Chinese underground smuggled medication in and I was lucky enough to get some. I heard some poor devils on the floor above us who weren't able to get any; it was too late for most of them anyway.

In early 1943, the first draft of prisoners was being shipped out of Hong Kong to P o W camps in Japan. My buddies who were on it came to say goodbye. I could hear them, but I couldn't make a sound or move a finger. I heard the orderlies saying I wouldn't live long, but that just bucked up my determination to make it through. I could also have sworn I saw the Lord, white light, beard and robes, looking down on me. I've had more lives than a cat, so I've always felt He must have been keeping an eye on me.

The first draft were mainly British, eighteen hundred of them. On their way to Japan, the ship was torpedoed by an American sub. When it was hit, they fought their way up from the hold, killed the Japanese on deck, and jumped in the water. The Japanese shot a lot of them in the water, and the current took a lot of them down, but about eight hundred got ashore in China. Most of them were rounded up later by the Japanese and moved to slave labour camps. I heard terrible stories about them after the war.

I went blind from malnutrition and diphtheria. As a result of the withholding of medical supplies, Hong Kong vets suffered the highest rate of blindness of World War II veterans. Doc Stewart of the Royal Rifles managed to get me some milk, a little egg and some vitamin shots, and little by little my eyesight came back. It took about twenty-one days. I was the only Hong Kong vet who got his eyesight back, as far as I know.

The doctor said I wasn't fit to go on the next draft of prisoners to Japan. I actually had a choice not to, because of the blindness, diphtheria, malnutrition, and malaria. I said to him, "It's Japan and they must be civilized there. Send me over." What a mistake. Once again, volunteering when I should have kept my big mouth shut.

The first one to see me getting onto the ship was the Kamloops Kid. He said, "You smart bastard. They'll teach you in Japan."

"I'm going to a civilized country, I hope. You've got the emperor there."

He just laughed, and said, "You'll see."

I said to him, again, "You're Number One on the hit parade when this war's over." At that point I didn't care a damn what he or anybody else did to me. After what I'd been through, what else could happen? I wasn't afraid of anything anymore. That was the last time I saw the Kamloops Kid.

On the way to Japan, we had five men die down in the hold. We had no food and not much water until we got to Japan after a fifteen-day trip.

There were five hundred of us when we arrived in Osaka. We were in rough shape, staggering and stumbling. We were marched through the streets to the train station, where we were each given a wooden box with fish and rice in it.

"Civilization!" I told myself. "We're going to do good in Japan. We're going to eat!" We were taken by train with the blinds down to Niigata, a northern city, where Camp 5B was located. We were moved to a temporary camp; 5B wasn't ready yet. That first night they served us red rice—all we could eat! I thought, "This is great! John, you made a good decision deciding to come."

That was the last time I ever had my stomach full in Japan.

We were there about a month, and then moved to our new camp. The huts were new, but it was already infested with vermin. We'd left the bedbugs in Hong Kong, but picked up lice in Niigata. It was winter and damned cold there—this was northern Japan, as cold as Canada. We were given a board to sleep on and one blanket. Without the buddy system, you couldn't survive. Two of you would lie together with the two blankets, and that, with the body heat and getting up and down at night to kill the lice, kept you going. Once a month, we were taken out to a bathhouse—even in winter—and were allowed to soak in a bath for ten minutes. The lice didn't like that much. On your birthday, you got one day off work to wash and clean yourself, but also had to carry in wood for the stoves in your hut, as well as for the guards.

"Foo Men" were the guards in charge of prisoners. They were soldiers who'd been wounded, and they represented the companies who paid the Japanese government for our slave labour.

The first job I had was unloading coal from ships with two baskets per man, seventy-five pounds each, up and down a ladder. A lot of the guys were too weak and collapsed trying to carry baskets that weighed more than they did. Then they'd be beaten by the Foo Men for not working. I wasn't too bad at that point, and would try and take half the weight of somebody else's basket on top of my load to help them out. I was beaten more than once for that.

The other job was pushing coal cars along a trestle. They didn't lubricate the wheels, and they were hell to push. You'd try and get on a two-man cart if possible, because the one-man carts were so tough to move. Some guys chopped off a finger so they wouldn't have to work anymore. That's how bad it was. Coming from a country like Canada, some of the things that went on in those camps were beyond your wildest imagination.

We were in groups of ten: if one of us escaped, the other nine got the "chop-chop." We wouldn't let the other guys out of our sight. We heard about three Canadians at another camp who'd tried to escape and were caught. They were dragged out and beheaded: no trial, nothing. Just "chop-chop." One of them had written a letter to his mother just before the escape. The letter and some other of his belongings are in the War Museum today.

Slowly, slowly, we were starving to death. One thing the Japanese gave us were pickled grasshoppers that they wouldn't eat. Somebody said they were full of vitamins. Me, I was always thinking up great ideas, so I put the grasshoppers in boiling water with soy to make a nutritious drink of sorts. When I dropped these pickled grasshoppers into the water, their eyes popped open and they started moving. I never went near another grasshopper after that. After the war, a doctor confirmed that they were indeed rich in nutrients, but I still couldn't have eaten those things.

Red Cross parcels were brought in, but the Japanese put them in storage and pilfered from them. They'd steal the chocolate to make hot chocolate, and Randy, one of our guys, was designated to carry food from the kitchen to the guards' barracks.

We'd all tested positive for dysentery, but the Japanese refused to acknowledge we were sick. "All in our imaginations," they said. I thought, "Okay. Let's test that one out." I arranged with Randy to put a positive dysentery sample into their hot chocolate, see how good their imaginations were. Of course, they all became sick as dogs, and medicine was

John Stroud (right) at Shamshuipo camp in Hong Kong in 1943, just prior to being shipped to Niigata prisoner-of-war camp in northern Japan. Stroud is smiling at a wisecrack a fellow prisoner has just made about one of the guards.

finally brought in for the guards and us. If they'd ever found out what I'd done, I would have been "chop-chop."

Another thing the Japanese lifted from the Red Cross parcels were cans of salmon. Somebody stole one back, and the Japanese searched the huts looking for it. They found the empty can under one guy's bed—James Mortimer—but it could have been anybody in that hut who'd eaten it. They took him out, tied him to a stake in the winter wearing nothing but his pants, and beat him if he tried to sit down. Finally, gangrene took over his arms and legs and he died. That was one of the deaths I remember most vividly.

Spear was another. He was an American P o W, and was a little kooky. Didn't matter how tough the work was, he'd go out and sing. The Japanese all thought he was nuts and just left him alone. Near the end of the war, rumours were flying that the Japanese were almost defeated, and Spear—in his mind—heard an American band coming. He walked right past the guard at the front gate and out to meet them. They charged him with attempting to escape and bayoneted him to death. They knew he was kooky, but it didn't stop them.

A secret diary was kept on every death in the camp. I didn't even know about it until years after the war. Approximately forty percent of the Canadian P o Ws in our camp died there. Prisoners in other camps apparently heard about the dreaded Niigata from guards who were transferred between the camps. Even some of the guards wanted to get away from our camp.

Somehow, hope keeps you going. Something had to give; the war couldn't go on forever. We knew that once the Americans got going in the war, with their capacity for building ships and armaments, they'd overwhelm the Japanese. Yamamoto, the Japanese general, had been educated in the United States, and spoke perfect English. He was against the Pearl Harbor attack, and was the one who said they'd be waking a sleeping giant if they attacked. He said, "Six months, then they'll be back." And they were.

The atomic bomb, for all its destruction, saved our lives and probably millions of other lives. First, had Hiroshima been clouded over that fateful day, Niigata was the alternate target. As well, all the P o Ws were to be killed in the event of the Allies invading Japan. So we were spared on both accounts. Second, there were millions of Japanese prepared to defend the Emperor to the death with pitchforks, knives, and even brooms. Their lives were spared because of the Emperor's ultimate capitulation. And third, the lives of hundreds of thousands of Allied soldiers, sailors, and airmen that would have been squandered in a final "nonatomic" fight were saved. The dropping of the bomb was terrible, without question; but the casualties of the war in Japan would have been much, much worse without it.

―――――

In August, right after the war ended, the worst guards fled the camp. The good guys, the ones who hadn't beaten us, stuck around and guarded us for our own sake. There were still a lot of die-hard Japanese around who wanted to carry on the war. We were the last to be liberated when it was finally over. September 1945 the Americans found us; they hadn't even known about the camp in Niigata. When they arrived and told us relief was on the way, those guys never got so many hugs and kisses in their life.

I'd never cried in my life until I saw all the parachutes coming down with food. We saw the planes coming over and they tilted their wings at us, which meant we'd been seen. Then there was this God-awful thud, and I found myself covered in blood. Rescued at last, then mortally wounded in a food drop!

I took a good whiff and a taste and realized I was covered in ketchup: a big drum of it had exploded when it landed. There were also chocolate

Japanese guards being marched as prisoners through the streets of Niigata following the liberation of the prison camp, September 1945.

bars, tinned rations, clothes, blankets, medication—the Americans must have spent millions of dollars dropping food and clothing to us. That night there were bonfires all over camp with the guys eating and celebrating. I weighed 87 pounds when we were liberated; we wouldn't have made it through another winter. For four years, all the guys ever talked about was food: steaks smothered with onions and gravy, with mashed potatoes. Not me; I had a crazy fixation on Kraft Cheese. That's all I could think about and I ate it like a chocolate bar when I managed to get my hands on some. We had a lot of food and supplies left over, so we took blankets, soap, and food to the Korean P o W camp, which wasn't far from us. But we didn't give a thing to the Japanese.

I have nothing but respect for the Americans: not only for the food they dropped, but also for bringing us home. We went to Hong Kong third-class and came home first class. They took us by train down to Yokohama at the end of September, cleaned us up, and gave us American uniforms. There were Red Cross girls at the station with coffee and doughnuts; this was the first time I ever tasted American coffee. On the ship home, they told us we could eat as much as we wanted. They even had ice cream machines on board! I can't ever thank the Americans enough.

I would like to have served my country more. All those years I felt I was actually serving the Japanese. I'd signed up to fight for king and country, and there I was, dying in a prisoner of war camp.

During my time in Hong Kong, there had been two exceptional displays of bravery that I vividly recall. When the Japanese attacked on Mount Butler, Sergeant Major Osborn cut them up for lunch with his Vickers machine gun. They threw grenades in our trench, and he tossed them back. He couldn't get to one of them fast enough, so he threw himself on it. He was killed, but saved the life of his men, and was posthumously awarded the Victoria Cross: the first Canadian to get it in World War II.

There was also the famous Sergeant Gander, a Newfie Dog. The Royal Rifles had adopted him when we'd been stationed at Gander. When we arrived in Hong Kong, all the Chinese were shouting, "Canadian bear! Canadian bear!" He was a great big thing. When the Japanese broke through at Lye Mun, he'd chase them off. They were terrified; they didn't know what he was. He was protecting the trench of a group of wounded Canadians, and in his final act of bravery, he'd pick up Japanese grenades and run them back to their lines, like a game of fetch. Sadly, on his third run, a grenade blew up and killed him. For that, he was awarded the Dickin Medal in 2000.

The Royal Rifle's mascot, Gander, leaving for Hong Kong with the regiment.

———

I still have nightmares; most of us do. You can't get it out of your brain. You watch a movie that has anything to do with the Japanese and the war, and the nightmares start all over again. I can forgive, but I cannot forget.

I've found that the best therapy for vets is talking about your experiences with friends or other guys who went through the same thing. We all knew what starvation, overwork, and having no medication was like. When you're sitting by yourself, you think you're the only one who knows how it feels. But when you start talking to other guys who've been through it too, it loosens you up. It's the best therapy: maybe the only therapy.

I used to take food and living for granted. I think most people do. Now, to me, food is the most important thing in people's lives, and it bothers me to waste it. Go through four years of starvation and then you'll know the importance.

Another thing people take for granted is the world they live in and the sacrifices made to preserve it. One of the things that's lacking with children today is an understanding of this history. Most have no idea where Hong Kong is, let alone what happened to us there.

We formed an association of Canadian Hong Kong Veterans in 1946. I figured there must be some reason I survived those four years and the least I could do was to serve my fellow veterans in return. I've tried to do that faithfully for the past fifty-five years.

My kid brother, Donald, and I were only a year apart in age. When we were young, we shared everything. After I joined up, he enlisted with the RCAF. He wrote to me from his base in England in 1943, worried about my health and how I was surviving. I received the letter in Niigata in 1944, but when I finally got back to Canada a year later, I found out he'd been killed on a bombing run over Germany in September of 1943.

To me, war is hell. I don't care where it is. There's no heroism in war: there's nothing but grief.

Dick Corbett

BIRTH PLACE: TORONTO, ONTARIO
RESIDENCE: TORONTO, ONTARIO
SQUADRON: 11 SQUADRON RAF
THEATRE OF WAR: BURMA

I WAS BORN IN 1921 IN THE WEST END OF TORONTO, THE YOUNGEST of four children. During the Depression, I didn't suffer an awful lot. We always had food on the table, but the Depression was all around us. My dad built our house by hand; he dug the gravel out of the pit for the basement and made the cement blocks. There's a street in Toronto's west end named after him—Corbett Avenue. It was a poor neighbourhood. Poor, but proud.

I was aware of what was going on in Europe. But I don't think I was really tuned in; it didn't seem to hit home. Even when the war first broke out, it always seemed like it wasn't going to last that long. I remember the Finns fighting and the Polish cavalry fighting against the German tanks, charging on their horses. In fact, I met a lady not so long ago whose grandfather had been a Polish cavalry officer and had died charging a German tank.

I never got involved in the politics. But it's a funny thing: when you don't get involved in the politics, you don't know what's really going on. It's hard for people to understand now, but you were a part of the events and yet didn't really understand what was going on, even if you read the paper and listened to the radio.

I wanted to get into the service to win the war! Everybody was hyped up in high school. I really wanted to fly, because I was an airplane nut. I took a lesson down at the Toronto Island Airport, to get a jump on things. The instructor was a gal named Harrison, who later became a Ferry pilot [ferrying aircraft back and forth between Canada and the UK]. She was terrific.

When the war first started, you practically had to be a university graduate to get accepted by the air force as a pilot. So I worked in munitions for a while before I was accepted into the air force in September 1941, maybe when things got a little lower in the barrel. My parents were against it, as any parents would have been, but never opposed it.

We did some boot camp in St. Thomas at the insane asylum. Lots of guard duty. They told us the Japanese workers from a local onion farm that belonged to Ontario Premier Hepburn might attack us at any time. There was this great surge of ethnic discrimination.

For instance, if anybody had a German or Italian name, people wouldn't buy vegetables from their stores. That really bothered me. I thought it was terrible, even at that time. These people were being lifted out of their lives. Even though some joined the Canadian army, they weren't welcome. It was terrible. But you tended to become oblivious to a lot of this stuff. Once you enlisted, you didn't think about anything other than what was right in front of you.

I was sent to Malton and learned to fly on Tiger Moths. That was my first plane and I loved them. They landed at about forty-five miles an hour, so really anybody could fly them. I wish I were still flying them today. I got myself into trouble, flying places I wasn't supposed to. I was anxious to get going, and had the bit between my teeth, so you get a bit wild. One time I dropped down to about a hundred feet and swooped down over Lady Eaton's garden party. All the ladies in those days wore these wide-brimmed hats and—well, you can imagine it. Fortunately, somebody else got blamed for that one, although another time I had to wash all the windows on the hangar for pulling a similar stunt.

In retrospect, I think the more daring you were, it almost stood in your favour. I eventually got my wings down in Aylmer and Billy Bishop pinned them on me. Everybody knew Billy. He'd travelled across the country as a morale builder and was a regular guy. A significant part of that graduation was the Rolex watch my parents gave me. It was a beautiful thing to have, and it played an important part in my life a few years later.

———

We were shipped off to England on the *Queen Elizabeth* in late 1942. There were about twelve thousand of us on that trip. You were keyed up the whole time during the crossing. I don't think I slept at all, which was okay because the sleeping wasn't great anyway. The ship didn't have any stabilizers, so it was a-jumpin' and a-movin' the whole time. I had a small single room with five other guys in it; bunks on both sides and you couldn't get into the washroom unless you were friends with the guy in the middle bunk. On deck, they had big long troughs for latrines. You always made a point of sitting in the middle of it, because with the ship going up and down, you can imagine the effect of being stuck at either end. You were served two meals a day, and it was a non-stop line-up. They'd finish serving the first meal, and the line-up would already be in place for the second one. The American army ran the provisions on the ship, which was just as well, because you sure ate better.

During the day, you just wandered around the decks, but it was kind of exciting because we were aware of the U-boat threat. American destroyers came out to escort us for awhile, but the *Queen Elizabeth* was doing something like thirty knots, so even the destroyers couldn't keep up for long. I don't think anybody was really scared, but you were always expecting something.

Rumours were the entertainment. I can remember one fellow who loved spreading them. He'd go to one side of the ship and pick on some poor guy, telling him, "You hear those engines pounding? They've got a scare on. They're taking evasive action." He figured it was a successful rumour if he gave it about fifteen or twenty minutes then walked around to the other side of the ship and had somebody else tell him the same story.

When we landed in England, we were shipped to Bournemouth. They didn't have any planes for us to fly, so for a while we were stationed with the 5th Division, which had a lot of Cape Bretoners in it. Now you have to remember that the army hated the air force: it was quite open. And these Cape Bretoners were pretty uninhibited about showing it. One night, they raked the top of our Nissan Hut with a Bren gun. Completely wild, those guys. But damn good soldiers, I bet.

Finally they found some aircraft for us and we were shipped to Millfield, where we started training on Hurricanes. It was a good plane, fairly easy to fly. We also did some training on Typhoons. At this point, we didn't know where we were going to be posted. Then we started getting injections for this, that and the other thing and were told we were going to someplace hot. We figured either North Africa or the East.

We shipped out in 1943 on the first convoy to go through the Mediterranean through Gibraltar. We were loaded onto trains and shipped across to the Red Sea. When you're young, you pick up friends on a day-to-day basis and just roll along with things. That trip was a little grim, but all part of the experience.

I find tough times like that are never sad in retrospect. It's a funny thing. Later in the war, when you came face to face with death and got away with it, you didn't think of it as sad: it was kind of exhilarating. I still tend to remember the good times, the happiest times. I think most people do, if you come out alive! Maybe it's just the joy of getting out in one piece.

We ended up in Bombay, which wasn't too bad. Except I got dysentery and landed up in the hospital, where the heat was around a hundred degrees. It was pretty horrible to be stuck in a ward with about a hundred other people suffering from the same thing in that heat, so when they came round to check if I was getting better, I said, "Yeah! I'm better! Get me the hell outta here!" But I probably had the damn bug the whole time I was in India.

Then we went to a place called Poona, where the British army was stationed. You'd think it was peacetime, because they played cricket and had afternoon tea. The Brits challenged us to a game of cricket, but refused to play when we turned up without our cricket whites. So the Aussies took the appropriate action and burned down their sports shack.

Dick Corbett (front row, far right) with members of the 11 Squadron RAF in India, 1943.

Dick and friends at the base in India, 1943.

Fair dinkum, I thought. I always liked the Aussies; spent a lot of time with them in the east.

I was assigned to 11 Squadron RAF, which was a mixture of guys from Australia, Canada and the RAF. We were sent to Bangalore, then to Madras, then down to a place on the coast. Our squadron was Lord Mountbatten's personal squadron and he wanted to invade the Japanese on the east coast of India, instead of going up and around. But we never knew what was happening or where we were going.

We were operational, but the Hurricanes we flew were just terrible. I don't where they got them from; maybe North Africa, but they'd had the hell beaten out of them. There wasn't a decent airport either, so we had to land in a flattened paddy field.

Typically a mission would be to fly down and hit the Japanese airstrips south of us. There wasn't any anti-aircraft fire, but the Japanese were great for concentrated rifle fire. They used to dig in below the trees as an air raid protection, and let loose at you with their rifles. It was perfect cover and you could never see them. We used to fly over the jungles and blindly fire off our machine guns, but we were always guessing.

The Japanese were very efficient. A couple of thousand Japanese soldiers could knock the hell out of ten thousand of our troops, because they didn't have any mess halls or mess tents or supply vehicles holding them back. They lived off the land and could survive on next to nothing.

Early in 1944, our communications weren't working half the time, because people were always stealing the wire. But this one particular day, things were working just fine and we got the word to scramble. A whole pile of Japanese planes were coming over and we had to get our planes the hell off the ground because they were all lined up on the paddies like sitting ducks. One of the English officers said to me, "To hell with them, Dick. Let's go up above and hit them from the top."

So we did. We got up as high as we could, then came diving down on them. I was banging away at some planes, and may have knocked down a couple, when all of a sudden another bunch of Japanese who were flying above *us* came down and banged away at us. I got hit in the leg. It wasn't too bad, but I lost some control of my plane. There wasn't much time to think, so instead of bailing out I decided to put it down in a paddy field.

It was the late afternoon, and I thought I landed on our side of the line. After I got my Hurricane on the ground, I tried to set fire to it. That was the routine: when you crash-landed, you were supposed to try and burn it. You had to take the crystals out of the wireless set, but I thought I heard someone coming and I was bleeding pretty badly, so I just got out of there into the jungle. The next thing I saw was a dugout near a tree with some men sitting around having a cigarette. I thought this was strange, because our group didn't usually operate like that. But they were smoking British cigarettes—Churchill cigarettes, I'll always remember that—but as I got closer I realized, "Oh geez, it's the Japanese," so I got the hell out of there.

I was within about a kilometre of my own lines, so I thought I would just crawl back. It was a strong moonlit night and I was aware I was in enemy territory. As I was crawling back, trying to figure out how to get back to my own line, an enemy patrol walked right in on top of me. Even though I had a revolver, I surrendered. I wasn't going to be dead hero. I think they were as surprised as I was when they stumbled across me. I shoved my Rolex up my arm and under my tunic before these guys tied me up to a stake.

In India at that time, there were about forty thousand Indian troops under the British that defected to the Japanese side. The leader, Subchandras Bos, was the Indian national leader of all these troops, but

PERSONAL

CANADA HOUSE,
TRAFALGAR SQUARE,
LONDON, S.W.1.

Dear Mrs Corbett,

    This is meant to tell you how deeply
my husband and I feel for you since we heard
that your son is missing, - we know what
these days of anxiety and doubt will mean
to you.

    Do know with what understanding and
sympathy we are both thinking of you.

    I had so hoped that I could write to
you in my own hand, but, alas, the pressure
of work here continues so great, that I
know you will understand and forgive a
dictated note.

    Yours very sincerely,

Alice Vincent Massey

I never knew any of this until I was taken prisoner. The fellows who were guarding me had British army uniforms on and were Indians. It's just amazing that this transpired. These soldiers were in kind of a phony war. They were wearing British uniforms, but working with the Japanese. But that didn't stop them from going over to our NAAFI and buying cigarettes and things, back and forth across the border through the jungle. They had the okay from the Japanese, but I don't know what the hell was going on, on our side. Our guys were probably sleeping.

I found out that my English buddy who I'd been flying with had also been hit and bailed out, but the Japanese had shot him in mid-air as he was parachuting down. Also, when I was being tied up, one of these turncoat Indians guarding me found my watch and took it.

It was devastating being captured, but at least I was still alive. From that experience I learned that the will to survive is something else. I was brought back to the Japanese lines and held in various work camps.

As a P o W, I was made to work as a coolie carrying rice, but I could never manage to carry anything on my head. We had to cross a river on one of those swinging bridges made of cane and if you dropped that goddam bag of rice, they'd shoot you right there. We always worked at night too, which was kind of scary.

There was another RAF guy in the camp with me who'd been shot down. They shot most of the army guys after taking them prisoner, but for some reason they didn't shoot us air force guys. The Japanese didn't usually take prisoners, so I was fortunate. Their soldiers didn't believe in being taken prisoner, either. They'd shoot themselves or cut their own throats before being taken alive.

I didn't know anything about the Japanese or what to expect, but there's no question they were pretty hard on us. They kept us caged up in a hut that you had to crawl into; you couldn't stand up. We were starved half the time. Guys with wounds were often shot. I'd bandaged my leg where I'd been hit, but it'd cleared up. They really were a lot tougher on the army guys than they were on us. Maybe because I was Canadian, they saw me as some kind of prize.

OPPOSITE: A sympathy letter sent to Dick Corbett's mother from Alice Vincent Massey, wife of Charles Vincent Massey, then high commissioner of Britain, after Dick Corbett was shot down over India.

They decided to move us out of India. They put us on a boat and one of our guys died there. They let us off the boat into this snake-infested mangrove swamp just long enough to cover him with some dirt and that was it. I didn't even have a chance to get his ID tags. That still bothers me.

We ended up in Rangoon, Burma, in the city jail. I was put into a cell by myself, where I learned my first Japanese word. It was "ohayu," which meant, "good morning." You bowed when the guard came and said, "ohayu." I figured I could remember that, because it sounded like the name of an American state. But I think at first I said, "Iowa," instead of "Ohio," and that's why I have a crooked nose now. The guard smashed me with a heavy bat and knocked me out cold. I always remembered "Ohio" after that!

Day to day, there were two of us in a cell. We were lucky, because we had two boards to lie on. No bedding or anything like that. There were bars on the window, but no window. If it got cool at night, and it did, you just about froze to death. All I had were the shorts and jacket I was wearing when I was shot down. When those wore out, I wore a loincloth made out of rags. About every second day, they'd let you out to dump the ammunition box you'd been given to use as a toilet. It was pretty rough. We got about a salmon tin full of rice every day and something that you might call soup, but I don't know what the hell it was.

We were isolated in this one section of the prison with only air force guys. The Americans were bombing Japan, so you knew it was just a matter of time until they were going to kill us in retaliation. Some of the guys went out of their minds with this hanging over their heads.

There was no medical attention whatsoever. We had one fellow who got gangrene in his hand and we had to cut his hand off. A Canadian doctor was allowed to come in, but no anaesthetic was used.

Most of the guys in our camp eventually died from disease or starvation. Every day bodies were carted out. There was another jail in town that five Americans tried to escape from. I don't know why they bothered. There was no place you could go. A white face in Burma and a thousand miles away from any refuge? When the Japanese recaptured them, the Americans were taken outside every day and beaten until they died; and they all died.

We were in that Burmese prison for about fifteen months before we were released. During that time, my philosophy of life changed. I'd had strong views on race and the world from kind of a limited point of view.

I eventually shared a cell with this RAF fellow who had a pretty good philosophy of life and I learned a lot from him. We weren't supposed to talk. If they heard you yakking to each other, the guards would come in and they'd give you a belt. But we still talked, which sure kept me sane.

This RAF fellow used to say to me, "Dick, you can't hate. Hate's going to kill you faster than anything else. So you got to take things as they come. I know you don't like those Japanese, but you have to try and stop hating them."

We'd talk for hours, trying to rationalize the Japanese behaviour. Basically, I came to understand that a lot of them had been at war for ten years and as a result, probably had a completely different philosophy of life from anything I would ever know. But they were still human beings, and that helped me immensely. It helped me in later life and has stuck with me to this day.

───────

One night, I couldn't sleep. I got up and was walking around and it became clear that the Japanese had left the camp. We were alone. I came across a note they'd left on the gate. It said, "We have guarded you with honour and hope to meet you again on some other battlefield."

So that was that. But then we were in for a few hairy days, because the British were starting to come into our area and didn't know we were holed up there. The RAF bombed our camp, so I had some of the guys get on the roof and whitewash a sign that said, "Japs Gone."

Lo and behold, the next day a Mosquito bomber flew over and dropped another bomb on us, which didn't kill anybody but sure shook me up. I figured we'd better get another sign up on the roof, something that the air force would understand.

I had the guys paint, "Extract Digit" ["Get your finger out of your so-and-so and rescue us!"] on the roof, which I figured was a phrase the Japanese wouldn't have known, but the Brits could decipher. And that's what did the trick. That was April 29, 1945. The British evacuated us from the camp and put us on a hospital ship to Calcutta, and finally we were flown back to England on an old DC-3.

When the tide turned against the Japanese, the Indian soldier who'd taken my Rolex tried to defect back to the British lines with a friend, but was captured by Gurkhas. Lucky for him he was wearing the watch, because it had my name engraved on it and they figured he must know something. But the Gurkhas killed his buddy.

The watch was handed over to the authorities and my family was informed that, at the very least, some trace of me had been found. This was enough to convince them I was still alive and put their minds at some peace. Unlike Europe, there was no Red Cross in India, and no communications with P o Ws. When I made it out of the camp and got my things back, there was my Rolex, still working. It stills works to this day.

———

I don't want to glorify war. It's a horrible thing. The kids see these things where the hero always gets out alive; or he gets wounded, but still makes it out. And war isn't like that. I've seen a lot of horror in my time and I just thank God that I'm still here.

I think the kids idolize people who've been in the war too much, so I try to keep away from that. I don't even have my medals. I remember after the war, being in London and talking with a Chelsea pensioner. I had this old uniform on that I'd picked up from someplace because I'd lost all of mine. This old thing had some remnants of ribbons on it and the old soldier gave me a hard time, saying that I shouldn't be wearing the such-and-such ribbon unless I had served in that particular effort. I told him that I didn't know anything about the decorations on this old uniform; that I'd lost everything when I was serving in the Far East. And with that, I took the jacket off and threw it in the garbage bin in front of him. I've never worn any medals since.

I had nightmares after the war for many years; memories of the Japanese, of things I'd seen and had happened to me. I still get them. There were about eleven Canadians in that prison camp in Rangoon and I'm the only one still alive. I get a little depressed when I think about those years. But the ones of us who survived with the best outlook on life are the ones who got rid of the bitterness. There are very few survivors who have bitterness in their souls. They don't seem to survive. Hate eats people away, and it sure killed a lot of guys who went through what I did.

Dick Bartlett

Birth Place: Fort Qu'Appelle, Saskatchewan
Residence: Victoria, BC
Squadron: Fleet Air Arm, 803 Squadron RAF
(HMS *Ark Royal*)
Theatre of War: NW Europe, Norway

I was born in 1919 and raised in Saskatchewan in a little place called Fort Qu'Appelle. My dad was an Englishman who had come out in 1910 and still regularly received *The London Times*. In the spring of 1938, I'd graduated high school and noticed a little ad in the *Times* advertising for pilots for the Fleet Air Arm. The RAF had supplied personnel to the Fleet Air Arm from about 1923 until 1938, when the Admiralty decided to take over, which is why they were advertising for pilots. And, of course, the war was in the offing. I'd always had a hankering to go to sea and thought I'd like flying as well, so I sent in my application. In the summer of 1938, I got an answer from England to come over for an interview, which I did and was accepted.

There were about thiry of us training as pilots. We were sent down to Portsmouth for three months of naval training and, once we'd completed that, we started our flying.

I completed my training in early 1939 and was then moved under the training of the RAF to get my wings. The Netherhaven air station was a funny old place. It had grass runways, no control tower, and no radios, so each day a pilot was selected for "air traffic control." If two aircraft were coming in for a landing at the same time and might collide, the pilot on duty had to got out on the runway and shine a Very light into the air. It was primitive, but a very pleasant life there through the spring and summer.

When war was declared in September, life changed entirely. We started working seven days a week, had airfield security patrols, and the planes and hangars were camouflaged, which had to be changed every other day. During this time, the Fleet Air Arm flew such aircraft as Harts, Audaxes and a new monoplane, the Harvard. I was transferred onto Swordfish torpedo-bomber biplanes and took a torpedo attack course. With the Swordfish, you'd climb to ten thousand feet, then point the nose straight down at the sea. You'd haul back on the stick when you were about a hundred feet off the water and hope the aircraft would level out at about fifty feet. If it did, then you flew straight and level towards your target and dropped your torpedo about a thousand yards from the ship you were attacking. Despite its archaic appearance, it was a beautiful aircraft to fly. But I must confess I wanted to fly something more modern.

Operations in Norway started early in 1940 and very quickly they

A Swordfish torpedo bomber taking off from the deck of the HMS *Ark Royal*.

began to run short of pilots. The Admiralty phoned down to our squadron one night to ask if any of us could fly Skuas, which I'd had a few hours on. So the next day I was sent down with another chap to do a two-week fighter course. The Skua was a fighter with two front guns that fired through the wooden prop. On occasion, the guns would literally fire into the prop, but as long as you didn't get too many holes in it, that didn't seem to affect it too much.

After this course, I was sent as a fighter dive bomber pilot to 803 Squadron on the carrier HMS *Ark Royal* for operations off Norway to support the British Norwegian expeditionary force.

When you went in on an attack from the *Ark Royal*, the carrier hovered about a hundred and fifty miles off the coast. We'd go off in flights of three Skuas, each carrying a 500-lb. bomb, or two 150-lb. bombs. The aircraft had four front guns and an old Lewis gun in the back seat for the air gunner. The Skua was a very underpowered plane, so its best feature was that it went "downhill" very fast. It was like flying a bathtub, but they could certainly take a lot of punishment. In fact, you were more or less expected to take some punishment. The captain of the *Ark Royal* thought you weren't pressing home your attacks properly unless you came back with some holes in your aircraft, which was fairly easy because the German flak always had a good whack at you.

When you returned to the *Ark Royal* after an attack, a screen of destroyers surrounded the carrier. We were on radio silence, so we had to use a Very light to identify ourselves, but this just seemed to make our destroyers angry. They'd see our lights and think they were being fired on, and they'd open up on us. Which meant we often had to fly through our own flak just to get back to the carrier. What's more, the closer you got, the more the destroyers thought you were attacking them. It's a good thing their accuracy wasn't any better than their aircraft recognition.

A lot of the English pilots surprised me when I first joined the Fleet Air Arm. Many had long hair, wore a bit of cologne and had handkerchiefs hanging out of their sleeves. I wondered what I'd gotten myself into. But these same types would come back from a rough attack saying, "Wasn't that fun! Let's go for a drink." Meanwhile I'd be thinking, "Geez, I'd better go change my underwear before I go for any drink."

The *Ark Royal* was operating at Narvik in the north of Norway in late spring 1940, and at that time of year it was daylight pretty much all the time. Operations were going twenty-four hours a day and we got tired very quickly. We were assigned to cover the evacuation of our army from Norway. Our job was to provide fighter patrols over the embarkation area. There would be two aircraft patrolling over the land area and two over the area where they were transferring troops from small boats onto larger ships. Each patrol lasted two hours and you had to stay up there for your patrol regardless. If you ran out of ammunition in the first ten minutes, you still carried on until the next two aircraft came to relieve you. We were fortunate, because there'd been some Hurricanes stationed at Narvik. If the German bombers came over and we dove at them, the Huns thought we were Hurricanes and quite often they split up and headed for home. Little did they know we often didn't have any ammunition in our front guns.

When that evacuation was complete, we heard that the RAF were going to blow up their Hurricanes, because they weren't equipped with arrester hooks to land on a carrier. If they'd been left in Norway, the Germans would get them. I went with some other pilots to the CO and asked if we could try landing them on the *Ark Royal*, but the RAF pilots got wind of this and came back saying, "Nuts! If anyone's going to try and land them on deck, we're going to." So they flew them to HMS *Glorious*, which was cruising alongside of us, and did a tremendous job of getting them down. The RAF was short of aircraft at that time, so the *Glorious* headed for Scapa Flow with the Hurricanes, while the *Ark Royal* stayed with the convoy. On the way home, the *Glorious* ran into the German battle cruisers *Scharnhorst* and *Gneisenau*. With only one destroyer escorting her, the *Glorious* and her destroyer were quickly sunk, with maybe a half dozen survivors from both ships.

As soon as we got clearance that the convoy didn't need any more air protection, we were sent to hunt the *Scharnhorst* and *Gneisenau*. The ships and their destroyer escorts had been spotted in Trondheim harbour. We headed in, the *Ark Royal* with her two squadrons of Swordfish and Skuas at the ready. Trondheim harbour was ringed with hills and mountains, solid with German anti-aircraft guns, in addition to the battleships and destroyers in harbour. There were also squadrons of German ME-109s and ME-110s on the Trondheim airfield, so the outlook was pretty glum. As we approached Trondheim, we learned that the Swordfish wouldn't take part in the attack, which was a blessing because they would never have survived a torpedo attack into that harbour. I can safely say there were some mighty relieved pilots.

But around midnight on the 13th of June 1940, fifteen Skuas were sent in to dive bomb the *Sharnhorst* and *Gneisenau*. I remember the date and the time all too well because I was one of them. The sun was just coming up as we approached land. We must have been a German fighter pilot's dream, because it was a beautiful, clear morning and you could see for miles. We were about ten miles away when the flak opened up from the harbour. About the same time, two ME-109s attacked me from the rear. The anti-aircraft flak coming from the German ships looked like an inverted solid cone of hot metal being thrust up into the air. On the first attack, the 109s knocked away pieces of my port wing and then on the second attack, they put quite a few holes in my starboard wing. A shell from one of their cannons hit the fuel tank just behind my seat, but, maybe because it was full, it didn't explode. Certainly an awfully close call.

Suddenly I felt like I'd been kicked in the side by a mule. When I looked down, I could see three bullet holes in my flying suit. The fighters came in for a third attack, but seemed to miss. I can't say for sure, because I started feeling woozy and my left side had gone numb. Blood was trickling down my leg and I thought I might pass out. I told my air gunner to get ready to bail out, but he'd taken off his parachute and said he didn't think he had time enough to get it back on. I knew I couldn't make it back to the *Ark Royal*, so I headed for land, attempting to manoeuvre around the fringes of the flak, and tried to get a grip on myself.

I put the old plane into a dive to drop my bomb and it seemed pretty sluggish. I remember thinking, "I don't think I'll be able to pull out of this." A few more pieces snapped off the aircraft as we dove. I didn't see where our bomb fell, but I know I missed the target. I reminded myself that I'd been struggling too much with the aircraft to get in a good attack. After much shuddering and shaking, the aircraft pulled up level over the water and I headed for the rooftops over Trondheim, thinking that they wouldn't shoot at us once we were over the town. By the time I got there, the engine was shaking so badly that I could hardly read any of my instruments.

Another surprise was waiting for us here, though. The Germans had placed machine guns on the rooftops, so once again we took quite a strafing as we flew over. A few miles out of town, when we were still at treetop level, the aircraft engine seized up. The Skua seemed to stand on its tail, then just fell out of the sky with a great shuddering jerk and slammed into a clearing in a farmer's field.

Both my air gunner and I made it out, but it's a dreadful feeling finding yourself wounded and on the ground in enemy territory. Just dreadful. I had trouble standing, and my head felt woozy, so I had to sit down. After a brief discussion, my air gunner decided to head for Sweden, which was only twelve miles away. But not much time seemed to pass before he came back with a German soldier holding a gun to his back. The next thing I remember was being in the hospital. I didn't realize it at the time, but I was very lucky. Only three out of the fifteen aircraft from our attack made it back to the *Ark Royal*, and very few of us who'd been shot down turned up in P o W camps.

I spent some time in the hospital in Trondheim, and then was moved to an air force P o W camp, rather than an army or naval camp. The Germans weren't interested in me, or any information that I might have had, so I was quickly moved to Stalag Luft I on the Baltic near Stettin, where I spent the rest of 1940. My main memory of that camp is hunger. Our daily ration consisted of two slices of very dark, sour German bread, one small piece of sausage, and a watery bowl of soup. And so we wasted no time in trying to escape.

A "Kriegie" P o W letterform from Dick Bartlett to his sister, Joan, 1943.

In early 1941, the Germans discovered our first tunnel. They moved fifty of us, whose rooms were closest to the tunnel, to another camp. When we got into the new hut, we were searched, with the ones who'd been searched lined up on one side of the room and the others waiting to be searched on the other side. The Germans had confiscated a pair of wire cutters from somebody and left them on the table. As I moved toward the table, I was accidentally jostled and my hand drifted across and those wire cutters found their way into my pocket. I then bumped into a guard and explained to him that I'd already been searched and had got on the wrong side. So he let me pass and I got away with the wire cutters.

That night there was an air raid and all the lights went out in the camp. It lasted about forty-five minutes before the "All Clear" was sounded. The next morning, the Germans told us that because of the raid, the boxcars we were to be transported in hadn't arrived and we'd have to spend another day in this camp. I spoke to my friend, Joe Hill.

"I've got these wire cutters; let's have a fling tonight. We'll be ready if there's another air raid tonight. We'll knock a hole in the floor, drop down to the ground—it was about two feet—and then have a crack at the fence. I'll pinch a bed board and you hold the wire up while I cut the wire."

Joe was from the prairies and used to barbed wire, so he had no problem with that.

That night, right on schedule, came another air raid and off we went. At this stage of the game, we were new to P o W camps and pretty damned inexperienced at escaping. We hadn't anticipated that the Germans would triple the guards and have dogs, which slowed up our whole plan. But the camp was in complete darkness, and we made it to the fence.

Our first snip on the old wire sounded like a rifle shot. I heard footsteps approaching when I was about a third of the way through. Joe was holding the board up to keep the wire from snapping down on me. As I cut the last wire, the "All Clear" was sounded. I kicked Joe.

"Get the hell out of here before the lights come back on."

"I'll wait for you."

He stayed and held the wire while I scrambled back inside. We both stood up just as the lights in the compound came on again. I think the Germans were more than a little surprised to see two guys standing there.

There was a bunch of shouting but no shooting, and as the searchlights started playing on us we dashed behind a brick garbage bin and ran to our hut. We'd pre-arranged that our guys would keep the shutters open as long as the windows were open so we could just dive through, which is exactly what we did. By midnight I was back in my bunk, but I'd learned quite a bit about trying to escape.

Our next camp was Oflag 9 A/H. This was an old castle surrounded by a dry moat with three wild boars in it, and floodlights constantly lighted the moat. The darn guards with machine guns were posted on the outer side of the moat and the camp seemed to be almost escape-proof. But this was just a temporary stop as the Germans organized their P o W camps.

We were moved from the old castle on a third-class train to Poland, sitting on hard wooden seats, not allowed to move except for one trip to the toilet per day. They were short of food, clothes, and water and it was generally miserable. I was sitting next to a window that was wired shut. I had a nail file and whenever the guard wasn't looking, I'd file away at the wire. After three days, I'd nearly got through. The plan was to fling a window open and dive out if the train went uphill and slowed down. The chap sitting next to me was supposed to nudge me if the guards came my way, but when we were getting close to Poland and time was running out, I became oblivious to everything except getting through this wire. At some point, apparently, my pal gave me a warning nudge, but I didn't feel it. The train was slowing to a stop, and there was a lot of shouting going on. When I looked up, a German guard was standing over me and I thought he was going to pin me right to the wooden seat. But it was too late anyway; we'd reached our destination.

The train had stopped near a clearing surrounded by German troops and personnel carriers with their floodlights shining into the centre of the circle. It looked quite sobering, I must admit. We were bundled off the train and escorted to an underground fort, which looked like it had been built in Bismarck's time. Big doors opened on the side of the hill and in we went.

Rotting potatoes had been stored inside, so the stench was awful. The rooms were like dungeons, cold and damp with no light, heat or windows. We were surprised to find quite a few British Tommies there, whose duty was to cook, clean up and generally maintain the camp. They told us that they'd made the Germans believe they hated all British officers, which seemed to make the Germans treat them a bit better, and might help us as well. These Tommies called us SOBs while they served us dinner that night, but the stew they gave us was the best food I'd had in Germany. They'd actually gone without rations for three days to make it for us. And that was their attitude from then on; they were tremendous guys.

In early May 1941, the German attitude towards us seemed to change for the better. We were allowed to go on top of the fort during daylight hours. To see the old sun again was a very pleasant experience. We had one sad sight that I can't forget. In front of the fort there was a line of old men, women and children being made to dig a ditch. There was a German guard with a 15-foot bullwhip. He'd walk up and down the line and every now and again, would stop and lash somebody. If they dropped their shovel, he'd keep lashing them until they picked it up again. To go to the toilet, these prisoners were only allowed to step out of the line and pull down their trousers or hike up their skirts. This guard took great delight in waiting till these poor people were halfway through and then lashed their bottoms with his whip to make them jump back into line.

From the top of the fort, we could also see and hear the constant flow of men and equipment moving east. In early June 1941, the Germans told us they were about to attack Russia. They seemed to think that when this happened, Britain would make peace with Germany and become allies to fight Russia as a common enemy, which likely accounted for their change of attitude towards us at that time.

In anticipation of this wishful amalgamation of England and Germany, we were moved to a huge camp where they had about two thousand British army officers from all over Germany. They were going to hold us all in one camp until peace was declared in the following weeks. Most of these officers were from the 51st Highland Division and a finer crowd of people you couldn't wish to meet. They'd held the rear-guard action at Dunkirk and had been ordered to stand and fight until they were overrun.

There were only about two hundred of us air force officers, and we were allocated two barracks. One was only about a hundred and fifty feet from the main fence. Our senior officer had a room in one of these barracks, so we approached him about digging a tunnel from his room, which he completely supported.

This tunnel went down for five or six feet, and then moved out horizontally from there. It was about two feet high and two feet wide, just large enough for one man. When I was digging, I'd crawl along on my stomach, sometimes naked and sometimes in old clothes I could leave down in the hole when I came up. When you reached the face of the tunnel, you would push the dirt underneath yourself to someone behind you who, in turn, pushed it behind him or hauled it out, depending on how long the tunnel was at that stage.

There was a tendency for the guy at the face to dig the slope upwards. I think it was a psychological need to get to the surface. I fought this by telling myself to keep digging down, so at least I stayed somewhat level. On a long tunnel, by the time I'd crawl to the face at the end, I'd feel exhausted and be in a cold sweat. It was a form of claustrophobia, especially rampant in those tunnels that had no shoring. The ground was frozen about two feet down, and you would hear a few plops behind you as bits and pieces of earth fell down from the top of the thing. If it collapsed, you would have been stuck down there. I'd have to talk myself down and into getting on with the work at hand.

For air, we'd bore holes the diameter of a broomstick up to the surface. This had a funnel effect and brought fresh air down, but as it turned out, it was also our downfall. On one very cold morning in the winter of 1941, a German was walking between the wire and the huts and noticed steam rising from the ground. The hot air was escaping through these holes and condensing into a

A tunneller in Stalag VIIIB. This tunnel would be typical of most escape tunnels. The exception to this is Stalag Luft III, from which the Great Escape took place. There, bedboards were used to shore up the tunnel walls and ceiling.

whole bunch of little steam chutes. And with that, the Germans moved in and shut us down, which meant eight months of hard work gone for naught.

In April 1942, I had the opportunity of taking part in an escape with five others from an internment cellblock just outside the camp perimeter. You'd get put in the "cooler" for minor things like not saluting a German. In their methodical manner, the Germans would let you know on Friday that you'd start your cell time on Monday. To get six of us in the cooler at the same time, we changed names with six army officers who were starting their cell time on the day we were going to head out. Every night, the Germans took each prisoner from each cellblock to the toilet, starting at one wing and working around to another wing. When everyone had gone to the toilet, the Germans locked the place up and went home.

The cells in the corridor were pretty dimly lit, so the first thing we had to do was create a diversion so that the guy who was returning from the toilet, was able to slip the bolt on his friend's door. That guy would hold the door closed tight until the guard had gone. For once, it all worked well, which was a pleasant and surprising change given my escape record to date. However, when we opened the cell door of the chap I was going with, his feet and legs were so swollen from fleabites that he couldn't get his boots on. He wished me the best of luck and I carried on by myself.

The building had one window that faced the compound and it was the only escape. I was the last one out, closed the window behind me then crept along the side of the building. It still surprises me that the Germans didn't see us. It was a bright moonlit night and with the odd searchlight reflection, I thought sure we would be easily seen against the building.

We'd been living on bread and water, two slices of bread per day and water. I hadn't eaten all day and was pretty hungry, but carried on and hoped I could raid a chicken house or find something. I would have eaten anything at that stage. There was still snow on the ground in places and in one place near a farm, I saw a big snow bank with running water and thought, "Oh, boy, something to drink." I stuck my hand in it and got part of a mouthful and realized that the snow pile was an old manure pile covered in snow. I choked and retched after that for quite a while.

I headed for a railway marshalling yard about ten miles away. It was about two o'clock in the morning and I didn't have much time because

I was after a train going towards Holland. I didn't make it, and had to hide in some bushes before it got light outside. I had a close call that day about three P.M. I heard voices and saw three German soldiers coming with guns and a dog on a lead. I didn't have much cover, so I lay on my stomach perfectly still and hid my face as best I could. They walked within thirty feet of me and the dog looked at me, but kept going. I couldn't move until I couldn't hear their footsteps any more. Since my heart was pounding so loudly in my ears, I lost track of how long I lay there.

That night, I caught a train and hopped off about three A.M. when it stopped. I'd had no food and was getting a bit desperate at this stage of the game. I approached a farmhouse, but the dogs started barking so I hid up for the day. Night came and I caught another train and stayed right on until dawn, when that train stopped. During the night I started to hallucinate. I kept thinking there was somebody with me and I'd turn to talk to them, then realize there was no one there. I knew if I didn't get to Holland pretty soon, I wouldn't make it at all.

I decided I'd better travel by day as well. I hid in the boxcar until I spotted another train going in the direction I wanted. I slipped out from around one end of the car and spotted a German guard with about three or four French workers working on the railroad not too far away. I hadn't gone more than three feet when he had his rifle levelled at me, so that was the end of it. I came close to ending up in the hands of the Gestapo at that time, but ended up being taken by heavy guard back to Stalag Luft III at Sagan.

I spent the summer of 1942 participating on the fringe of a number of escape plans, keeping track of goons and that kind of thing, but basically just coping with camp life waiting for the Allies to arrive. There was always a crystal set wireless in the camp, which brought us the BBC news every night at eleven o'clock. Coded messages from England were also sent through these broadcasts. In the spring of 1943, I was asked with two others to guard this secret radio—the "canary"—in anticipation of the large-scale escape that was being planned.

The Germans were suspicious that a radio was in the camp and kept trying to find it. If they suddenly broke into the compound, my job was to eat any messages, destroy the coils as best I could, then hide the radio under the toilet and sit on the seat. Because of this, I wasn't able to help dig any of the tunnels ["Tom," "Dick" and "Harry"] which were being built for a mass escape, but because of the work I was doing with the radio, my name was on the list as one of the ones who was to go out.

I was teamed up with a Norwegian fellow for the escape and learned to speak a bit of Norwegian so we could get to Norway together. Just before the tunnel was complete, however, another Norwegian arrived in camp and he was a friend of my partner. Because of my faltering Norwegian, we agreed that they should go together and I'd drop out of the escape roster. It was a strange twist of luck, because, sadly, these two men were both among the fifty who were shot by the Gestapo after the Escape in April 1944.

D-Day came and went and I lost enthusiasm for escaping and decided to just wait it out, since the Allies were obviously on their way in. We'd also been warned of severe repercussions for any further escape attempts. In January 1945, Russian guns could be heard in the distance. The Germans marched us west, away from the camp. They were starting to realize the game was up, and were stalling for time. But I think they knew their fate with the Russians would be a lot worse than with the Allies. On that march, there was about two feet of snow on the ground and it was one of the worst periods of my four and a half years of P o W life. Quite a few of the people didn't survive that forced mid-winter march.

After several weeks, we arrived at a former navy P o W camp outside of Bremen, just before the British army crossed the Rhine. When the Germans knew the Brits were approaching, they marched us northeast to just outside Lubeck. During that leg of the march, our column was strafed a few times and we lost a few more of our guys. At Lubeck, we were living outside in the fields, sandwiched between the Russian and British armies. Fortunately, the British 2nd army overran our camp first. By this time, we were a pretty scruffy looking lot and the British colonel explained that he would have to hold us all for a couple of weeks while he documented us, one by one.

By nightfall of that day, I think the camp was almost empty. Nobody was sticking around for paperwork. I headed out with a group in a truck within about two hours of the British arrival.

Within a day of leaving that camp, we made it to a British air base just south of Holland and the next morning at dawn were bundled into a squadron of Lancasters headed back to England.

Tom Lane

Birth Place: St. Boniface, Manitoba
Residence: Guelph, Ontario
Squadron: 10, 35 Squadrons RAF (Pathfinder)
Theatre of War: NW Europe
Decorations: DFC

WHEN WE LANDED IN ENGLAND, I DISCOVERED IT WASN'T FIGHTER pilots they were short of, but bomber pilots. At that time, bombers flew with two pilots, so every time a plane went down, they lost two pilots. I volunteered to transfer from single-engine aircraft to bombers, and by the time I was flying operations, they'd dropped the crew down to a single pilot.

Once I graduated, I eventually ended up assigned to 35 Squadron. I was crewed up with four members of a group who'd been on operations together. They'd lost their pilot, engineer and bomb aimer in a crash landing, so I was fortunate enough to be teamed up with them. It was a

blessing, as they were an excellent crew, and we've continued to stay in touch with one another since the war. I lucked out. They were all English, and I was the only Canadian, but we melded extremely well. I think you have to have confidence in yourself to be a good bomber pilot, and have the capability to make quick decisions. You have to understand the significance and importance of all the crewmembers, and to understand their abilities. In training, I'd flown a few operations as a

Tom Lane (third from left) with his crew from 35 Squadron RAF (Pathfinder) in England, 1942. They were one of the first pathfinder crews.

second pilot, so I had some experience in battle already. All in all, we made a good team and started flying operations in July 1942. By August 1942 we'd become a Pathfinder crew.

The Pathfinder Force formed a new squadron under Don Bennett, who selected the operational crews from several squadrons to form the new crews of the Force. While we weren't a tremendously experienced crew in terms of number of trips, Group Captain Don Bennett, who oversaw the Pathfinder Force, saw the potential in our particular crew.

Pathfinders were the crews who'd fly in at the head of an attack and lay down marker flares to guide the bomber stream to their targets during a raid. We trained on new H2S equipment, which was like RADAR, and a significant advancement in terms of being able to look at features on the ground, even with a thick cloud cover. We were the only squadron ever allowed to fly over London during the war without being shot down, because we were testing this equipment.

As the first ones in on a raid, this responsibility held certain obvious dangers. It was a special honour to fly with the Force, and we relished the challenges of it, which sometimes meant being at the head of things. In December 1942, our crew was frequently called on to be the leader of a raid. The danger of what we did was occasionally in my mind. I don't think I ever went on any trip where I wasn't somewhat dubious or scared. I remember sitting in a pub in London, and someone from Coastal Command coming up to me, and asking what my special "wing" was. I explained to him what we were and what we did. Years later, I met up with him by chance, and he said, "I never expected to see you again. At least not alive."

When the Pathfinders led a raid, two aircraft would go in together, then a couple of minutes later two more would come in, to keep the target continuously marked. More than once I was chased miles off target because I'd been "coned" in the searchlights, and had to take evasive action to get out. When that blue searchlight hits you in that cone, it's very, very difficult to get out. You have to violently throw the aircraft around to do it; you certainly can't baby the aircraft. Then you have to come around again and remark the target.

But the enemy wasn't the only obstacle. I remember a mission over Hannover, and running into a severe thunderstorm where the aircraft was bouncing up and down, five hundred feet each bounce. You'd finally get the plane down and discover you had a quarter inch of ice all over everything. As much as anything, the violence of some of those storms we flew through will forever be ingrained in my mind.

There was always the danger of other aircraft as well. A Canadian pilot, Hank Melkin, got badly shot up on one of the raids to Germany. He took aggressive evasive action to get out of the flak, and just barely missed clipping our plane. I can still see the red-hot exhausts of his engines flashing past me, close enough that I could almost reach out and touch them.

When we were selected for the Pathfinder Force, that meant signing up for two tours of sixty trips in total (twice as much as other crews). After we'd been flying for a while, they came to the conclusion that sixty trips were just too much, and that forty-five was more appropriate. When you think of all the people who were lost on the bombing missions, however, realistically we had a pretty small chance of even making our full tour of forty-five. But when I'd signed up, it was for sixty. We could have called it quits before that without any question of Lack of Moral Fibre, but we were just too good. We wanted to keep flying!

When we reached the end of our tour on our forty-fifth mission, we'd planned to take our Elsan, the onboard toilet, and drop it over whatever city we were bombing. I planned to transfer to Mosquitoes on the Pathfinder Force once my crew's two tours were up. Mosquitoes were twin-engine aircraft, very fast, and could get up to tremendous altitudes. I didn't want to go become an instructor or sit around on my duff. I think that was fairly typical of most of the pilots and crews: they would have been back up and at it again, with the possible exception of those who were married with families, or some of the older guys. We were young and fearless. The ones who bought it boiled down to luck of the draw. We didn't catch it until that fortieth mission.

On June 22nd, 1943, we took off on our fortieth, feeling very confident. We were one of the leaders going in on that raid. We laid our markers down with no problem, and we were on our way home. It felt like an extremely successful mission. As it turned out, a third of our squadron didn't make it back that night. We were within ten or fifteen minutes of the Dutch coast when a night fighter hit us. What bothers me most about this still, is that with all our intelligence, at that point in the war no one seemed to know about the Germans' upward firing cannons.

For the life of me, I still cannot understand why we didn't know. Of the six crews that were shot down that night, forty-two men, only fourteen of us survived the war, seven of whom were my crew.

Our port engines were hit, and then the wing caught fire. My engineer tried desperately to extinguish it, but couldn't. He and I decided to give up trying, which left it to me to give the crew the signal to bail out. When it came to these young men on our crew, their behaviour under this critical situation shows just how professional and on top of things they were. They did things absolutely by the book and with cool heads.

First, my rear gunner called in that he was okay and was going out the rear hatch. Then the navigator and bomb aimer came up from down below, and signalled me with their thumbs that they were going out; my wireless operator was right behind them. My mid-upper gunner checked to make sure I had my parachute harness on. My job was to hold the aircraft steady while the others bailed out. Then the gunner and the engineer went out after the others, and I was alone.

I had a great deal of difficulty in getting myself out at that point; I'm lucky I was able to. The aircraft was on fire, and extremely unstable. I had to get out of my seat, move across to the empty co-pilot's seat, climb down below, and go out the front hatch. I was taller than most of the guys, and got stuck in the hatch, eventually ripping my flying gloves to shreds scrambling to get out, and carrying my smaller parachute in my arms as I went. In my memory, I can still see the small rear wheel of the aircraft just skimming the top of my head as I went down and out. I'm sure a lot of pilots were killed escaping this way. If they did what I did, most would be fortunate to get out at all, and even more fortunate to not get hit by the undercarriage of the aircraft as it passed over you.

But I'm a survivor, and feel very fortunate to be so. That's what we all felt on our crew. To have the whole crew manage to safely bail out of a burning aircraft was certainly pretty rare. Of course at that point, I didn't know where anyone had landed or if they'd injured themselves when they landed.

I probably bailed out at 17,000. My parachute opened immediately, and as I started floating down, I watched the aircraft go down burning, and crash. In the bright moonlight, I could see the outline of the coast of Holland, with water everywhere in sight. Being a non-swimmer, my main fear was that I was going to land in the water and drown; we didn't have any life vest or anything.

I remember hearing the drone of the other aircraft going home over the Channel, and thinking how unlucky I was. I still didn't realize that I was several miles inland from the water. In a parachute at night, as you drop down to a hundred feet or so, things suddenly go dark, even on a bright moonlit night, because you're into the shadows. So I dropped down into what seemed like a pitch-black void. I was pretty athletic back then, and managed to avoid landing in a canal, hitting the ground properly in a farmer's pasture. Out of nowhere, a white horse appeared, which scared the devil out of me. At first I thought it was an apparition, but I must have scared the devil out of it, too, because it bolted away.

So I'd managed to land safely with no injuries, albeit in enemy territory.

I hid in a cornfield for a day, watching a woman milking a cow, and keeping an eye on where she went. I waited until around ten o'clock at night, and then went up to her house to look for some help.

I knocked on the door, and was greeted by three very surprised and nervous people who didn't speak any English. They may have been alerted that the Germans were looking for a pilot, because they invited me into the house, but then reappeared a few minutes later with a gun. The woman picked up a pitchfork, and I was marched into the village and handed over to the authorities.

I have no animosity towards them. Their lives were much more in danger than mine, if they'd been caught aiding an Allied airman. The Germans knew our crew were in the area, and were actively searching for us, so the Dutch family had done the sensible thing.

I was taken to an interrogation camp in Amsterdam, but didn't learn anything about the fate of my crew. A German officer who spoke far better English than I ever did interrogated me. He asked me my name, rank and serial number, which I gave. Then he asked for more information, but I kept quiet. The next day he returned with an RAF magazine in which my DFC [Distinguished Flying Cross] had been written up. He showed me the article, and said, "We know all about you, and everything you've done." They certainly knew that I'd just finished one tour of operations, and the particulars of the missions we'd flown. It was astonishing. He knew more about my squadron and me than I knew.

They interrogated me daily about details of our missions, but treated me well enough. The biggest scare I had was being transferred from

Amsterdam to Frankfurt. When we arrived in the city, the guards escorting us had to turn their rifles on the crowds because the people were fighting to get at us. We'd bombed Frankfurt only a few weeks before, and had done a lot of damage. So they wanted their revenge right there, and were dead serious about it. And I could understand that. Maybe the same thing happened in England after the Blitz, or maybe it didn't; but you could understand why when you looked at both sides of it.

From Frankfurt, we were sent to Stalag Luft III in Sagan, Poland. I ended up in the North Compound, which is where the Great Escape was made from. This was the summer of 1943, and the camp was relatively new. There were several fellows from my own squadron, so I was taken into the camp right away. A lot of fellows had to wait for someone to vouch for them—often for days at a time.

The camp was comprised of a series of numbered huts, with each hut having several rooms that held eight men. The compound was surrounded by barbed wire fences and guard towers. About ten feet inside the main fence, a wire ran around the perimeter. If you even touched that wire, you'd be shot—or, at least, shot at. During my time at the camp, men were certainly shot just for accidentally touching the wire.

The men I shared rooms with were always a broad mixture: an Australian rancher, an English lawyer, a Welsh economist, a fellow from Northern Ireland, a young man from Oshawa, and Kingsley Brown, who'd worked on the *Winnipeg Free Press* and a paper in Paris.

As far as I'm concerned, I have no regret at having been a prisoner of war. Being a farm boy, I learned to shut up and listen—and learn. But if anything about agriculture came up, maybe I could offer something to the discussion. I remember one debate, which was whether or not we should become German paratroopers. They'd have these things just to keep your mind alive, and to hear some of the guys arguing their points of view was wonderful.

What you learned to do in those small rooms was to back off; to only go so far with people, whether it was in sport or in a debate, and then you'd back off. All the time I was in prison camp, I saw some tremendous arguments, but somebody would always reach the breaking point, and say, "That's enough." I never saw a fight the whole time I was in there. As far as I'm concerned, that was a great part of my education.

We all had duties in the hut, whether it was cooking, keeping things

Roll Call at Stalag Luft III, 1943.

clean, or whatever: everyone shared the duty roster. There was a fellow in our room we called "Black Pat." He was a very morose and moody guy, and when it was his turn to make breakfast, he'd turn downright ugly. I'd say to him, "I want my breakfast first," and he'd launch into an awful tirade at me. But it was the best thing I could have done, because he vented all his frustrations, and I'd get my breakfast first to boot!

———

While I was in the North Compound, the Great Escape—as it later came to be known—was being planned. I was a "Goon Watcher." My job was to keep an eye on the guards and where they were in the camp. We'd be able to signal one another around camp if a guard was getting to close to a hut where a tunnel crew were working. I used to stand in Hut 104 (which is where "Harry" was dug from) when one of the guards dropped in to have a coffee with one of our guys. If the guard came out of the room quickly, our job was to knock him down to distract him long enough to get the guys out of the tunnel. They could clear a tunnel in less than a minute if they had to.

A prisoner-of-war room in a Stalag Luft III hut.

In January 1944, word came that they were moving some prisoners to a satellite camp, Belaria, three miles north of Stalag Luft III. They asked for volunteers, and about fifty of us went up there. This was a camp that had been used for the foreign workers. The facilities were the barest of bare, but it was still full of bedbugs and lice. We had no utensils to speak of, and the materials the Germans gave us were negligible, so we'd make what we needed from Klim tin cans. It was a spartan life, but we kept reasonably happy.

We had a guard by the name of Paul who knew what war was all about. He'd been on the Eastern Front for a couple of years. He'd probably been wounded, and ended up as a guard at our camp. He was an unpretentious fellow, who we were able to bribe with chocolate and cigarettes for small amenities we needed.

Two of my roommates, Brown and Martin, were very friendly with him; Martin could speak a bit of German. Paul was worried, because the town his wife and children were in had been bombed and he hadn't heard from them.

"When was the last time you saw your wife?" Brown asked.

"More than two years."

"What do you have to do to get leave?"

"It's almost impossible. One way is to catch someone escaping; then the Kommandant might give you a break."

Brown and Martin decided Paul needed a holiday, so they arranged an escape. They would hide in the washhouse; then he would find them, sound the alarm, and turn them in. The plan went like clockwork, although Brown and Martin were at first a little unnerved by the enthusiasm with which Paul flourished his pistol and shouted to the other guards. I heard later on, when they were all brought up in front of the Kommandant, they could see Paul biting his lip to keep from giggling. Brown and Martin got a couple of weeks in the cooler, and Paul went on leave and saw his family.

Just prior to the escape from the North Compound, Wally Floody, who was the technical director of the Escape, and George Harsh, who was the security officer, were moved out of the North camp and up to Belaria in my room. The Germans knew that tunnelling was going on, but didn't know any of the details. Floody and Harsh—as well as a number of other men who'd been suspected of being prime escape instigators—were moved in an attempt to quash the plans. Had they stayed in North Compound, they would have been doomed. Both had been slated to be in the first group escaping, and virtually all of those guys were captured and then later shot by the Gestapo. So fortune shone on them, although they didn't feel that at the time.

Wally was a very down-to-earth fellow, although someone you didn't screw around with. George Harsh was a different story. I've never seen a fellow with eyes as steely-blue in my life. He was older than most of us, with white hair and a trim moustache. He was tall and trim, and carried himself with an absolute sense of inner security and assurance. Apart from Wally, I don't think anyone knew much about him. I came to know him much better after the war, and only then did I learn the whole story.

I found passing time to be a fairly easy thing in camp. I was one of the ones they'd call a "Three Games a Day" man. If it were possible to play three games of something, I'd do it. Baseball, football, hockey, soccer—it didn't matter. I was probably the fittest I'd ever been in my whole life during the time I was in there. If the weather was no good, I'd do circuits around the compound. You had to keep active, and couldn't dwell within yourself. And you had to take other people into consideration, or they'd put you to the test. As far as I'm concerned, those two years out of my life were very rewarding in many ways.

The other thing I'll say about prisoners of war is this: when we're together at a reunion, if you go with your wife she has to understand you're in another world. You have to live it to know it. There's such a bond, it's tremendous. It's the same kind of bond I have with my crew: it's something you can't explain.

All I can tell you is that I experienced it; and those of us who experienced it for any length of time have a camaraderie that's almost beyond understanding. The only thing that will ever beat it in the long run is marriage and family. But that depth of understanding is just immense. P o W life brings you back down to earth.

In January 1945, Wally, George, Kingsley Brown, myself, and the rest of the Belaria camp were marched out as the Russians moved in from the east. The guys who were in the North Compound in the main Stalag were also marched out, but went off in a different direction. Our march was quite rough, but my training stood me in good stead. Other than being cold and hungry and wet, I had no problems.

We finally ended up in Luckenwalde, about twenty-five miles south of Berlin. We got there in February, and the camp there was nothing less than a hell-hole. Triple-decker bunks, no food, and swarming with bugs: it was foul. I finally started to get sick, developing jaundice from malnutrition. Our doctor told us not to shower, because we were in danger of losing too many body oils and vitamins through our skin.

That was a tough time. There were probably twenty-five thousand of P o Ws in that camp—Canadians, British, Russians. That's when we really saw how much the Russians had suffered. I saw them cleaning out the garbage dumps for anything they could find, and there wasn't much we could do for them. I saw our own officers fighting over the scraps in the bucket of barley glop that was brought to us as food. You'd see them getting up at the crack of dawn to scrounge for cigarette butts. We'd been there for several weeks, when finally the Danes brought in some food in March.

At the end of the war in April, the Russians overran our camp, and then surprised us by putting more guards on us than the Germans had. An American captain arrived in his Jeep with 120 trucks to take prisoners out of the camp, but the Russians fired their machine guns over his head to warn him off. So they left. But the captain came back the next day with five trucks, and as we were walking the camp's circuit, we heard him arguing in Russian with a Russian colonel that he wasn't trying to pull anything; he just wanted to take a few guys back to the Allied line. As they continued to argue, I said to my friend, "Let's go."

We walked out the front gate, around the corner of the camp, and over the hill to the trucks. We hopped on, and they moved out a short time later. When we tried to cross the Elbe River, the Russians were there again. They had all their guns and armour on the east side, and were saying, "We're going right through to the English Channel." They made it tough getting back to the American side, but our drivers didn't stop for anybody. They just kept saying, "Let's get the hell out of here," and I think I was back in Canada before most of the rest of the other guys even got out of the camp.

———

I'm extremely proud of my war experience. Under the same circumstances, I'd do what I did again. I'd seen Coventry, as well as a lot of the other damage that the Germans had inflicted on England and Europe. I'm also extremely proud of being a Pathfinder, and having been on the leading edge of some of those thousand-bomber raids.

The war years certainly changed me and matured me. There's no doubt about the fact that my military service allowed me the opportunity to go to college. I simply didn't have the resources, particularly as a farm boy from the prairies. We are a generation who respected what it was like to get such things. There just isn't the same fervour and commitment to community that we had.

I believe one of the problems with today's society is that they want a home, two cars, a fridge, and pretty much everything else, almost without having the resources for them. I was five years out of university before we owned a car. When my wife and I were married, we didn't have curtains on the windows; we didn't have any living-room furniture.

I'm not being judgmental. It's just that it's the age of entitlement. I feel the younger generations missed our opportunities, and as a result, rarely have the chance to develop a real sense of appreciation.

John Weir

BIRTH PLACE: TORONTO, ONTARIO
RESIDENCE: TORONTO, ONTARIO
SQUADRON: 403 SQUADRON RAF
THEATRE OF WAR: NW EUROPE

IN THE 1920S AND '30S, MY DAD HAD OCCASION TO GO TO Germany for business and I was fortunate enough to go with him. The first memory I have is of the Hotel Metropole in Wiesbaden, looking out the window, and saying, "Those people down there look just like us." Dad said, "You'll learn in time that they're a lot different." We found that out pretty soon afterwards.

Four years later we were in Cologne. And I wandered into the town square as some Blackshirts went by. Everybody gave the "Heil, Hitler" salute, but not me. This captain came over and blasted me, said he was going to throw me in jail. My aunt, who was a fiery Nova Scotian, just like my mother, came walking round the corner. She saw this and marched up to this guy, using every filthy word in the English language and a fair number in German, which caught his undivided attention. The one way to get the Germans to respond was getting face-to-face with them and screaming. The guy saluted and walked away.

In 1936, we were in Frankfurt, and I was looking out a window at thousands of people demonstrating against the tyranny of the SS and the Gestapo. By that time, Dachau and the other camps were filling up with the Jews, Gypsies, and malcontents—meaning anybody who wasn't a Nazi—and people were just disappearing. At one end of the street, a bunch of Blackshirts showed up with a water gun truck. One of the officers took out his flare pistol, fired two shots into the crowd to divide it, then blasted the protestors with the water cannon, and that was the end of the demonstration. Very efficient.

On our final trip in 1938, my father and I went to the Koïnstadt, which was a big amphitheatre.

"I want you to see this," he said.

There was a Nazi rally warming up. I'd never seen so many flags in my life. Hitler hadn't arrived yet, so we quietly slipped in at the top to have a look. I was about to take a snapshot, but Dad stopped me and said, "Don't. Don't do anything." Then we walked out, because we would have been challenged if we'd stayed. But it was an amazing, frightening sight; fanatical Nazis as far as you could see, like something out of ancient Rome. Everyone was absolutely swept up in the building furor. If they'd been told to hit the person standing next to them, they would have done it in a second. Hitler often said, "When you're talking to a crowd, it's like talking to a woman in love. They're hysterical and easy to sway."

Every time my father returned from Germany during that period, he wrote letters to Ottawa and England, warning them of what he'd seen. Ottawa brushed him off as a warmonger, and the Brits said, "We're trying to make peace." They didn't want to upset the nest, didn't pay any more attention.

My dad had been a colonel in a machine gun regiment in the First War. He joined as a lieutenant the day it started, won the DSO [Distinguished Service Order], was gassed at Mons, got out the day it ended as a colonel, but was stuck in the front line trenches the whole time, which was awful! He talked about the horrors of trench warfare and

Hughie Godefroy, John Weir's best friend, with whom he signed up in 1939.

the abominable living conditions. So when war broke out in 1939, I made up my mind to join the air force: I thought, "Let the 'Brown Jobs' do the dirty work; I'm going to have a clean shirt and be home every night in a nice comfy bed." I also figured if I got hit in a plane, I'd be killed and wouldn't have to worry about being maimed.

War was declared on September 3rd, and I joined on the 4th. Just turned twenty. It was incredibly exciting because they were going to pay me to learn to fly—I would have paid them! And I sure as hell wasn't going into the trenches. My best friend Hugh Godefroy and I joined up together. He wanted us to break the news to my father first; his father was Dutch and didn't want Hughie running off to get himself killed. That night, Dad came back from Ottawa and said to us, "I just got both you guys commissions in the Governor General's Horse Guards."

I said, "No dice. I'm not fighting in some mud ditch." Hughie and I both wanted to fly, and what's more, we both liked the idea of flying fighters.

I arrived in England in the middle of an air raid during the Battle of Britain. We'd watch the vapour trails of the Junkers 88s and the ME-110s coming over, then our fighters going up to engage them. You didn't see one vapour trail, but hundreds of them. Then every so often you'd see one of the planes come down. It was an eye-opener after doing nothing but training flights for months.

I was in London during the Blitz and it was a real mess. The rule was that if you got caught out in the open during an air raid, you got to a shelter or at least a doorway; but you did not run! During one raid, this guy was running ahead of me up Regent Street from Piccadilly, and I yelled at him to take cover just as a bomb hit. The bomb blew a piece of cornice off a building and it simply took off his head. Educational, to say the least. So I always made sure I got myself into a doorway.

In those early days, I was told the life expectancy for a fighter pilot was about six hours. But that's all I wanted to do. I never thought I was going to get shot down; I don't think any of our guys did. The first fighter I flew was a Hurricane, which was built like a truck; it took a hell of a lot to knock it down. It was very manoeuvrable, much more manoeuvrable than a Spit[fire]. A Hurricane was like driving a cheap car, whereas a Spit was like driving a really top-of-the-line racing car. It was smoother in the air than a Hurricane, but it was like a junk heap on the ground. When you taxied a Hurricane, it was smooth; when you taxied a Spitfire it coughed and sputtered. But a Spitfire was a beautiful thing to fly.

Don Blakelee, an American member of 403 Squadron RAF, who became a famous fighter leader and ace with the USAAF.

The German Junkers 88s could fly faster than anything we had. One guy nearly bought it because he had a Junkers on his tail as he came in to land. When he touched down, the Junkers let loose with its guns, but luckily our guy landed badly and bounced off the tarmac so all the Junkers' shots went underneath him.

God, it was fun flying back then.

We flew alone at night because we couldn't see each other. When you saw a ring around the moon, you knew it was a sign of fog, and was going to be a bitch to get down. Landing at night with fog is hit-and-miss. But still we loved it; all the guys did. By seniority I got first crack at some of the missions, but there was never any argument about who was going to go. We all wanted to. We got pretty good at flying in all kinds of conditions and operations. We didn't get much time off. Things were pretty one-sided, even in late '41. We were just beginning to hold our own.

We did "sweeps." You'd fly over as a squadron and fly low to attack buildings, trains or truck columns, and rake the enemy. Or a bunch of us would go up and try to knock a German flight out of the sky. If we saw a squadron on the floor, we went down and gave them a nice welcome on the ground. We were always trying to get the German fighters up in the air so we could beat them up, just looking for trouble.

What makes a good fighter pilot? The main thing is that you want to be one. You need good reflexes and you can't be too concerned about your own skin. That's why I didn't want to be on bombers, because I'd be concerned about the guys who were flying with me. But on fighters you didn't have to worry: you were alone. The other day, my wife, Fran, asked me if I was ever afraid. I told her, "No, I've never been afraid. Ever." A lot of guys felt that, "If your ticket's not punched, don't worry about it. If your ticket is punched, it's too late to worry anyhow."

I think that's an important part of it. If you're afraid, you're not going to be objective—and when you're fighting you've got to be as objective as hell. You've got to really keep your eyes open. If you're busy worrying about your tail, then you're not worrying about everything else that's up there.

I don't say all pilots weren't afraid; but I don't think Hughie was, or Ormie. We had some guys who were, one guy that was fairly senior. And we got rid of him. He used to regularly turn back with all kinds of

Flight Officer Neal (left) and Pilot Officer Ian Ormston (right). Ormston, aka
"Ormie," is and was one of John Weir and Hughie Godefroy's closest friends.
Taken at the 403 Squadron base, 1941.

excuses: bad engine, oil pressure, anything he could think of. They transferred him out of the squadron, but if he hadn't been the rank he was—a
Squadron Leader—he probably would have gone to the "Glass House."

The Glass House was a place for dealing with guys who were branded
LMF: "Lack of Moral Fibre." This was their regime: you'd get up in the
morning at five or six o'clock, you'd run to go to the can, you'd run to
breakfast, gulp your meal, go for a run with your pack, run to lunch, run
back to the can, run to pack drill in the afternoon, then run to go to bed.
That's it. They did a job on you; they were brutal.

I went to visit a guy who was sent to one of these places. I wanted to
see what it was like, because I wanted to tell some of the guys who were
showing a bit of queasiness. I told them the story. I said, "You think the
Germans are bad, well we're pretty bad to our own people." Especially at
that time, because we only had a tenth the number of planes the Germans
had, and less pilots, too. The purpose of the Glass House was to cure the
buggers so they wouldn't be afraid to fly, and some of them came back and
were good pilots after that. They didn't fly as free as a person who had

never been in, because they had that fear. But the punishment overruled the fear, and that was the objective.

It could be damn dangerous if you lost a man to nerves. In those days we'd fly three and three—but if one guy left and you were his number two, then you have to go with him, so that's two gone. You'd reduce your chances because there were fewer of you, and you become a target.

Hughie had been delayed for a few months getting over, and what a delight when he showed up. As soon as I saw he'd been posted to our flight and was down at Sutton Bridge, where I'd trained, I flew down, walked into the mess at lunch, and said, "Is there a P.O.P. Godefroy here?" Hughie turned around his jaw dropped.

"Hughie, we're in the same flight."

He didn't know; you weren't supposed to know.

"And what's more, we're in the same squadron, so I'll see you in about four days."

"You're kidding! Do we fly together?"

"You're damn right! I'm not letting anybody else on my tail anymore!" We pretty much flew together from then on, until I was transferred to A flight and Hughie stayed in B flight. If only he'd been on my tail that one day, I don't think I would have been shot down.

We could fly up to 30,000, but we flew around 25,000 because the Messerschmitt had an automatic two-stage turbocharger that shifted automatically at 24,000. When they did that, they lost power and let out a big puff of black smoke, so they were easy to get—well, easier to get. In those situations, we usually got more of them than they got of us. If your plane got hit, the odds were pretty good the pilot would get out unless he was badly wounded.

I got hit at 25,000 feet in November 1941 because I pulled rank.

Our flight had been badly wiped. We lost ten guys out of twelve one day, then lost nine guys the next. Near the end of the week, the whole squadron—except for four of us—were replacements. There was Jeep, Ormie, and myself—Hughie was on leave. That particular day, our flight were to do a sweep of Normandy, but I wasn't supposed to be flying—I was supposed to have a wisdom tooth yanked by an English dentist.

Well, English dentists were probably better as vets than dentists. They were terrible! I said, "Screw that. I'm not getting my wisdom teeth

A spitfire from 403 Squadron RAF flying over Kent shortly after Weir had been shot down.

chopped off by this guy." Then said to one of the new boys, "You're staying, and I'm taking your place."

The new guys were flying so soon because we were so short on people. They didn't have anything like the combat time we'd had, not to mention any practice with us.

Which is how it came to pass that I had a freshman behind me. It was probably my fault as much as anybody's. I was nurse-maiding him and should have been more aware of what was going on around me. There's the point about a guy who's afraid: he's watching himself, so he's not really paying attention. A bunch of us got shot down that day. I was worried sick about this freshman, so I wasn't paying proper attention. Then he bought it and I was shot down. A whole bunch of us were.

I was hit over Abbéville in France. I knew the area well from having been at summer school in Dinard not too far from there. I thought it'd be duck soup when I got down: I'd just head for my old schoolmaster's house and I'd be home.

I got hit in the gas tank, which even though it was self-sealing, exploded when it was hit, and flamed back over me in the cockpit. I was badly burned on my hands, neck and face, and most of my instruments were gone, so I jumped right away at 25,000 feet.

Everything happened so fast, I didn't have the time to do anything but move, but I never lost consciousness. When I bailed out, the first thing that happened was my boot went shooting off, which made me mad because my gun was in there.

I landed near Abbéville, buried my parachute, and met a guy on a bike. In training they'd told us never to talk to anybody with someone else around; always pick someone alone, because you never know when you'll run into an unfriendly Frenchman who'll turn you in. I told this guy who I was and asked if he would help me.

"I'll come back in an hour or so, you keep heading south," he said. So I did.

About an hour later I came to a road and he was waiting for me. But he looked at my face and said, "*Merde. Ce n'est pas possible. Vous êtes* blind."

At that point I could still see if I tilted my head far back, but my burns were starting to swell and my eyes sealed. He sat me on a tree stump and he said, "You never saw anybody; you've been blind since you landed."

"I understand."

Not more than twenty-five minutes later, I heard dogs. The Germans had been following me all along. They took me to the hospital and gave me decent treatment; no anaesthetics, but they did a pretty good job on the damage.

After Christmas, they cut my eyes open. The doctor said, "*Lieber Gott, er kann sehen*," or "Good God, he can see." I could speak German and French, which was useful. I never told them, and that came in handy a couple of times.

After being in an interrogation Dulag, I was sent to Stalag Luft I at Barth. I made up my mind there that I was going to escape. They were digging tunnels at that time with no shoring at all, and they were all collapsing. Somebody got me a good map of Stettin, which is the biggest port west of Barth in Pomerania, right on the Baltic. We had these topographical people in the camp; some of these English guys had more information than you could ever imagine. They told me, "There's a slope up from Barth before you get to the switching yard that goes south to

Berlin, and there's a station there that they usually stop at." I don't know how they got that information, but it was accurate. My plan was to get to Stettin and onto one of the boats in port—it was a bitch of a cold winter that year—but I could hide until the ice broke, or at worst be taken over to Sweden or Norway.

They decided to move us by train to Poland—Stalag Luft III—and when we were put in the cars, I noticed the windows weren't nailed shut; they only had wedges in them. I spent about half an hour loosening one, then changed seats and loosened another with some help from a couple of guys who were coming with me: a fellow named Michael and a guy from the Red Cross.

The train stopped right where the topographical boys had said. After this, the train had to climb a slope, which meant it would take a while for the engine to start. I whispered to Michael, "I'm going to drop the window, jump out and you come too." We had a pack with some food. Out we went, but the Red Cross man lost his nerve and slammed the window shut behind us. Michael and I were left standing in the snow in northern Germany with two chocolate bars and nothing else. So off we went.

We made it to Stettin across a railway bridge, and I said to Michael, "If we see anybody, don't say a goddamn word."

We passed a guard who said, "*Guten abend.*"

"*Guten abend.*" Michael kept his trap shut, and we weren't challenged. We walked right into the centre of the port and started looking for a ship. We found one with a hawser slung down to the pier, but my hands had been burnt so badly that I couldn't climb. I told Michael to go up and find someone who could come down and get me. Michael had climbed about halfway up when I spotted a German standing guard up on deck with a rifle, then noticed the barbed wire strung around.

"Michael!!" I whispered, as loudly as I could, and gestured frantically for him to come back down.

"What?"

"It's a prison ship!"

We took off fast. One of the guys on the train had told us that there was a whorehouse in Stettin that was full of girls whose parents wouldn't kowtow to the Germans. In retaliation, these girls had been rounded up and stuck in this house to service the troops. Needless to say, they hated the Germans. If we could find it, chances were they'd hide us.

Four or five days without food, just those two chocolate bars, and God, was it cold! Eventually, about four o'clock in the morning, I saw a light. I said to Michael, "That's got to be the whorehouse. Why would anybody else have a light on at this time of night? I'll go in first. It's probably a standard house plan where you walk right to the back, then a stairway goes up towards the second floor from there. There'll be a bar or a lounge on one side, and then a room for the girls on the other. Just walk straight through and do not turn your head. Just keep on walking."

I walked in and wasn't challenged. Out of the corner of my eye I could see a bartender and one man at the bar. Nothing; piece of cake.

I got halfway up the stairs and from behind me I heard, "Halt!!" Michael had come in and couldn't resist, he had to take a look.

I heard a pistol being cocked behind me. I turned around and it was the officer from the bar. He was SS and was wearing a Gestapo badge, so I thought, "Well, I've got shit coming out of my ears now."

He took us back to the bar and I whispered to Mike not to answer any questions. The German turned out to be not a bad guy.

"*Vo sind sie?*" "Where are you from?"

I said I didn't speak much German, but he persisted, so I said, "*Kriegsgefangener.*"

"What are you?"

"*Franzosisch,*" and pointed to the battered French uniform I was wearing.

"Mmm-hmm. What about your friend?"

"*Dumbkopf.* He can't speak."

We talked for a while. Then very casually, he turned to Michael and said in perfect English, "And whereabouts do you come from in England?" and Michael said, "Surrey." With that, we all burst out laughing! But for the privilege of that shared joke, we spent two weeks in a Gestapo jail, which was an education.

They beat the crap out of us. Michael didn't speak German, but they didn't believe him. In the jail, you went into your cell, where there was a bunk folded up along the wall. It stayed up till they told you to put it down, so you had to be on your feet. Michael didn't get that, put it down right away and climbed into bed, then got beaten up for it. The next morning, we were given a pot, which you put through a square hole in the bottom of the door for them to put your food in, then they'd open the

Four Canadian prisoners of war who worked on the tunnels at Stalag Luft III. John "Scruffy" Weir (right), Ted Sangster (left), Wally Floody (front left), and Henry Birkland, (front right).

door, and you could go to the can. Again, Michael didn't understand. I said, "The pot goes out first, the food comes in next, then you go to the can with me." Whammm! I got hit across the back for talking.

I forgot to tell him that we got drilled twice a day, at eleven o'clock and three o'clock. They took you out into a square, lined you up in a circle, and the guy with the whip said, "Walk." Michael didn't know what the hell they were saying, so I whispered, "Just do what they do." Whammm! They hit me again. Michael started to walk and bumped into the guy in front of him, so he got hit. Then they told us to turn around, Michael didn't understand, and whammm!

And so it went.

When those two weeks had passed, we were sent down to Sagan and put into solitary for two weeks, which was wonderful! The food was certainly better than the Gestapo jail, which had been practically nothing.

Finally, I ended up at Stalag Luft III. This camp had just been opened and we were the first ones in. There was one compound for the Non-Coms, and another one, the North Camp, for officers, which is where we did the tunnelling from.

There were a lot of guys in the North Camp who were some of the finest escape artists in the air force, so escape plans were already under way. Four of us—Wally Floody, myself, Henry Birkland, all Canadians, and a Polish guy by the name of Minskevic—had worked in the mines at one time or another. We went to one of the "Big X" meetings about tunnelling, because they'd had failure after failure at Barth. It was the same type of soil at Stalag Luft III, sandy and wet. The contribution the four of us made to the plan was the suggestion that they start building the tunnels like a mine: with shoring, air pumps and the whole works.

We spent the better part of a year digging. A Norwegian fighter pilot who was a surveyor did the triangulation and figured out how far we had to go: about 420 feet to get to the trees. When we dug the tunnel, we first went down thirty feet and shored it up with boards from our bunks. Jens designed a one-man air pump out of a duffle bag and suggested we connect Klim tins to make an air duct, and then bury it underneath the railway track. I don't know who suggested the railway, but I think it was Pappy Plante. He was a great guy, always looked as if he didn't have more than two eggs in his basket.

We put bed boards across the top, sides and bottom of the tunnel, then put plugs in and nailed them to hold them in place. Pappy suggested, "Why don't we do it the same way we make drawers?" In other words, tongue and groove so that they fit into each other without any nails. Which was great, because the Germans could hear us hammering, and with the tongue and groove shoring we never had a cave-in.

At the bottom of the entrance shaft, we started tunnelling out towards the woods. It was hard to crawl quickly down to the face of the tunnel, so we dug it on a slope down to the middle of the tunnel, which we called Piccadilly Circus, then it sloped up again to what we thought was the thirty-foot depth at the far end. That's why we had two slopes: the guys at the face could ride the railway back, and the guys at the pump station could pull us up the hill, so we could get back in very short order.

The organization was great. Goon watchers were placed at all corners of the cabins where any tunnelling was being done. They were damned important, as they were our only warning system. But they couldn't be obvious because we didn't want the Germans to know for sure that we were digging. If we got the signal, we had to come back down the tunnel and up into the hut in under a minute.

At first, the Ferrets used to crawl underneath the huts to listen, but after a while they couldn't because we'd dumped so much sand there. We had Penguins dumping it all around the compound. Unfortunately, the sand at that depth was bright orange and the dirt on top was grey. So the

Penguins had to learn to pull the plug and scuff their feet. But they were good; they got rid of a lot of sand.

The digging was soft and wet. The water table wasn't far below us, so it was easy digging. But I had a very bad habit of digging left and down. So until we got things straightened out, we had to keep filling in my errors.

To do triangulation you have to have three points of vision, which we didn't have, so we had to guess. We'd dug the face of the tunnel down steeper than we'd planned, and as a result the tunnel was something like thirty feet deeper at its end than we'd anticipated. Ultimately, the guys had to dig up those additional thirty feet the night of the escape, and then found themselves about sixty feet short of the woods, just outside the wire. Someone scrambled out of the tunnel across open ground to the woods with a rope. He'd tug on the rope when the guard had passed, which was the signal for the next man to climb out and run to the trees.

But I hadn't been there when the escape took place. Around Christmas 1943, the Red Cross came to me and said, "You're going to Frankfurt to have your eyes operated on."

I didn't want to leave because, hell, we were getting close to the escape. But I had no eyelids because of my burns. They said, "Are you sleeping with your eyes open? It's just a matter of time before you'll get an infection." We couldn't get rid of the sand from the tunnels and everything had come a stop, so I said okay.

I went off to Frankfurt to get my eyes taken care of, and was there for about five months. Meanwhile, the escape went ahead at the end of March. Fifty of my guys were murdered; I heard about it through the grapevine in the hospital. The Red Cross doctor told me, "You're going back to something that's not so good."

"Jesus! Has the escape happened?"

"They've murdered fifty of your guys. Nobody is talking to the Germans anymore in this hospital, and nobody is talking to the Germans at Stalag III. We think it's going to spread to the other camps if we can get the information out."

Which was fine with me.

Most of the escapees who'd been shot had a higher education than me. If I'd been one of the escapees and had been caught, I would've told them what I told everybody else; that if it hadn't been for the war, I would have failed at university anyhow, so the war saved my bacon. That would've probably saved my bacon with the Germans, too, because they'd think, "Here's a dum-dum, we'll let him go back." The guys they killed were the ones that had what they considered to be "leadership qualities," like education and languages.

Two guys may have been killed trying to get on a bus or a train; they had run and had been shot. Roger Bushell's goose was cooked right from the beginning because they knew who he was. After the interrogation, he and five or six other guys were taken out on a truck—there was a guy on a motorcycle behind them with a machine gun—let them stretch their legs, then machined-gunned them down. We know how that happened.

Henry Birkland, my roommate in camp, was a great guy. When he escaped, he decided that instead of going west and south like all the other guys, he'd go east into Poland, less chance of being caught. Sadly he was caught and shot.

The other ones are very difficult. We know they were murdered because the Germans were so methodical. They put four men in a cell, then they'd take two out and interview them, then put them back in different cells. So now our guys would know who was still alive, and when they were moved, and they'd pass the information along. From that, they established that every one of them was alive in this jail; they weren't shot while trying to escape, as the Germans claimed. Every guy had been witnessed as being alive. Then they all came back cremated, which meant the Germans were hiding something. So it was murder, just straight out-and-out murder.

After the war, we discovered that a lot had been shot in the back of the head. During the war, undertakers in Europe kept two books—one for the Gestapo and SS, and one for the "Fraternity," as they called it. In the Fraternity books, which had been hidden, they told it exactly as it was. If a guy came in shot in the back of the head, it was written down— his name and everything else. We were able to trace quite a few that way. They were all butchered.

When I returned to the camp, the atmosphere was one of brassing off the Germans at every turn. Not talking, not cooperating. When they asked for a parade, they got a parade that a bunch of morons would be disgusted with: guys with their pants undone, peeing in the lineups, fist fights, anything to get things going. The Germans hated roll call. Every time a German came into the compound, the guys would all walk up close to him so he'd be afraid to move. We never touched him, because if we did, the Germans would shoot. But we intimidated them and kept the Germans pretty much off balance.

There were some bright spots. We had our famous booze party where Minskevic showed us how to make gin out of apples, sugar, raisins and spit. We had barrels buried underneath the huts. They used a trombone, a heater and a cold shower to get it to condense. When the liquid came out and the flame burnt blue, you could drink it, but when it burnt yellow, you had to let it burn off. We collected the good stuff and someone—I think it was Pop Collett—got a bet going, saying, "Two squares of chocolate to any guy who can drink a glass from the vat and still be standing in five minutes." Naturally, I took the bet, even though I wasn't a drinker.

I swallowed mine and managed to get my glass back down on a table. Then the strangest thing happened. My glass slowly started towards the floor, hit the floor and fell apart in slow motion. And that's the last thing I remember. I came to about an hour or so later and saw everybody was sick. They had to get a fire hose and wash out every room. That was the kind of crazy stuff we did. We made it difficult for them. But nobody else ever escaped, because they'd told us, "Anybody escapes and gets caught, they're shot. No trial, nothing."

Around New Year's 1945, the Russians were closing in from the east. The Germans wanted to hold onto us to negotiate, so they moved us out of the camp on foot. The march started in Poland and went west, where we were taken by cattle car to Bremerhaven. The car next to us wasn't organized very well and was full of guys sick with dehydration from diarrhea. At one stop, I got off the train and ran to the engine to get some hot water for them. The engineer watched with a big grin on his face—he wasn't going to do anything—then I ran back as fast as I could and dropped that off. On my way to get some water for our car, one of the Ferrets who we called "Red Face"—he was a miserable son of a bitch—tried to shoot me underneath the car as I ran past, but I made it back before he could hit me.

Our cattle car had great organization on that trip. These cars were built for four horses or twenty men. We had forty to fifty guys in each one. Pop Collett, who was older than most of us, said right off the bat, "A third of you, stand up; a third of you, sit down; and a third of you, lie down. And you stay that way for four hours. We're gonna carve a hole in the floor right here, so if you're going to be sick, try to get over to there, and if you've gotta do anything else, do it down that hole." He also said, "I want all the food that anybody's got of any kind. Anybody that tries to hide food, you know what'll happen to you. No spare chocolate bars or anything like that; I want the whole works. We're going to ration it." When we got to Bremerhaven, we were in good shape; we were pretty clean, and with the extra water I got every so often, we never had any trouble with dehydration.

At Bremerhaven, the Germans realized that the war was all but over, and we were going to be freed by the approaching 8th Armoured Corps, so they moved us north on foot to Lubeck.

There were over two thousand of us and we clearly couldn't be fed. The first night on this march, eight of us built a sod hut and were the only ones who stayed dry. I'd been taming a Goon in Bremerhaven ever since we got there—giving him a little coffee, a little sugar, a little chocolate, maybe a cigarette here and there—and was getting information in return. I found this Goon and said, "I've got a deal for you. There're four of us, and we'll all sign a letter of amnesty, so you won't be put in a cage, you'll go straight home."

"Yeah?"

"In exchange for that, we want a cart, a horse, a driver, and you are to be our guard, with your gun. Any time it looks like somebody's going to question you, you turn the gun on us and the story is that you're taking us to a P o W camp."

"I'll think about it."

"Well, think about it right now, otherwise I'll find somebody else."

"I'll think about it."

"Okay, I'm in the mud hut over there. Four o'clock in the morning we take off." If we left then, we could travel the rest of the night and all the next day and get well ahead of the others.

Just before four, my Goon came over and gave my foot a kick. So four of us took off. I'd picked Sam, Ed, and Henry to travel with, all for different reasons. Henry was much more stable than we were, Sam spoke good German—he was Icelandic, from Winnipeg—and Ed was beautiful, blond, pink skin, blue eyes, five-feet-ten, a typical Aryan, so he was going to be very useful with the women. And me, I'd been trained for this type of unconventional action, so off we went.

We travelled all night and all the next day; we didn't stop. I figured they couldn't move two thousand guys on foot at much more than two miles an hour, whereas with the cart, we could do six or seven miles. So we got well ahead of them. The German guard had to change the horse and cart every two days because we didn't want anybody to notice us. We kept to country roads parallel to the autobahn to avoid getting lost.

We ate high off the hog in the country, eggs every day. We used Ed to charm the housefrau, then Sam would go around one side of her house and I'd go around the other, and Henry would stay on the road ready to whistle if anything happened. We shared our food with the guard and driver, so they were happy.

There were a couple of close calls, though. One day, we came up to a bridge, and one of the guys said, "Let's have our lunch under there, it'll be nice and cool in the shade."

"Just a minute."

I crawled up top of a knoll and peered over the edge of the ridge, just to check. Sitting under the bridge were about a hundred Germans having their lunch. I crept down and said, "We've got to—" and I only got that far, when we hear this *thrub-thrub-thrub-thrub*. Ed yelled "Tiffies! Hit the dirt!" We dove into the ditch just as two Typhoons flew over and let loose a barrage of rockets. They didn't blow the bridge apart, but there wasn't much left. All the Germans were killed. Those Typhoons did a hell of a job.

We took off fast and kept changing direction for two days; we couldn't take a chance of being caught after an attack like that.

The second close call happened about a week later. It was my turn to ride in the cart and I was dozing in the straw with the other guys walking behind. I woke up, looked over the top of the horse's rump at what was coming towards us on the road up ahead.

"Oh, shit!"

It was a grey German field car with an officer's flag flying.

"Christ, we've had it. Tell the guard to assume P o W position, get in behind the cart and for God's sake look hangdog or sick. Or both! But don't look at anybody."

The car stopped. There was a major, a colonel, a captain, and two guards. Our guard was sweating and had turned as grey as their damn car. But it was hot, so these guys didn't catch on. The colonel wanted to know where they were and the name of the next village, so our guard told him. Then the colonel asked, "What's all this? What's goin' on?"

Our the guard said, "I'm taking these prisoners of war to the Luftwaffe camp in Lubeck."

"Ahhh! Carry on." And off they went, satisfied.

We didn't know there was any such camp there, but our guard did. Thank God. Just to be safe, we doubled back south for two days, and then headed back up.

Near Lubeck, we were walking parallel to the autobahn. I saw four cars heading west, and in the front car was Admiral Doenitz, the man who succeeded Hitler.

"It looks like they're going to a meeting of some consequence."

That was about ten or eleven o'clock in the morning. Around three o'clock, they came back. The next day, the procession headed towards Lubeck again, but didn't return.

"Boys, the game's over," I said. "We've gotta find our gang. We're not staying out by ourselves anymore, it's too damn dangerous."

We scooted on up to Lubeck, where we caught up with them. That was the only time I was really nervous, because if anything went wrong the four of us would have just disappeared. At the gate to our compound, I saw Bill Jennings, the 2IC, who looked us up and down and said, "Scruffy, where the hell have you been? Geez, I wish I had been with you."

We were well-fed and healthy as sin, since we had been able to do what we had to do to survive without our guard giving us a whimper. They'd had a particularly rough go; no food, not much shelter, and sure as hell no cart and horse.

Now the war was over. There was a cage outside Lubeck for the Germans, and our army was having trouble keeping the Germans under control. Since we hardly had enough food to feed ourselves, they had to feed themselves and report in at seven in the morning and at night. But they weren't doing it. Our guys wanted to make an example of one of them and asked me if I'd come and finger someone that we'd like to get rid of. I said I sure would: one of the Ferrets, Red Face. I won't say what they did, but there were no more problems with the Germans from then on.

Not long after, one of our guys asked, "Did you sign a piece of paper for some guard?"

"Yup."

"Did anybody else?"

"Yeah. Henry, Sam, and Ed. With our serial numbers."

"Was it torn?"

"Yeah. We signed it and tore it in half, gave him half and promised to give him the other half when we were freed."

"Okay. Then there's your man." He pointed to our guard, now inside the cage.

"What are you going to do with him?"

"Well, we hadn't made up our minds. When a German has something like that on him, it looks like he got rid of the four of you."

"No, we're all here. He did us a real service."

I waved at the guard, gave him a thumbs up, and he was released and gone before you could even see dust. I never knew his name, and never knew where he came from. Frankly, the less I knew about him, the better. But it was great to have had something like that work out.

———

Most people wouldn't believe what I went through, or what I did during the war. I enjoyed the challenges, but they certainly changed me. While I was naïve, I probably knew more than most people did about what was going on. Yet even after all I'd seen, I still found it hard to believe that the Germans would go as far as they did.

Even though after the war they were always saying, "I wasn't a Nazi," or "I was Swiss," they all knew. They did. I'd been taken out of camp at Sagan once to get my teeth fixed, and noticed ten black carts on the railway track. There was a bunch of girls—Poles, Gypsies, and Jews—standing by the tracks. I said to the dentist, "What are those black carts on the railway track?" And he turned grey. They were gas chambers.

By the time I came out, all those girls were dead. The carts were still there, but the girls weren't. There wasn't a sound. I told one of the guards what I'd seen, and he said, "Don't ever say anything. Ever! I saw it too, but I would never tell my friends. That's how you get it yourself."

The world was basically uninformed. They'd been told about Dachau, but didn't believe what they heard. There are guys still writing about it, saying that the Holocaust was a figment of the Jewish imagination. I went to school with one of them, and I've done everything but kill him, he makes me so mad.

So I'm proud of what I did during the war. I'm sorry I wasn't better at shooting down planes, and there were some things I did that I'm not proud of, but in those situations it was a case of them or me.

ke Patterson Bomb-Aimer

Johnny Tovatt Navigator

Dave Balchin Gunner

Clement Pearce*

BIRTH PLACE: TORONTO, ONTARIO
RESIDENCE: TORONTO, ONTARIO
SQUADRON: 101 SQUADRON RCAF
THEATRE OF WAR: NW EUROPE

I'LL NEVER FORGET THE WAY THE WAR CAME HOME TO ME. IT was Sunday morning and my parents were due back from a holiday that afternoon. There was a knock on the door and a telegram delivery boy stood there, whistling. This was quite an event: we'd never received a telegram.

"We regret to inform you that Sergeant Basil Vincent Pearce is missing in air operations over Germany. Letter to follow."

It was a long afternoon waiting for my parents to arrive home. When they did, I murmured to my father, "Come out to the garden with me."

He read it quietly, and then had to go back in to tell my mother. To this day, I can still hear her shriek of anguish. I was sixteen, six years younger than my brother Basil, and it was at that moment I decided I had to enlist in the air force.

———

Two years later, I was an air gunner in England. My squadron in England was the famous 101 Special Duty Squadron, which specialized in airborne RADAR jamming to disrupt German night-fighters' interceptions. The squadron was so secret, the saying went, "that they hated to pay us."

Our crew had a brilliant skipper, Gene Atyeo, who was only twenty-two. But since I was eighteen, Gene was an old man to me. As the youngest on our crew, I did all kinds of necessary things prior to a mission. Frequently, I'd pick up parachutes for some of the other guys who were busy with their pre-flight duties. Our wireless operator, Johnny, was thirty-one, which seemed very, very old. He was a lovely, quiet Mennonite fellow from out west. It was on our last flight together that he said, "Clem, I'm going up to signals. Would you draw me a parachute?"

"No problem."

The parachutes were packed in canvas. Of the two I picked out, one cover was khaki, and the other was dark brown. I brought them to the aircraft and held them up for him to choose.

"What'll you have: vanilla or chocolate?"

He laughed, and said, "I've always loved chocolate," and took that chute.

That night, we were shot down and had to bail out. I later discovered that the Germans found Johnny's body in the morning, buried four inches into the ground. His chute had opened, but hadn't deployed, which paratroopers called a "Roman Candle."

Another man on our crew was a German Jew who had fled Germany with his parents before the war, then volunteered to fly on this secret squadron as a radio operator. That night, he was the last one to bail out. He was one of the bravest men I ever knew. Imagine being a German Jew, and having to bail out over Germany. The last thing I knew of him was visiting his grave in Germany years later.

When the plane was hit, Gene gave us the order to bail out. The aircraft was exploding, the oxygen bottles were exploding, but I couldn't seem to function; I couldn't move! There I was, only eighteen, terrified, and going down in the aircraft that had killed my brother. I wanted my mama.

I couldn't find my parachute. I crumpled into a fœtal position on the floor of our Lanc, which was quickly turning into an inferno. As I lay there, I looked up and coming through the smoke and the flames was an airman with a familiar face and voice.

"Don't worry, Clem. It's going to be all right."

A great peace descended on me. I got myself together, managed to get to my feet, find my chute, then bail out. As I was floating down, it suddenly came to me: that airman had been my brother.

I've tried to explain that, to rationalize it away, a thousand times, but there it is.

I landed in a cornfield, and buried my chute. When I'd bailed out, my flying boots had been torn off, so I was in socks that had been torn to ribbons. We'd been told to avoid any built-up areas, but I thought, "It's three in the morning. Aw, to hell with playing it safe," and I set out for the Dutch border. It was a fatal mistake.

I walked into this little village, which looked like a safe enough bet. I turned a corner and strolled right into the arms of a bunch of young Germans who'd been out drinking; they were big strapping, healthy kids, and I was exhausted with nowhere to run.

They took me in tow to the local jail, and the Luftwaffe was called in to pick me up. The next day, I was put on a train to the Dulag, and was now officially a prisoner of war.

It was now the end of August '44. On the train to the P o W camp, we heard that Paris had been liberated. I thought, "Boy, they're really

A Dakota that has been hit starts its downward spiral.

moving now! Won't be long before we're out of here." I was only off by about eight months.

It was a gorgeous summer. Even though we were prisoners, we were alive, and being treated pretty well. We arrived at our camp, which was still in the process of being built. There were Red Cross parcels there for us, and everything was new. God, if this was what is was like to be a P o W, I couldn't believe our good luck.

In the camp, life was fairly relaxed. The guards treated us well. But there was one standing order: if you had to answer the call of nature at night, you flung your hut door open, waved to the chap up in the sentry box. He then trained his machine gun on you, and you made lots of noise as you walked to the latrine. You did your business, then waved like mad at him as you came out, and he'd follow you in his gun sight back to your hut. Then you slammed the door shut.

If an air raid was sounded during the day, our instructions were to immediately clear the field, move into our huts, close the shutters and doors, and stay put until the "All Clear" came. This one particular day, there was an air raid. We heard the "All Clear" down in the village, but not in the compound. One of the lads in our hut was reading, and when he heard the "All Clear" in the village, without thinking he tossed his book down, and simply walked out to the latrine. He was shot immediately.

Everyone dashed to the door, and one of the officers said, "Don't go out or they'll shoot." We stood there watching him, unable to do anything. When the "All Clear" finally came, we waved at the guard in the tower, then brought him inside. This poor kid kept saying, "Mother, Mother, I'm so cold, Mother." Just like in a movie. Then he died. I was still a teenager, and his voice and the look on his face has always haunted me.

In January, we could see artillery flashes from the approaching Russian army. Word came that we were being moved west, and had a half hour to pack. We took the slats out of the bed and we made rough sleighs, and then piled on everything we could. And with that we started our march west.

We walked. And we walked. They didn't have food, water or shelter for us. At night, we'd be put in barns if there were any farms around; and in the morning, if we were lucky enough to find livestock on the farm, we'd fight them at their troughs for turnips or anything else edible. From this, the inevitable happened, and a lot of us, including me, got dysentery.

I remember one point on this dreadful march, curling up in the snow, and just wanting to die. I was in agony and couldn't move and frankly didn't care what happened to me. These two army men found me; they were glider pilots from Operation Market Garden who'd been captured at Arnhem. They pulled me to my feet, and said, "Look. Your mother's lost one boy. She's not going to lose two." And with that, they dragged me between them, slept with me one on each side, and generally hauled me along on this march, and so saved my life.

We finally made it to Luckenwalde, about thirty miles south of Berlin. Here we were put into a terrible camp, which was more or less for civilians. Terrible food, bugs, miserable cold. The morning of April 22nd, we looked up and saw that this big tank had knocked down the front gates.

"Comrades, you're liberated." This was Marshall Koneve of the 1st Ukrainian Army. They were great, but were still under Russian orders, and so they kept us under close guard. We waited. And we waited. A few days later, about a hundred American trucks rolled up to rescue the Americans among us who'd been captured in the Battle of the Bulge. This was tremendously exciting, and so we all ran out to greet them. All of a sudden, the Russians started firing their machine guns over our rescuers' heads.

"Turn around! Go back!"

We were appalled, but couldn't do a damn thing. So we started marching dejectedly back to camp. I was walking with Wally Floody and a bunch of other guys when an American major rolled up in his Jeep. He didn't want to get shot by the trigger-happy Russians, so he was getting the hell out.

He spotted my Canada flashes on my jacket, and said, "That's close enough." He hauled me into his Jeep, and I was home a month before everybody else.

But probably the best luck I ever had was yet to come. I was scheduled to fly back to England from Brussels. There were two planes ferrying the lot of us back to England. There were a lot of Brits who'd been taken prisoner at Dunkirk in 1941 and they ended up on a Lancaster, which I envied, since I was stuck on a slower Dakota. But when we reached England, the other plane hadn't made it. The survivors told the story.

Inside a Lancaster there's a release cord that runs the length of the plane. If you had to crash-land in water, you pulled it and a life raft popped out of the wing and inflated. On the flight home, there was an army boy who didn't know anything about this. When they were about a thousand feet over the airdrome, climbing. He reached up to this cord, said, "Ding, ding! Next stop, Piccadilly," then pulled it. The dinghy popped out from the wing, then wrapped around the tail, and the Lanc went down into the North Sea, killing most of the guys on board. That was as sad as anything I heard from the war. God knows how long he and his buddies had been locked up in their camp. And to get that close to home! There but for the grace of God...

———

During the war we were never attacked by fighters and so I never fired my guns in anger. All I wanted was revenge for killing my brother. It gives me no pleasure to think what carnage our bombs did when we dropped them, not for one moment. But it was an eye for an eye. They're doing it to you, you're doing it to them, and that's pretty bloody terrible, no matter how you look at it.

No one wanted to kill innocent civilians who may not even have known what Hitler's policies were. It's hard to justify, but it was a necessary evil. If we hadn't taken action, what else might have happened to other innocents?

It was only after the war that we learned about what had happened to the Jews and all the other people in the camps. I can only hope that a mother, her child in her arms, being forced into a gas chamber, could hear the roar of our Merlin engines coming to kill and hurt and maim those who had persecuted her and her family. You sow the wind; you reap the whirlwind.

Nora Cook

MY NAME IS NORA B. COOK. I WAS BORN IN UPPS TOWNSHIP, which is five miles from Lindsay. There were seven girls and one boy and we lived on a farm. My father died when I was four years old and my mother had to manage the farm, had to do everything herself with the help of the girls and my one brother. But we had farm help and we managed. We had a very enjoyable life, actually. We never had a lot of money, but we were very close.

We didn't seem to miss the money. We enjoyed each other, played a lot of cards, made our own entertainment. All of us were going to school and university when our time came. When I was eighteen, I decided that I'd had enough school, so I decided to go into nursing because I always enjoyed helping people.

I put in a few applications and I was accepted at most of them and ended up at St. Joseph's in Toronto. It was a very good hospital at that time. In nursing, you started off as next to nothing—as a "probie." There were only thirteen in our class. We went in February and got to know each other very, very well, but the nuns were very, very strict; we worked very, very hard. But it was good training. We had to take our classes in our time off from the wards. We used to have to wash bedpans and all these things that nobody else would do now. We used to call it slave training.

One of our little pleasures was zipping off and going to swim at the lake at Sunnyside. We didn't have time for much of anything personal, between going to class and working all the time. We were so intent on trying to graduate that the war didn't mean that much, really. We were so involved in our own little lives, in our own little group. All the boys were gone, that was the sad part. Once in a while, the air force boys would come into the yacht club and we'd go on dances and so forth, but that didn't happen too often.

After we graduated, I worked at the hospital for about six months. I worked on the private floor as a head nurse. All my friends and my brothers-in-law were joining the army, and I thought it sounded kind of good, so I applied and I was accepted.

When I was accepted, I was put at Chorley Park, which isn't there any more. It was a military convalescence hospital overlooking the Don Valley on the edge of Rosedale; it used to be the Lieutenant-Governor's residence, and was a beautiful old building. I was there about three months, then they sent me to Hamilton, to a school that had been taken

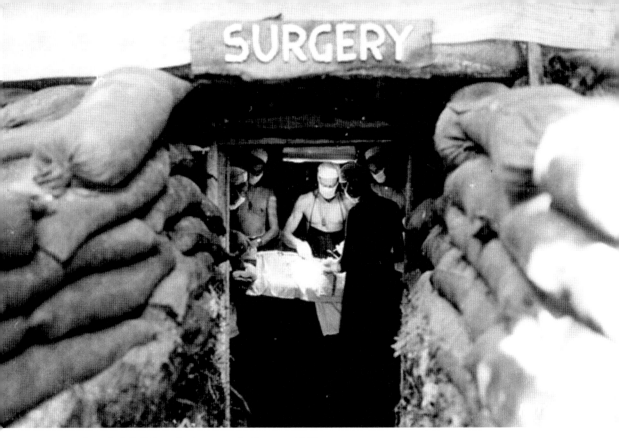

SURGERY

A typical field hospital surgery in France, 1944.

over as a hospital. It was just for the boys that were militia, not that sick really, and I think more than likely were looking for time off more than anything else.

I was only there for about three months when my friend and I got word that we were going overseas as nursing reinforcements. It was November 1943, which was a pretty tragic time to leave—just before Christmas—when you've never been very far away from home. I didn't want to go any more. I'd also met this lieutenant in Hamilton, and we'd become engaged. But he was going over with the artillery, and so we decided to meet in England.

We were shipped to Halifax for a week so they could check us out and make sure we weren't pregnant. They had to make certain about such things, because they didn't want to have to send us back home again.

We got on this ship, which looked like just an old tugboat. There was a whole gang of nurses and NCOs going over, and we had fun on the way over. At least at first. We started being chased by submarines, so instead of being a five-day trip, it took five weeks. We had to zigzag non-stop all the way across. I think we went as far south as Bermuda and as far north as Iceland. Most of us were sick as could be on that awful trip over. After that trip, they docked this old ship and got rid of it because it wasn't fit for anything more. We were its last trip.

We landed up in Watford, which was quite another shock. We'd come from Canada just before Christmas, and in England, everything was so bleak. We'd all been looking forward to this adventure, and everything was so dark and dreary, not to mention the constant blackouts. The Canadians had taken over a mental hospital and we had these little huts, which was where we had to look after these patients. It was quite a come-down from what we'd known in Canada; it was a shock more than anything, because we'd never had to do anything like this before.

I met my two brothers-in-law about two weeks after we arrived and they said that I was still green. They said, "My God, what happened to you?" The trip and those first weeks getting used to England were unbelievable. And I got word that my fiancé had been killed in France. It was a rough time.

———

After about three months, they decided that we needed more training, because the boys were going into France and we needed to build up our strength. They sent a whole group of us up to a place called Scott's Corners, near Richmond Hill. This sergeant major was to whip us into shape, and whip us into shape he did. It was just awful because we had never had to do anything like this before. It was exercise, morning, noon, and night. He yelled and screamed and hollered at us. Then he'd load us into trucks and drop us off about two miles away from camp with these great big double packs.

We'd just received food and gift parcels from home for the first time, so we had to take all that with us, then haul it back again. It was something else for a bunch of nurses. Anyway, we made it through it okay. I look back at it now and think how thankful we were for the exercise, because if we hadn't had that training, I don't think we could have gone through France the way we had to. We wouldn't have had the stamina, because we were all sort of soft.

———

When they took us over, we landed at Dieppe, which was just being taken over by the Canadians again. We had to go in by little boat to land, since no proper harbour had been established. Our field hospital was just some tents pitched in a farmer's field. There was so much rain and mud, no food, and basically no drinking water except for the rain.

We got everything set up and it wasn't long before we got patients flooding into us. This is the sad part, all these kids coming back. It was so tragic, all these boys with arms and legs blown off. You can't explain what it's like to try and deal with all these casualties. They were filled with shrapnel and had every imaginable injury. I think they were just glad to see a nurse, a friendly face, after what they had been through. To be able to lie in a bed with sheets, and to have some loving care, so to speak, get a little tenderness: I know it meant a lot to them.

We bandaged them, sewed them up as best we could, and kept them for maybe twelve hours at the most, then shipped them out to England, as quickly as we could. It was just a constant thing, with them coming in all the time. We worked about twelve hours straight, had a rest, and then went back for another twelve hours. There was no time off; you just kept working. The doctors, too.

You'd get off work and be exhausted after eighteen hours straight looking after all these sick boys. You'd think, "If I could just have a little bit of relaxation and a drink…" There was always a bit of booze around.

Then a call would come through: the air force boys were back from a mission and needed some companions. They posted a list for a get-together and if you wanted to go, you put your name down. But everybody was so darned tired that nobody wanted to go, so it would be, "You go." "No, you go." "No, you." Then before you'd know it, the air force drivers would roll up in this great, big truck and zip a bunch of us off to their base for a dance.

We usually had a good time when we got there, but it often was that extra something we didn't need. But it helped them, the air force boys. Oh, God, what they went through was unbelievable. It was non-stop mental pressure. So we cheered them up as best we could, had some fun, and they needed it.

It wasn't just the anti-aircraft and the night fighters that got to them. They had to fly these missions dropping these damn bombs, and it bothered a lot of them. They'd say they didn't want to, but didn't have any choice.

So we didn't get much sleep—but when we did go to sleep, which was rare, we used to wear these helmets—I don't know how we managed to do it—but we had these damned helmets on all the time, night and day, come hell or high water. We were bombed once by the Americans—it just was an accident and it didn't do that much damage—but it could

Wounded Canadians being loaded into an ambulance Jeep in Germany, 1945.

have done a lot of damage and certainly made us nervous. It was a good reason to keep your helmet on. We had dress uniforms, but in the field, we wore these khaki things with great big pants. They weren't pretty, but they were very practical.

Our hospital was the first one to get penicillin when it was made available, and we used to just move up and down the wards giving injections, all day long. In the hospital, everything had to be boiled for twenty minutes. We used the same syringe for everybody; you didn't have any choice. But it did miracles. There would have been a heck of a lot more loss of life if it hadn't been for that penicillin.

It was very sad, difficult work, but you always had your friends with you. They supported you. Everything was all so new and so different. Thank goodness, we had a very, very good unit. Everyone was very supportive, except for a few snobs and oddballs. The friends you made were good friends.

If you were working a long shift and exhausted, then had someone come in that was all cut up and was all dripping blood, telling you his problems—you'd get so down, so sad. You'd go back to the unit and meet one of your friends and they'd cheer you up. All the togetherness we had, and we became very good friends that really lasted for the rest of your life.

In this farmer's field, we lived in tents, and at that time, it was just rain, rain, and more rain. There was canvas on the floors of the tents, but that didn't help much. I remember one time that someone, with good intentions, sent over a great big load of beautiful, blue wool blankets. We'd put them on the beds, but there was so much water on the floor that these beautiful blue blankets were a wreck in no time. And the mud—oh, God, I never saw so much mud in all my life.

For food, they had these big tables set up and you had your tray and you would go along and get your meal. But the food—well, there was no decent food—it was bully beef and hard tack. Occasionally they might get something decent like dessert, but they'd just plunk it down on top of the other stuff. It wasn't difficult to lose weight.

The other thing about France was when we first went in, they gave us a shot for malaria, which we never had a problem with. What everybody suffered from was diarrhea. We had these toilets—so to speak—about six rows of them down at the far end of the camp. There was always a line-up

A field hospital in France. Nora Cook (extreme right) with colleagues and friends.

because, with diarrhea, what do you expect? The air force boys would fly over where we were lined up, which was most embarrassing, but after a while we finally got some medication.

As the front line kept moving towards Germany, things got better, because we didn't get nearly as many casualties. We went from France into Belgium, then Germany. We were there almost eighteen months. After the winter of 1945, in March and April, we had a lot more free time. We did get some leave, but I don't think we went many places, just off to a town or village nearby. When we moved into Belgium, we took over a great, big place that had been a mental hospital. It was much easier working there. Everything was inside, so we were able to get rid of the tents. And that's pretty much where we were 'til the end of the war.

I had a leave to go to Ireland. I had my plans made, because we weren't that busy, and things were quietening down. V-E day came and we had a big celebration—patients that were in the hospital and everybody—we were all just so happy. Some people stayed on after and took trips around England and Scotland. But I didn't go on my trip to Ireland. I decided I wanted to catch the first boat home that I could.

I remember being greeted when I came back. I had six sisters and a brother and all the relatives there to greet me, and I was treated like a hero. But I didn't feel like any kind of a hero at all—I just did what I was supposed to do. I think a hero does great things. I didn't do great things; I just kept going.

———

The horrible parts of the experience—like seeing all these young kids coming back so badly wounded—never leaves you. These boys had joined up with a desire to serve their country. They joined because they wanted to, not just for an adventure, but because they wanted to help. Then they came back from battle wounded in every possible way. It was unbearably tragic. When peace came, we were all just so happy to get out of it and get home that most of us tried to forget about it.

One of my best friends was a nurse in France as well, and we never talk about the sorts of things we saw and had to deal with over there. We block it out of our minds, which is natural, I think. You try to remember the good times.

Don Cheney

BIRTH PLACE: OTTAWA, ONTARIO
RESIDENCE: OTTAWA, ONTARIO
SQUADRON: 106,630,617 SQUADRONS RAF
THEATRE OF WAR: NW EUROPE
DECORATIONS: DFC, RCAF OPERATIONS WINGS

I BECAME AWARE OF THE APPROACH OF WAR IN HIGH SCHOOL, WHEN I WAS fifteen or sixteen years old. I remember listening to Hitler's speeches on short-wave radio. Hitler spoke extremely fast, very passionately, loudly and forcefully. We understood quite a bit of it and it was frightening. In addition, I could see my dad getting worried about what was happening in the news and he'd drop the odd comment.

By the end of the summer after high school in 1939, war was declared, I was only seventeen but was already thinking about signing up as soon as I could.

I'd always wanted to fly, from the time I was a little wee guy. I still have my scrapbooks, page after page, squared off in pencil, with pictures of various airplanes that I drew. Underneath each one, I'd list their speed, ceiling, what their armament was, and so on and so forth. Thus, I built an air force on paper. I used to dream about flying. I used to dream I could fly!

Two days before my eighteenth birthday, I was accepted by the RCAF and allowed to sign the papers. I was fortunate enough to be channelled right through as a pilot. I was an only child and so my mother was very distressed, but kept a stiff upper lip. I know my dad's heart ached as well, because he knew what was ahead. It was only twenty years since the last war, and he had a premonition that we were in for another war as bad, or worse, than his "war to end all wars."

———

Once in the service in 1941, I spent about four weeks in manning depot to obtain my uniform and kit, and then spent another four weeks doing guard duty where we were drilled and taught the elements of service. Only then did I begin training in the fighter pilot stream.

I was then posted to ITS [Initial Training School] where there was no flying, only classes in navigation, meteorology, airmanship, and Link Trainer (which was an early flight simulator). I passed the ITS satisfactorily, and was then posted to EFTS [Elementary Flying Training School] on the Fleet Finch biplane equipped with skis, as it was wintertime. Later in the spring, the skis were converted to wheels. With the wheels, we flew from a grass field.

At last, with about forty hours of dual and solo flying on the Fleet Finch, I was sent to the SFTS [Service Flying Training School] in Yorkton,

Saskatchewan, for wings training, to become a qualified RCAF pilot. My course arrived at the SFTS as the last of the single-engine Harvard trainers were flown away, and were replaced by twin-engine Cessna Cranes. At that point, we knew that there would be no Spitfire fighters for us. We were being streamed for bomber command.

At the end of the eight week course at SFTS, I was given my wings test by an officer on the training staff. The officer put me through all the manoeuvres, capped by a blind flying test. A hood was put all around you so that you could not see outside. All you could see were the instruments and controls and no view whatsoever out the windscreen. It was a weird feeling at first, but very effective because it was much like flying in cloud or in darkness.

In those days, flying in fog or clouds was a hair-raising experience, because you could easily lose your orientation. Even enormous Lancaster bombers, with a crew of seven, had been known to have the pilot become totally disoriented and fly upside down.

As the instrumentation became more sophisticated, it became a little easier, but it was always dangerous. Flying operations over Europe in the winters of 1943 and 1944 threw all kinds of weather conditions at us. The temperature outside could drop to minus seventy degrees, which had its own dangers. Occasionally, a rear gunner might go to sleep over his guns and his head would come down and touch the breech block of the machine gun and freeze to it. Oxygen masks could freeze up, cutting off supply and rendering a pilot unconscious. And there were other hazards as well. For instance, the electrically-heated suits could malfunction, running the risk of the crew freezing to death.

———

Following two weeks leave, orders came through to report to Halifax for embarkation. I landed in England with many of my air force colleagues in the early autumn of 1942. After debarkation from the *Queen Elizabeth* in Greenock, Scotland, along with 12,000 other members of the Canadian armed forces, the aircrew were sent by train to Bournemouth on the south coast. Before the war, it was a lovely vacation resort. But during the war, all civilians were evacuated and the hotels were used to house newly arrived air force personnel. Almost daily, a Focke-Wulf 190 or Junker 88 would come sweeping over the Channel at low level and strafe the buildings. They'd get under the RADAR by coming in at sea level, then lift up to about fifty feet and fire their cannons at the buildings and let a couple of 500-pound wing bombs go. That put the wind up us for a while, because we were just the new guys. You'd realize, "They really mean it. This isn't Canada any more."

There were hordes of Canadians, Australians, and New Zealanders there, all impatiently waiting to be assigned to operational squadrons. After a couple of weeks we were moved to training bases with RAF instructors who were mostly familiarizing us with the aircraft, air traffic control, and topography, because from 15,000 feet England looks an awful lot different than Canada. After about three months training on twin-engine Airspeed Oxfords came some weeks at OTU [Operational Training Unit], where I began the process of "crewing up."

We practiced fighter evasion, night flying, and cross-country navigation on Wellingtons, an aging twin-engine bomber, from a grass field. From there, we were sent to the HCU [Heavy Conversion Unit], where we learned to fly the really big planes. At the end of the course, we did our first flight over enemy territory, dropping leaflets on Paris, and returned safely. That was our last flight in the Wellingtons, and we were happy to be moving on.

They were introducing Lancasters onto 106 Squadron shortly after we arrived. We needed to add a flight engineer to our crew because somebody had to watch all the instruments. We were given a once-over with an instructor, and then he hopped out and said, "Okay, off you go."

Down the runway we went, and started climbing. I called to flight engineer to pull the wheels up. No response.

"Wheels up, flight engineer, wheels up!"

Still no response. I looked over and saw poor old Jimmy, the Scottish engineer, holding onto the bar on the window, staring at the ground. He was a mechanic and had never been off the ground before. I gave him a poke on the shoulder, and said, "Get those bloody wheels up," and he did. We climbed up a little further, and sure as hell, a big trail of black smoke emerged out the back of the starboard engine. I radioed the tower.

"I got an engine fire!"

A very calm WAF voice on the other end said, "Oh, don't worry too much. It's probably just glycol. You'll be okay. Circle around, we'll give you priority to come in."

We circled around, came in with our engine flaming. Out came the fire brigade, doused us with foam and that was the end of our day. Never a dull moment. But you were too damn busy to let that kind of thing unnerve you, because you'd be up in the air again first thing the next morning.

As production of Lancasters increased and as more trained aircrew became available, the Air Ministry formed new squadrons. They'd take two or three seasoned crews from established squadrons and put them in the new squadrons to help the "sprog" [novice] pilots and crews become accustomed to operations. We were posted to 106 Squadron the week that Guy Gibson left to form 617 Squadron [the Dam Busters] in early May 1943.

Don Cheney (front, centre) with his crew from 106 Squadron RAF in 1943.

A new pilot joining a squadron would have to do a "second dickey" [final apprentice] trip with an experienced pilot, just to settle you in to the routine. My second dickey was with a lovely Dutch pilot. (His aircraft was shot down and the entire crew killed on a subsequent mission. I learned this much later, to my great sadness.) It was a relentlessly sad business. It was a great strain on the crews, but you just dealt with it. You put it out of your mind and just went on. Before you knew it, there would be a replacement on the squadron and you were getting on with the job. What you didn't realize that it was telling on you, all the time. The pressure was always there: get on with the job, and don't look back. Just get that plane and crew back to base after each mission

The Germans developed a nasty new weapon on their Junker 88 night fighter, which they called schrecklichmusik, or "horrible music." It was a cluster of four machine guns mounted back of the pilot. The Junker 88 would fly from behind and lurk fifty or sixty feet directly underneath you. The pilot would turn these guns upwards, press the trigger and the shells would fire straight up into your gas tanks, wings, fuselage and everywhere else on the bomber above. They were a nasty piece of work.

Sometimes we'd be sent out on a moonlit night, which meant it was a shooting gallery for night fighters. Or, if they didn't spot you right off the bat, the German searchlights would "cone" an aircraft. There'd be ten or twelve searchlights in a group and one or two would catch your plane. Then the rest of the searchlights would join up and lock you in the apex of all the lights. The interior of your plane would be so bright that you literally couldn't see anything. You were totally dazzled. Once they coned you, the flak opened up and frequently that was that.

We only got coned once. We had a full bomb load aboard. When it happened, I stuck the nose of the aircraft straight down. We dove five or six thousand feet straight down, then twisted, turned and pulled with all my force on the control column, climbing to a near stalling speed, then pushed the nose down again. We were weightless for several seconds; my bum came right off the seat and I was hanging in mid-air in my safety straps. It was all I could do to level out and push the controls forward, but we managed to get out of it. A lot of guys didn't.

———

In the summer of 1943, I received orders to report to the HQ of Air Vice-Marshal Sir Ralph Cochrane, who was the air officer commanding RAF Five Group Bomber Command.

"Oh, boy, I must have done something pretty bad," I thought. "I guess I'm on my way home in disgrace."

I was brought into Sir Ralph's office with a couple of officers on either side. I saluted, tucked my cap under my arm and came to attention. He told me to relax, sit down, gave me a cigarette, and lit it for me.

"I want to ask you something. Not a favour, really, but I want your thoughts."

"Yes, sir?"

He got right to the point. "You've got a good record. We're rebuilding 617 Squadron after the losses from the dam raid, and we're looking for experienced aircrews to fill in the holes, because we have other plans for the squadron of a special duty nature. We want to train these crews to high efficiency for various objectives, which shall remain nameless. We'd like to have you and your crew join them."

"My God, 617 Squadron," I thought. They were known as the "Death or Glory Boys" throughout the RAF. They were a low-level flying squadron who took terrible losses during the Dam Buster raids on the Ruhr in May 1943. They'd gone back into action with the few airplanes they had left and were being hit pretty badly. Now they were planning new types of operations and were looking for new crews to fill in their losses. New aircraft, specially fitted with large bomb bays, were being delivered.

"Well, sir, it's a great honour, a great honour indeed."

"It is, I think. The leader of squadron is Wing Commander Leonard Cheshire, who is probably the finest bomber pilot in the world. He is absolutely fearless, a wonderful leader. He's got the heart of a lion."

"If I may, sir, I would like twelve hours to discuss it with my crew."

"I would have considered it a mistake if you didn't."

I called a meeting of my crew. We were nineteen, twenty, twenty-one; the oldest guy was twenty-two and we considered him almost too old. We got a bit drunk and hashed it around, then agreed we'd go. The lure of low-level daylight raids was very attractive. It was challenging, exciting and daring, all those things guys our age went for. So off we went to 617.

Cheshire himself was only twenty-four. He had the face of a preacher, very solemn, but warm, easy to talk to, and an absolutely marvellous person. He knew everyone on the squadron, including all the mechanics, the WAFs, intelligence, and everybody in the control tower. A great leader, the kind that comes along once in a century.

We trained as a squadron all through the winter of 1943 and were put through weeks of practice with "practice bombs," which were little six-pound white things. We got pretty damned good. Our squadron could hit a target with an error of margin of about twenty yards from a height 20,000 feet, which was unreal. And our crew's accuracy was one of the better ones on the squadron. This accuracy of bombing dovetailed beautifully with the development by Sir Barnes Wallace of the Tall Boy, a 12,000-pound armour-piercing bomb. The "earthquake bomb" became our principal weapon.

Its fins were designed so that once it was released, it would start to revolve and when it hit the ground it had become supersonic and was going like a bullet. Not to mention that it was extremely accurate. We developed a special bombsight on the squadron. These Tall Boys would bury themselves up to 200 feet in the ground and then explode, literally causing a local earthquake. They were devastating for ships, and extremely effective against heavily reinforced bunkers and underground targets.

Our first target and the first use of that bomb in operations were against a railway tunnel in southern France in April 1944. This tunnel went about 200 feet underground, right through a hill and out the other side. It was the main line between southern France up to the Normandy beachhead and the Germans were sending tanks and heavy vehicles on this rail line at night.

That was a night raid, and Wing Commander Cheshire flew a Mosquito loaded with red and green flares. He flew fifty feet off the ground at night, travelling a couple of hundred miles an hour, straight down the railway track to the mouth of the tunnel. Only then would he let go of his red flares, then pull up as hard as he could over top of the tunnel. This done, he'd radio, "Okay, A Force, start bombing red flares. They're right in the mouth of the tunnel."

Half our force would track in one after the other and start letting the bombs go. Cheshire knew how many were going to drop and as soon as the last one was gone, he flew back in across the mouth of the tunnel to see what had happened.

"Jolly good show, chaps. We got a couple of hits and two near misses."

The after-effects of a Tall Boy bomb attack on Saumur railroad tunnel near Toulouse. This was the first use of the Tall Boy bomb.

After that, he called up again on the intercom. "All right, I'm going to make a run from the other end." So, around he went, flying down the track from the other direction and dropped green flares on the far side in the mouth of the tunnel, then circled around to watch.

"Okay, B Force, you drop yours now," and another eight or nine of these enormous bombs went down. Two of the bombs went right through the tunnel and blew up inside, blowing the track and everything else straight up and out the top of the hill. The whole area was pock-marked with giant craters.

Cheshire won his VC [Victoria Cross] for "continuous and consistent acts of daring," not for any one particular act. The American general Jimmy Doolittle put in a good word for him with the Americans and they gave him a Mustang fighter. Cheshire taught himself to fly this damn plane. I watched as he took off for the first time with the instruction book in his lap and the plane bounced off the runway like a grasshopper. He had an awful time getting the wheels up, but finally succeeded and flew around for about a half an hour, then came and bounced a few more times as he landed and taxied in.

We thought, "Oh, God, there goes the Wing CO for sure." But he was just fine and kept us all in stitches that night over drinks in the mess talking about trying to find the bloody lever for the wheels. He armed this Mustang with marker flares so he could get even closer and faster to the targets. It reached a point where on a raid, he'd leave an hour or so after we would. We'd lumber over to the target while he was sitting in the mess, relaxing. In due time, he'd climb in this Mustang and zip over to mark the target and be back sitting on the ground waiting for us when we finally got home. What a guy, and what an inspiration for the squadron. That's the kind of thing that always made you want to achieve more and reach higher.

On the night of June 5, 1944, our squadron engaged in what was probably the biggest spoof ever pulled off against the Germans: the highly secret Operation Taxable. It was based on a material called "window," which was simply long strips of aluminum foil, shiny on one side, black on the other and which was dropped in bundles. As they were dropped, the bundles would break open and release hundreds of thousands of strips, which confused the German RADAR. Dropped at carefully calulated timed intervals, heights, and air speed, the window would very accurately resemble an approaching convoy of ships as it fell.

We flew a straight course for five minutes, did a fifteen-degree turn for a minute, dropping the window all the way down this leg, and then stopped. On the way back, we'd drop window all the way. With each subsequent run, we'd advance our track a little bit so that we were moving a little closer each time to the Calais and Dunkirk beaches, which is where the Germans expected the landings would come. They were fooled right up until daylight on June 6th. According to German sources, they had their guns ready to open fire on what they thought was a very large convoy and to their consternation, they saw nothing. Absolutely nothing.

We practiced that operation for three weeks. The idea for it was worked out by two fellows on the squadron, one of whom was my roomate, Don McLean, a Canadian. Because the airplane was just packed with great big bales of window, there were two pilots and a crew of ten. We had a couple of gunners to defend us and the rest of the guys were all there just to keep heaving this window out the door when we gave the orders.

Submarines were sinking tremendous numbers of merchant ships coming in convoys from Canada and the States. The Germans had their sub bases all along the French coast, and after the invasion these became even more of a menace. At Le Havre, the Germans had a large flotilla of E-boats, which were huge motor torpedo boats, heavily armed and extremely fast, certainly bigger and faster than anything we had. Prior to D-Day, the Americans, practicing amphibious landings off the coast of England, using a couple of transports and landing their troops in a simulated attack. One of these E-boats came racing among the ships and sank both transports and killed about seven hundred of the American soldiers. This threat had to be removed and quickly.

On June 14, in a daylight raid, two hours before darkness, my squadron headed a bomber attack against them and the entire fleet was wiped out. I think one E-boat got away, but later gave up. Had those German E-boats been able to attack the troop ships during the next few weeks, there would have been absolute carnage.

After D-Day, we targeted V-1, V-2 and V-3 bases. The V-3 was a winged bomb launched through a tube 150 feet long. In this tube, a special type of propellant was fed at certain intervals, so that as the projectile moved through, the propellant was ignited and increased the velocity of the V-3. When it left the tube, the bomb was supersonic and aimed right at London. The Germans had three or four of these installations right on the coast and it would have been a matter of a few seconds to fire them across at the city.

The V-1 and V-2 bunkers were massive things. Had they been able to complete them, the potential devastation is beyond comprehension. German scientists like Werner von Braun had been developing the V-2 rocket from the war's outset. They were ten years ahead of us in the development of propellants, trajectories and speeds, and construction of rockets and launch technology.

We were able to destroy some of the sites and significantly delay repair of damage or the construction of new ones. After the breakout from the beaches, the Allied armies quickly outflanked and overran these launch sites and they were abandoned by the retreating enemy.

August 5th, 1944, was a clear day. I was flying a daylight raid to France. We were flying at 16,500 feet and cut across the Brittany peninsula to make the Germans think we were going to one of three targets. At the last minute we altered course and headed to Brest. There was the target straight ahead of us and the defenders didn't have time to start their smoke screen. It was clear sailing, absolutely beautiful. We had to fly at very precise assigned altitude and speed, which meant we were flying straight and level for about eighteen miles.

Our target was one of the biggest German naval bases near Brest. The Germans knew exactly what altitude and course we were on and put up this wall of flak, which we had to fly straight into it. I'd never seen anything like it.

We received four direct hits, which knocked out an engine, set our starboard wing on fire, and seriously wounded three of the crew. We were within seconds of dropping our bomb when I saw huge holes in the wing and flames belching from it. With three of the crew badly wounded, I was absolutely petrified that the aircraft was going to lose that wing or the petrol tanks would explode, in which case no one had a chance. We were in flames. My job was to hold the plane steady so the others could escape. Before I gave the order to bail out, the navigator, Roy, who was badly wounded, managed to stand beside me and hold up a card on which he had written the next course to fly. But by then it was too late and I gave the order to abandon the aircraft. The escape hatch in the nose jammed, so everybody had to push one another out. Everyone made it except for Reg, the wireless operator, who was hardly able to move because of his wounds, and me flying the plane. The only way I could get him out was through the nose. I climbed out of my pilot's seat, held onto the control column with my left hand and got a grip on him. He was barely able to move but I managed to get down the couple of steps to the nose of the aircraft. I pushed him into the escape hatch in a position where he could wriggle himself through.

Reg looked at me as I grabbed the control column, and motioned frantically for me to get out. But how?

I couldn't push myself out through that hatch, and I didn't have time to get to the rear door.

The airplane was still under manual control because I'd turned off the automatic pilot for the type of bombing we were doing. My mind racing,

I reached up and twisted the handle on the hatch that you used if you ditched in water. I put the plane in straight and level flight as best I could, stood up on my seat, and then climbed up on the armrests. I could sense the plane starting to dive. I pulled back on the stick with my foot and levelled the aircraft a bit, then got a hold of the edges of the hatch. But I couldn't get out because my chest pack of the parachute was too big.

There was a slab of armour plate behind the pilot's seat for protection. I got my feet up onto the top edge of the armour plate and forced my chute pack out into the slipstream by lifting it up off my chest. With my chute pack out, I was able to get my shoulders and upper part of my body through the hatch, my feet still planted on the armour plate.

I grabbed the edge of the hatch opening, and got one foot out onto the fuselage of the plane and gave the most almighty push. Then I just prayed.

I'd taken an awful chance, because if the mid-upper gunner hadn't depressed his guns before he bailed out, I would have been impaled on them. As the slipstream caught me and threw me back, I just skimmed the aerial wires to the two tail fins. One kind of scraped me across the cheek as I went past.

I remember those two big fins flashing by, and then all I remember is tumbling in the air, tumbling and clouds, ground, then clouds, then sea, then, ground, and then "whoom," and silence.

I found myself hanging in my parachute, drifting along in the sunshine in complete silence. I couldn't see the other guys' parachutes, but I'd been quite a while getting out. The plane had dropped down from 16,000 to about 6,000 feet before I got out. I could see our squadron in the distance going home. Then I heard the crackling noise of a Merlin engine as a Spitfire throttled back and flew past me about thirty feet away. It was a beautiful sight. The plane could have been marked with black crosses, I thought.

The pilot looked over at me, waggled his wing and I gave him the thumbs up. He gave me the thumbs up, then swung around and followed me all the way down until I was just above the water, then scooted off.

I hit the water, but that didn't bother me; I was used to water. I got a mouthful and a nose full, of course, but came up and was all right. I turned on my back because the water was fairly choppy. I released the buckle on the harness and the whole chute just left me and went scooting off across the waves and sank. My Mae West inflated and I could feel it tighten up against my chest. The water was surprisingly warm.

I'd landed off the coast of one of the most popular French summer resorts. I could see the beaches and a spit of land and what looked like a town in the distance. I was a good swimmer, but wearing a Mae West and clothes, I couldn't make much speed towards land.

As I was paddling along when I heard some "peep, peep, peep" noises in the water. I could see the beach where the Germans had anti-tank traps as well as small bunkers with machine gun crews in them. So now these guys were taking pot shots at me.

"Hell, this is no good," I thought, and started swimming back out to sea.

A French dentist had seen my plane come down and watched me from his house as I dropped into the sea. He ran to the shore and helped direct a small fishing boat that had come to look for me. He was fired on and he had to duck for cover.

I was about three quarters of a mile from shore and after about an hour and a half in the water, I had begun to feel quite cold. It was bright sunshine, but there was a spanking breeze and every once in a while I'm taking a mouthful of salt water.

An old wooden fishing boat started chugging towards me with six guys in it. They pulled up beside me and a couple of big arms pulled me in over the side.

I looked around the boat for a German uniform, but saw only friendly faces grinning at me. Then in my high school French, I asked, "*Ou sont les boches?*"

"*Ah ha, les boches kaput!*" came the answer, with a throat-slitting gesture of the hands. The boat turned around and headed for the town in the distance.

The German garrison of the town had gone off on an exercise in the morning and the underground had taken over the command post and captured the Germans that were left. They opened up the arms lockers and armed everybody and then barricaded the town. When the Germans came back from their exercise they couldn't get back in!

Talk about luck. It was during that time that I was picked up and brought back to the jetty of the port. I sat there on a big stone and a lady came along and offered me an open can of pilchards. I was shaking and bewildered. A small crowd had gathered around me. I took one, just to be polite, and promptly threw up because I was full of sea water. Another lady came along with a pear and I thanked her very much, but tucked it in my tunic. I heard voices saying, "*Canadien! Canadien!*"

Shortly thereafter an old truck came along and I was motioned to get in the cab beside the driver. Then another guy got in beside me with a Sten gun in his lap. Two more resistance fellows rode on the running boards on either side of the truck. More resistance members, all armed with everything from hunting rifles to Sten guns and German Mausers, were in the back.

We pulled up in front of a house and they shoved me out the door. Two of the men took me up a quick flight of stairs and a very pretty French lady with jet-black hair opened a door at the top.

"We've got an Allied aviator for you, Madame," the men said.

"Come in, come in."

"We won't stay. We're going to get out of here," and with that, they went back to the truck and took off just as quickly as they'd come.

The woman brought me some of her husband's clothes and said, "You go into the bedroom and change."

She made me a sandwich and gave me some fresh fruit. They even had butter, because they were very close to a farming area. Being a fishing port, they had lots of fish too: sardines, herring, and such. So while I was there over the next few weeks, I used to have a nice fried herring every morning for breakfast, which was lovely.

The local priest came every two or three days with fresh fruit, books in English and a little brown paper bag. In that bag were strong, black French cigarettes, like Gauloises and Gitanes. But they sure tasted good! The priest would go around to all the resistance groups and cajole them into contributing a few cigarettes for "*l'aviateur Canadien*," so I was being kept in tobacco by the French resistance!

Whiling away the time, I used to play checkers with Madame or her daughter, Paulette, who was fifteen. Unfortunately, they were too good for me and I always lost. I hid there for over a month. Once in a while the German soldiers, who'd reclaimed

Don Cheney with Commandant de Marine's daughter, Paulette Québriac, in France, 1944. The Québriac family hid Don Cheney for over a month in 1944.

control of the town, came to this house and tried to browbeat the woman's husband into coughing up information and sometimes they took him to headquaters for questioning. From upstairs, I could look down the stairwell and see German soldiers when they came in. The husband, Aristide, was the harbourmaster and held the rank of Commandante de Marine in the French navy. The Germans respected him, and anytime they were going to come anywhere near the house, they gave him notice. He'd come tearing up the stairs and quickly don his uniform, and warn me. If necessary, I'd climb out the back window, down to the shed roof and into the back garden, then duck in behind the woodpile where there was a loose board with a hook on the inside. I could reach through and undo the hook and the board swung out so I could crawl in and close it up again behind me, but I only had to do that a couple of times. I sometimes wonder how long it would have taken the Germans to find me in my hiding place.

The Germans kept accusing him of being the head of the resistance, but invariably he'd vehemently deny this, saying, "No, no, I run the harbour! I'm just trying to keep my people from starving." But, in fact, he did command about eight hundred armed resistance members in that region. His name was Aristide Québriac. After the war, he was invested with virtually every decoration that the French government had. We remained close for the rest of his life; his daughter still lives in Paris and I keep in touch with her and her husband.

Through that summer of 1944, the Germans became very disorganized in that part of Brittany and the Americans were advancing on Brest. Aristide came to me one day and said, "It's time to go, Donald."

Without a word I went. We drove to the nearby city of Quimper, where some German military were still in evidence. I can remember them going up and down the steps to the city hall. I'd been directed to find a Citroën, which I climbed into. In the car, in addition to the driver, there was an American flier, Ralph Hall, who'd been hiding up the street from me and we'd met once in a while for a drink. There were also four French guys who'd been in the air force and were on the run from the Germans. We drove into the country as fast as we could go, and at nightfall pulled into a farmhouse where some people were waiting for us with food and sleeping cots.

The battlefront was fluid and we never knew whether we were going to run into Germans or Americans. So from that point on, we travelled at night until we got close to where we'd been told the Americans lines were. Finally we made contact with General Patton's 5th Armored Division, which was bivouacked in a pear orchard.

An American colonel was sitting in one of these folding camp chairs with his big boots up on the track of a tank. Ralph and I came up to him and saluted. He looked over and said, "Who the hell are you guys?" So we told him and asked for transport to a repatriation depot.

"Jesus. I don't want anything to do with you fellows," then called to the MPs.

"Get these guys out of here."

We hurriedly got back into our car, and drove away, arriving in the railroad station in St-Brieuc mid-afternoon. There, in St-Brieuc, among the ruins of trains and buildings, we were received by a Canadian intelligence officer, a major, who two years previously had been parachuted in to work with French resistance and organize an escape line for allied fliers. He arranged for us to get on the only freight train heading north that afternoon, heading for a larger city called Rennes, which was firmly in American hands. Our driver passed a few words with the major, waved, and then drove away. We travelled all night, sleeping in a boxcar, and arrived in Rennes the next morning. The major had supplied us with US K-Rations, cigarettes, and some French money. We hitched a ride on an American army truck to the big USAF base outside Rennes, where Ralph and I were given a meal and room together in a barrack block. The French lads were kept under guard someplace else on the base.

They fed us breakfast. Ralph went off for about an hour and came back in a new uniform.

"Where the hell have you been?" I exclaimed

"They've got me all fitted out. I'm flying out this afternoon to England."

"What about me?" I said.

"I don't think they want any part of you. You'll have to find some Brits, I guess." And that was the last I saw of Ralph.

A sergeant came along.

"We're going to take you down to the gate and put you on the road there. Every once in a while a RAF truck goes by and they may pick you up."

It was hot, really, really hot, and there was a lot a traffic and dust on that road. I was eating dust all day as I walked into Rennes.

Almost in the centre of the city, I stopped to ask directions from a kindly-looking gentleman standing in the doorway of the jewellery shop. Suddenly, there was this great commotion.

"Ah, ah," he said, and pointed. The resistance were parading the "collaboratrices" down the main street. There was a line of women with their heads shaved, with armed resistance guards escorting them. Apparently this was done at the same time every day to those who had befriended the German invaders. To add to the confusion, there were still German snipers up in the steeple in the church and every once in a while they'd let off a shot or two and everybody would scatter, then find their way back. It was pandemonium.

At the end of this bizarre parade there was a band playing "La Marseillaise." The jeweller and I both stood to attention and shouted, "*Vive la France!*"

I said I had to get moving and asked the way out of town. He pointed me in the right direction.

"Go that way and you'll see more trucks."

After about a mile of walking, a little RAF regiment pickup truck came bumping along and I stood in the middle of the road waving. They pulled up and asked, "Who are you?"

"I was shot down over Brittany and am making my way back."

"Oh!" they said. "A walker-back."

"Yeah, I guess so."

"Okay, hop in. Where do you want to go?"

"Anywhere there are some English or Canadian troops that will accept me. The Americans won't have anything to do with me."

"Hop on. We're on our way to Bayeux. That's the best place for you. That's where they repat the walkers back."

So I hopped on.

The RAF guys drove me into Bayeux, right into a camp and up to the sentry. The duty officer was called and he came and placed me under arrest.

I was taken off by two MPs and locked in a mobile trailer without a word, just, "In you go."

I sat in the trailer for about two hours. The door opened and a corporal said, "Here's some coffee and a little something to eat." Then I waited.

Finally, the corporal came in again and said, "I've got the sarge outside. He's going to take you to see the colonel."

Right, fine, I go to see the colonel. Progress.

He's a guards colonel from the old school. A full colonel, with a waxed moustache, ramrod stiff. This was no cartoon, but a real soldier who had been tested under fire. An obvions leaders. I came to attention and gave him my very best salute.

"Well, Chinny," he said, "Walker-back, are we?"

"Yes, sir."

"Identification?"

"No, sir, I lost it."

"Yes, we hear that story quite frequently. Yes. Who was your commanding officer? What kind of plane were you flying? What was the serial numbers and call letters of your aircraft? What was the horsepower of the engines? What were the names of your crewmen? How many were there? What was your flight commander's name?"

On and on and on he went with questions about the base and every other possible thing. Then back into the trailer I went. Eventually they got on the wireless and got in touch with RAF intelligence in London and London got in touch with the squadron and the squadron signalled back. That's Cheney, all right."

I didn't know this, of course. I was shut back up in my little trailer, where I spent the night. The next morning after breafast, the door opened again and the colonel climbed into the trailer.

"Sit down, Chinny."

"Thank you, sir."

"You're going to have a nice flight home."

"That's wonderful. I guess that means they've confirmed my identity."

"Yes. We're going to fly you over to Northolt and from there you'll be in the hands of British intelligence. I'm putting you in charge of a plane load of walkers-back."

"Thank you, sir, for your hospitality. And thank you for not shooting me as a spy."

But he never even creased a smile.

———

During the war, we believed we were saving civilization from barbarians, which the Nazi party certainly was. We were proud to be taking the war to Germany long before the invasion force was ready. And we kept hundreds of thousands of enemy troops engaged in air defense in the west who otherwise would have been available for the eastern front or an assault on Britain.

We felt no remorse and took pride in what we did in service of those who needed us. We believed in what we were doing, and I know it made a difference, albeit at a great price. I also owe a huge debt to the French people who sheltered me at the risk of concentration camp, torture, and death of themselves and their families.

As a final note, something that is fundamental to my experience is that three of my crew were killed in action, and that's with me every day. They're with me every day. They're still alive and they're still twenty-two years old.

The graves of Don Cheney's crew members, Noel Wait (rear gunner), Reg Pool (wireless operator), and Roy Welch (navigator), in Trésboul, a suburb of Douarnez.

Jack Gouinlock

Birth Place: Swansea, Ontario
Residence: Toronto, Ontario
Squadron: 432 Leaside Squadron RCAF
Theatre of War: NW Europe

IT WAS THE NIGHT OF MAY 27TH, 1944, AND WE'D JUST DROPPED our bombs and turned to go home when a German night fighter caught us. The rear gunner spotted him first. He frantically called a warning over the headset, but a split second later, before we could react, our engines were on fire. I popped the front escape hatch, was shoved out by my bomb aimer, and was out of the plane in a matter of seconds. My boots got stripped off in the slipstream, so I found myself floating down from six thousand feet over enemy territory in the dead of night in my stocking feet.

Actually, the biggest fear I had was landing on top of our burning aircraft below me, but I managed to land in the middle of a field a quarter of a mile away.

Standing in my socks somewhere in occupied Holland that night, all I wanted was to get away. I headed in the direction I thought was south, to try and walk down through Belgium and France into Spain. To be honest, I didn't expect to make it, anyway.

Dawn broke. I came across a solitary figure working on his farm. He was friendly at first, then got very nervous about helping me when he figured out who I was. But at least he gave me a pair of shoes and a coverall to wear over my uniform.

"To get to Belgium," he said, "you have to cross a bridge not far away. But watch for the guards."

I thanked him and off I went. After a few miles, I spotted the bridge in the distance. I crept up and could see the guard, but saw no way of getting past him.

"To hell with it," I thought. "I haven't slept and I can't think straight," so I hid myself in the bushes by the side of the road and fell sound asleep.

When I woke up, I didn't know where I was. Slowly it came back to me. I looked for the soldier again and could see he had fallen asleep, too. So I grabbed the moment, took off my shoes and crawled across on my hands and knees in front of his guardhouse. Halfway across I started hoping there wasn't another guard at the other end.

There should have been, but there wasn't. Now I was in Belgium and felt much better. It was still enemy territory, but one country closer to safety.

———

Crossing that bridge had given me courage, so I brazenly walked down the main road as I headed south. Whenever anybody passed, I just stared straight ahead and kept moving. It took about two miles for that flush of bravado to wear off, and I started thinking about finding some help. You always look for an isolated spot. I found my way into the woods and came across a good-looking farmhouse with a whole gang of children and adults outside.

I took a chance, went straight up to the house and flat out told them who I was. We'd been given a little foreign phrase book for just such a situation, but I didn't use it. I acted every bit as lost and scared as I felt and seemed to make a connection with this family: for whatever reason, they trusted me. Communication was difficult, but they invited me in and gave me some food.

Still, I needed to find somebody who spoke English. Two members of the family went off on their bicycles—maybe to fetch the authorities, I didn't know and was too tired to care at that point—but not long after, two young girls walked in. They were the teenage daughters of an Englishwoman in the next village, and they spoke perfect English.

"You stay here, we'll come and get you tonight and take you to our home."

That night they came and led me in the dark to their upper-class home. Their mother, Lillian Smetts, was a widow whose husband had been in the diplomatic corps, and her two daughters sat quietly listening while she asked me all sorts of questions.

"Where were you stationed?"

"Just outside York."

"Where's Betty's Bar?"

Fortunately, that had been a favourite of ours, so I was able to answer easily. She went on with detailed questions about specific spots in London, all of which I could answer. I didn't understand at the time, but realized later that she was interrogating me to see if I was a German infiltrator. But I managed to convince her that I truly was a Canadian navigator.

I spent the night there, but was told that her father-in-law's house across the road had been taken over by the Gestapo. I couldn't take the chance of staying any longer. Through her Resistance connections, she made arrangements to move me to a new "safehouse."

The bedroom in which Jack Gouinlock was hidden in Belgium, 1944.

The next night, I was taken to the farm of an elderly family, the Vanderhoedoncks: Martin, his brother Freddie, and his sister, Helene, who was my guardian angel. If someone ever came calling, Helene was the one who'd tell me to get out of sight.

In the room I'd been given there was a bed, a small table, a cupboard I could hide in, and a window. The window had curtains so I couldn't be seen, but unfortunately it had bars on it too. Whatever happened, I was trapped.

However, when Germans did come to the door, all they ever wanted was something to eat. Helene always made a point of being friendly to them to get rid of them quickly.

On the 6th of June, 1944, Helene came into my room absolutely ecstatic. She'd heard on the radio that the Allies had landed and it would only be a day or so before Belgium was liberated. I was a little dubious that it would happen that quickly, but what did I know? They were beside themselves with excitement and hope.

It was many more months before liberation came, so life quietly went on through June into July.

The night of July 24th, I heard a tremendous crash outside my window. I looked and saw a Flying Fortress had just crashed down into the forest. A rumour came round that the ten American crew members were in the area, which meant there'd be a house-to-house search by the Gestapo. With that the Underground made the decision to move me to the city of Liège. The Resistance made all those decisions, and if you wanted to save your life, you did what they said with no questions.

Not knowing what was going to happen or how bad things would get, I wrote a farewell letter to my mother and father. I buried it in the farmyard with the understanding that when liberation came, the letter would be mailed back to Canada.

The next day found me riding a bicycle along the highway with Lillian's two teenage daughters, and Freddie riding in front of us as a guard. We rode right through the military camp that our squadron had bombed. I'm thinking, "Gee, this doesn't feel too safe." But on we went, and I was taken to a delightful elderly couple, who said, "This is just temporary. You're to stay here until the Underground move you again." That's all you were ever told. I thought I'd be hiding in their tiny attic for the next few days, but that evening they came up to fetch me, and said, "We're going out to visit the neighbours. Here are some clothes."

"Out to visit…?"

Feeling a little stunned, off we went. I put on the clothes I'd been given—but held onto my dog tags just in case. We didn't just go to meet the neighbours, though; we went to a dinner party in the middle of the town. There were German soldiers walking around everywhere—I was sure I would be stopped at any moment—but the atmosphere was casual and nobody looked at me. It seemed the Germans just didn't pay any attention to people out on the street. At the dinner everybody was drinking brandy, toasting Churchill and Roosevelt. I met all kinds of people and had a wonderful dinner. But I couldn't get rid of the unbelievable feeling of being an airman in hiding at a noisy dinner party in the middle of enemy territory.

Three days later, someone from the Underground took me through the countryside, finally ending up at the home of the head of the

In a Farmhouse in N E Belgium.
Sunday morning June 25 1944

My dearest Mom and Dad:

How strange it is to write those words again — yet never did they mean so much as now! It seems years since I wrote you altho' actually my last letter was written just four weeks ago yesterday and I mailed it when Don and I went to mess for what was to be our last meal in England. You have been in my thoughts constantly and I could imagine the sadness with which you read that last letter, received, no doubt, several days after that fateful cable from Air Ministry. I have decided to write down a few thoughts and experiences since that night and will have these good people hide the letter and mail it to you when the war is over. Of course, I hope to be with you in person to tell you all these things but in case I'm not, I want you to know. I will not go to great length to give you all the details — I have done so in a narrative to Air Ministry and this will be more personal.

We had just dropped our bombs that night, May 27-28, when the boys spotted a German night fighter. Before Howie even had time to start evasive action, the fighter opened fire and I think set the engines and gas tanks in the port wing on fire. Howie almost immediately gave the order to jump. I cannot say whether any of the crew had been hit as I was the first to jump — my seat is directly over the escape latch — and I hope and pray I was quick enough to leave the other fellows time to jump. I never moved so quickly in all my life though, so I feel they must have had time. We were fairly low, only 8000' so the air was warm. My chute opened perfectly and I drifted gently to earth. Except for a slight nauseating feeling due to the swinging motion of the chute,

The farewell letter Jack Gouinlock wrote to his parents in 1944 while in hiding in Belgium.

178

Underground, Arthur Shalemberg. I spent the night there, and was joined by one of the gunners from the American plane, as well as a German deserter. He didn't want to play soldier any more, so he'd joined the Resistance.

The next day Arthur drove me on the back of a motorcycle into Liège, where there was another big dinner party in a church in the city's centre. I was told that everyone there was either a member of the Resistance or an airman in hiding. Once again, the Germans outside the doors seemed to be incidental, of no consequence.

I was paired up with the American gunner to be put into a safehouse, but he made me uneasy. He was extremely jittery and if the Germans had done a search, I felt sure he'd give us away.

I spoke to Arthur about this and he had me moved to the home of a couple that owned a cigar store in the suburbs. All these safe houses received funds through the Underground to help offset the expense. Wherever I went, the treatment I received was incredible. In all these places, I ate so well it was embarrassing. I actually put on weight!

I stayed there happily through the rest of the summer. In late August, the Germans were beginning to retreat from Liège. The Allies were starting to get too close. During this period, two German soldiers disappeared—a not-uncommon incident in occupied cities—and in retaliation, the Germans decided to take action. They were going to force the Underground to release the hostages.

The Germans went house-to-house, pulling out anyone they wanted and lining them up in the street. I was nervously sitting in my room above the cigar store, listening to this commotion outside. I suppose I could have hidden in the cupboard, but if I'd been found I would have been shot immediately, as would the couple who owned the shop. They were absolutely terrified as the round-up was happening and they fled with their young son. I sat in my little room with the hope that maybe the Germans wouldn't bother coming upstairs with the shop empty down below. I'd just managed to convince myself of this when a burly soldier kicked open the door, pointed at me, and said, "*Sie.*"

They took forty of us hostage—no women or children—and marched us out of the village, me still wearing slippers. The whole village was watching us. René, the son of the shop owners, ran in among the hostages and forced a bag on me, then ran off again. I don't know why they didn't stop him. In the bag was a pair of shoes and some bread. I'll never forget that.

We were marched past the house where the American was hiding. Everybody looked out their windows, but there was nothing they could do.

They marched us across a bridge out of town, up into the hills to a deserted farm. Again, they shouted at us to tell them where the missing soldiers were. I didn't know anyone else in the group and I sure didn't know where the soldiers were. No one answered.

They grabbed two of men from the line and beat them badly. We were then all herded into a barn. The officer announced that they would shoot some of us the next day unless they got answers. Then they bolted us in.

We didn't have much of a sleep that night. The other thirty-nine men were all civilians: none from the Underground, and none I had ever met. They were curious to know why I wouldn't talk to them, but I thought it was safer just to keep my mouth shut. More than anything, I was afraid the Germans would find out who I was and shoot the whole lot of us.

In the morning, they herded us out, lined us up and handed each man a shovel, then told us to pair up and dig holes. I got myself together with this one older man, thinking maybe I could convince him not to give me away. Maybe he'd be a loyal Belgian. As we started digging, he kept talking to me and I kept answering in my broken French, finally he said to me, "You're not Belgian, what are you?"

"A Canadian airman in hiding."

That put him through the roof. I thought he was going to have a heart attack. He didn't speak to me again. He knew the Germans would never have believed that he hadn't known. So we dug in silence.

One last time the Germans asked if anyone would co-operate. Nothing. Then an officer announced that unless he received information, we were all going to be shot. So we silently continued digging our graves.

About eleven o'clock, we were told to stop.

"Line up!"

We all lined up with our backs to the holes. I was scared to death. The Germans walked up and down the line, waiting for somebody to say something. Nothing.

They stopped in front of the two men who had been beaten the night before, looked at them intently for what seemed like an eternity, then shot them. Just like that. Their bodies fell backwards into the graves. Then just as unceremoniously the officer said, "You're free to go."

We marched away in a line as a group. As we approached the village, a lot of the men took their white shirts off and waved them to let anyone coming our way know we were a peaceful group. We crossed back over the bridge into town, and there was little René waiting for me. He led

Jack Gouinlock (standing, far left) with members of the Belgian Underground as well as other Allied evaders, immediately after Liège was liberated in September 1944.

me to another safe house for the night and the next day the Germans were gone.

That day the American armoured corps arrived, and the American flyers came out of hiding. I was the only airman who'd been part of the digging party. If the Germans had done a complete house-to-house search and found that jittery American, it might have been a different story up at the farm.

The farewell letter I'd buried back on the farm had been dug up and mailed to my parents. They had it in their hands before I was able to telegraph them to let them know I was all right. I can only imagine what went through their minds when they read it.

———

Dozens of people in the Underground risked their lives to help me, some of whom I knew only for a few hours. It's still unbelievable to me. That kind of selfless bravery—you never forget it.

Forty years later, René came to visit me in Canada. I stayed in touch with his family, as well as the other people who'd helped me.

Hilda Ashwell

—

BIRTH PLACE: VARS, ONTARIO
RESIDENCE: WINDSOR, ONTARIO
REGIMENT: RCAFWD (SECTION OFFICER), 6 BOMBER GROUP
THEATRE OF WAR: NW EUROPE

MY NAME IS HILDA ASHWELL, AND I WAS BORN IN A LITTLE VILLAGE near Ottawa on December 1st, 1919. The village was named Vars, and that was my father's home. He was a soldier in the First World War, and my mother was a bride in England—an English war bride. My father was very jolly, just sort of kept things lively—he would sometimes get up and do a sort of a step dance and make us laugh.

Growing up in the thirties was hard, because I was the oldest. I had a sister, two and a half years younger, and two young brothers. My father was a carpenter. He was with the Walkerville Lumber Company, which closed down during the Depression, so he was on relief for two years. But because he was a carpenter, our landlord had other homes, so if there was a broken door, or a baseboard needed repair, he sent my father to do the work, and he never paid him. He just took it off the back rent, so at the end of the two years when my father got work, we weren't in a great deal of debt like so many other families.

My dad never talked about his war experiences. It was very unusual for him to say anything about it at home at all. He was sent from Canada to England, but never went over to France.

We started learning about the possibility of war at school and at church. Our teachers started talking about the situation, and ministers preached about it. We read the papers. I think we were very aware because we had a father who'd been in the army. We knew that there was a great deal of trouble in the world.

I was working at GM, doing the payroll for 750 men at the plant. Different ones would always be leaving to join up and that affected us. We knew the families who were our neighbours might lose a son overseas and that would affect us. There was great sadness about so much of it all. The war was a part of our life.

I enjoyed my work at GM, but I knew as a woman I couldn't get advanced in the office and there wasn't anybody who was going to retire and make room for me.

My sister was the first to join. She was clerking in a store and didn't have a career. Then she joined the air force and came back at Christmas, very enthused. So I talked to her and that got me thinking and I joined the air force in January 1943 and was in for three years. After an IQ test or an aptitude test of some kind, they chose me to go into secret service— coding and cyphers.

I took a course at Guelph University. We were behind barred windows and couldn't take any work home to our rooms or even out of the building. It was very secretive that way and quite exciting. We'd been sworn to secrecy. From there, we were sent to Halifax for ten months, decoding messages. We knew there were German subs right off the shores of Canada, because that was coming through in the messages we were handling. And no one knew what the messages said until we broke the code. We changed our code every twenty-four hours, and

WRCNS coders at work in Halifax, Nova Scotia, June 1944.

it was really thrilling to me because it was something very unknown and very secretive and I thought that no one could ever work out these codes.

And it was frightening to know that the Germans were so close. It was upsetting to see the shiploads of soldiers and sailors leaving Halifax and knowing what they were going to face, even going across to England.

On the way out to Halifax on the troop train, I met this fellow, Al Ashwell. He was from Toronto, and was always full of fun and laughs. He was a nice guy, but I didn't see much of him because he was heading out to sea. I only knew him for about two months and didn't see him again until 1945.

Some of the Canadian WACs in Halifax gave us women in the service a bad reputation. Some of them had gotten a little wild with their new freedom. A lot of the girls who joined up were only eighteen and had never been away from home. I don't know what training they had, but they certainly did not know how to conduct themselves. As cipher clerks and sergeants, we were a separate lot. But you were aware of how some people might initially react to you.

After ten months in Halifax, I was stationed at Canadian Air Force Headquarters in Ottawa for a few months. Then I took officer training in Toronto and was commissioned as an assistant section officer. After graduation, I was sent to Yorkshire, England. There was a need for secret coding clerks.

The troop ship overseas was a crowded, nerve-wracking experience. Six in a room built for two. We were only given two meals a day. We ran near some German subs and had to detour north, nearly to Iceland, so we were late landing in Liverpool.

I served with the 6th Canadian Bomber Group in Yorkshire and that was a troubling time. I was there for D-Day when the planes were going over, just like swarms of bees going over to Germany. It was very disturbing.

Bomber Six Group was a different experience from what I was used to. They had huge blackboards the size of a room that would list the pilot, the co-pilot, the gunner, the navigator, and the time of departure. You'd wait to fill in the time of return and, of course, they didn't all come back. We could volunteer to get up at two or three in the morning and greet them as they came back with a breakfast or a cup of tea. But they couldn't talk to us about their experiences at all and we couldn't ask them any questions. After they had a bite to eat, they were taken to a private room and debriefed there. But we were most aware of those who didn't come back.

We'd been made officers when we went to England, to give us an equal footing with the other English women. Being officers, we had more privileges than some of the others, and mixed quite a lot with the bomber crews. The work in Yorkshire was quite a bit more difficult than in Halifax, because you were so much closer to the action, and working with people who were actually flying into the war every day and frequently not coming home.

The coding work we were engaged in was processing information from the missions, like the places the planes had been to, how many bombs they'd dropped, that sort of thing. But you'd read it, process it, get it to where it was going, then forget about it. Which was just as well, because there was always the danger that you'd hold onto details and dwell on them. Heartbreaking details.

After I'd served in Yorkshire for about a year, I was sent to headquarters in London. That's where the pressure became quite a bit more intense. We worked day and night; our office was never closed. It could be disorienting, because there were the bombings and the blackouts. In the office, you wouldn't know how long the bombing raids went on, because we were underground in what they felt was a safe office. When you came out, you didn't know what you would find or what changes there would be. Time was all spun around.

A blackout's very black, very, very black. Because all the windows in all the homes were black, and there were no streetlights and no car lights. Sometimes, going home, you'd just have to feel your way along the street in pitch dark until you found your way to the tube station. Down you'd go and find yourself stepping over people who were sleeping there. They might have a small suitcase beside them and that was all—all that was left of their belongings. They were homeless and had nowhere else to go.

There were no barracks in London; we had to find our own digs. I roomed with Vera, who was a very good friend of mine. We'd graduated together in Toronto. I went off one day to visit my aunt, and when I came back the whole area was roped off, and the policeman asked where I was going.

"I live down there."

"Not anymore you don't. It's gone."

"But I have to go and check."

"Then go around the block, 'round the other way, because these buildings are very unsafe."

I went around and the roof was all gone and plaster and glass were shattered all over everything. There wasn't anything left. And I didn't know where Vera was. As it turned out, she'd been at the office. But now we had no place to stay, so they put a cot down in the basement for us until we got another place.

We eventually found a new place, but the raids and the terror of the bombing never stopped. The sirens would go, we'd run to the stairwell, because our new flat was the second and third stories of a house. We'd simply run to the stairwell where there were no windows. We'd hear a loud bang, the whole building would shake, and our kitchen window would be sucked out from the bombs exploding in the next street. Once that happened, you never got new windows; you just got black tar paper, because it could happen again the next day. Bit by bit you felt the edges of your world were being closed off.

I went through a time when every time the sirens went and the blackout came, I became angrier and angrier with Hitler. Finally, I'd become so irate with it all that as a sort of mental reaction, I became paralyzed from the waist down. Fortunately, Vera was there and got help for me. They took me to a military hospital and finally, with some bed rest and talking to me, I was able to walk out. But the power of hate took my limbs away from me for a time. That was terrifying.

But we supported each other and had fun. We used to laugh and say that Churchill didn't know what was going on in the war until we got his messages decoded. We knew what was happening before he did.

There weren't a lot of things to do on what time we had off, because being on shift work our whole routine was disrupted. We had to sleep sometimes in the daytime to go to work all night. Another thing was that we were on British rations. We had very little food and would get a little square of cheese and maybe two eggs for a week. Clothing rations as well. Sometimes everything on the table was a gift from my mother or Vera's dad. I often wondered how the British people got along.

One time about six of us took a leave and went to Ireland. The Irish were neutral and we had a wonderful time in Dublin. We went to the fancy restaurants and were eating ice cream and peaches and all those rich foods that we never got back in London. We had so much of it that we all broke out in hives. But the break made it a little easier to come back to the war.

When we got back, they'd started the V-1 attacks. We saw those buzz bombs coming, heard their engines shut off, and we knew that that was it, they were on their way down. We were lucky never to have been directly caught.

The morning after a bombing raid in London.

But I did have one experience quite near to my heart. As I say, we had had no air raid shelter where we were. We just camped out under the stairs. I had an aunt and uncle living not far from London, and they had no air raid shelter either, but had a steel-topped table that was issued by the government. When the sirens would go off, they'd just dive under the table.

One time, my aunt took me to visit her mother, who was deaf. Her four-year-old grandson had been staying with her. When the raids would start, he'd pull on her skirt and tell her to get under the table. But this one time I guess she didn't make it and he did. When my aunt and I got there, the house was nothing but a pile of brick and rubble. That's all there was, just a pile of rubble. They'd got the little boy out but her mother had been killed. That hit me pretty hard. It made you wonder if you would ever get home.

Al and I had met up again eighteen months after we'd met on the way to Halifax. We'd kept in touch by letter, but hadn't seen each other for all that time. We got engaged in Edinburgh on a leave, and I knew then that all I wanted was to get home, to get married. That kept me going until things were over. And just doing my work, just keeping on going, day by day, doing your work. I knew I couldn't dwell on any of the tragedies that I'd seen or the anger that I felt anymore.

———

And then suddenly the war was over. We were so excited. On V-E day, London was chaos, just chaos. You couldn't move for people. Wall-to-wall people in Trafalgar Square and in front of Buckingham Palace, people singing and dancing and hollering in the streets. It was the greatest feeling ever, just wonderful. I can't explain what the feeling was like—it was so great. Then we were sent to Torquay to wait for a ship to go home. With the terrible experience going over on a troop ship we wondered what the trip would be like coming home, and we came home on the *Queen Elizabeth*. It couldn't have been better.

I'd been quite shy and reserved when I first joined up. Then after you take showers with no doors on with all the girls there, you lose a little bit of your self-consciousness. I became more outspoken and better able to express myself.

I was coming home to marry Al, and that was wonderful.

V-E Day in London, 1945.

———

England suffered so much that when I came back to Canada I was ashamed of people back home complaining about not having enough sugar or having to use uncoloured margarine. The English really had had a very, very bad time, and that made it difficult to see people getting upset about unimportant small things.

———

I think younger generations need to take pride in what our forefathers, and our fathers and we ourselves have done for the country. When I went to school history lessons were fairly simple, but now it's the whole world. The children have so much to learn, but they have the facilities to help them learn, that we didn't have. Of course, with computers and television—we didn't grow up with that, so I think they have a wider knowledge of the world than we had.

Joe Gelleny

BIRTH PLACE: HUNGARY
RESIDENCE: AURORA, ONTARIO
REGIMENT: SIGNAL CORPS, SOE (SPECIAL OPERATIONS
EXECUTIVE)—BRITISH ARMY
THEATRE OF WAR: ITALY, HUNGARY, YUGOSLAVIA

I GREW UP IN WELLAND, WHERE I LIVED UNTIL ABOUT 1940. WHEN I was seventeen, I moved to Toronto and attended a special training course at Central Technical School to help the war effort. Everyone in the city seemed to be in uniform, which got me thinking about joining the service. I could have stayed working at Anaconda, because it was war work. But what I wanted to do was to be a paratrooper. In 1942, I'd turned nineteen and decided it was time to join and by age twenty I was in the service.

I enlisted in the army down at the CNE cow palace and ended up assigned to the signal corps because I'd had experience with ham radio in high school. That meant shipping out to Vimy Barracks in Kingston for basic training, but it wasn't what I wanted to do. I'd been told I could get into the paratroops if I transferred to artillery, so that's what I did, ending up in Petawawa.

I hadn't been there long when someone discovered I spoke Hungarian. I'd come over from Hungary as a boy with my family. This information must have caught someone's attention, because I was asked in for an interview, not knowing what it concerned.

The people who interviewed me were recommending that I consider volunteering for a transfer to a special British army unit. I'd never heard of it: the SOE [Special Operations Executive.] I had no idea what the transfer meant or what they did, but I was told it would speed up the move to parachute training, so that sounded good to me. And it would give me the chance to see some action in Europe before it was all over.

I was sent down to Toronto where a Captain Bushell interviewed me. He promised all sorts of benefits from this volunteer assignment: interesting work, the chance to jump out of an airplane, and that it would be a quick route to getting my commission. This would involve a temporary transfer to the British army, SOE, and then back to the Canadian army with my British rank when the war was over. If we made it through basic training at this new camp, we'd be made sergeants. When we passed the parachute-training course and went overseas, we'd become second lieutenants.

It all sounded too good to be true, so I was happy to sign up. Needless to say, it was too good to be true. None of the promises were kept, either by the Canadians or the British. Once the war was over, they weren't that fussy about following through with these things for you. Which is typical.

But I didn't know any of that then, and when you're twenty, it's all a big adventure anyway. The next curious thing that happened was that the RCMP starting doing background checks on me, on my family, and everyone I knew. They gave me all kinds of tests: psychological tests, personality tests, IQ tests, none of which I really understood or cared about. But everything must have been okay, because I was told to meet a certain car in a certain place in downtown Toronto to be picked up.

I met the car—or the car found me—and after about an hour, I found myself being driven down country roads to a place about twenty miles east of Toronto. I had been assigned to the mysterious SOE Camp X in Oshawa. The training camp was officially known as Camp STS. 103 (Camp X). The turning points were all but unmarked and the driver of the car did an elaborate doubling-back routine before he actually entered the gates, which were guarded.

The camp was an unimpressive collection of wooden huts and outbuildings out in the brush. It had very tight security around it, despite the fact that there didn't appear to be anything of any particular interest or value there.

When I arrived at the camp, I was made a part of a group who were largely Canadians with Hungarian backgrounds. I also met some Yugoslavs while I was there, but we pretty much stayed with our own because that's the way it had been arranged. The camp trained their agents in cultural groups because of the language and knowledge of the culture. For instance, Yugoslav-Canadians, French-Canadians, and Hungarian-Canadians were grouped with one another, and trained for work in their parents' countries of origin. The objective was to drop Camp X agents behind enemy lines in various occupied areas of Europe.

Two things struck me about the recruits I was with. All but one of the guys were older than me and, in addition, most of them were from the communist party, or at least were communist-oriented. I don't think it was that way when the camp first opened, but after Germany invaded Russia, communists were actively recruited. I wasn't a communist, then or now, nor were any members of my family. But it seemed that a lot of agents-in-training in 1943 were communists. From what I understand, it was the same with the French and Belgian resistance.

Basic training at Camp X lasted a few months. The first objective was to be in absolutely top shape. We had a tremendous amount of physical exercise: running, jumping out of towers, climbing, scaling walls—anything and everything. Then we were given training on a whole range of weapons, including German guns of all kinds. We had to know them inside and out, how to load and fire them, and how to dismantle and reassemble them blind: Sten guns, automatics, whatever, which we did over and over and over again.

Then came explosives. It was important to our repertoire of skills that we know how to attack such targets as trains, roads, bridges, and transmission lines. For this, we were trained in the use of plastic explosive, which was a Czech invention. It looked harmless enough, like putty, and had to be detonated with a specific detonation trigger. For instance, a gun wouldn't do it. You could shoot through it, but it wouldn't go off. You could also chew the stuff, then afterwards—as I did once—pop it out of

A training session at **Camp X** demonstrating how to use all senses to ward off an attacker.

your mouth, attach it to something, then detonate it. It was a very powerful material and perfect to derail a train, as we were shown.

All officers at Camp X were British, with the exception of the Adjutant Captain Bushnell and most of the NCOs [non-commissioned officers], who were Canadians. A British instructor taught us how to shoot properly from the hip, which was faster and more accurate. We were shown how to string a piano wire across the road to disable or decapitate a man. And we learned how to kill a person a dozen ways, including how to do it without your victim being able to make a sound.

We had to learn to recognize German uniforms, planes, vehicles, whatever. We were shown how to disguise ourselves and how to stop someone from following us. In short, we were taught anything you could possibly need if you were working behind enemy lines.

As a final exercise, we were dropped off blind in the bush, twenty miles from camp, with nothing to work with, then told to find our way back. There'd be a time limit, but it was a lot of fun. We never had any problem getting back. By the time I finished the course, I have to admit I was in terrific shape. I'd added ten pounds to my legs and arms, but I didn't look any different.

We were shipped overseas to the UK for the final stages of our training. Our first base was a large commando-training centre in Arisaig, near the Isle of Skye. We spent twenty-some days there and never once did we see sunshine; it rained every day at least once. We had a great commander, though, a Scotsman who was very liberal with his whisky. He'd serve a small glass of it, neat, every day for breakfast. The first day at the camp, he addressed us in Gaelic—although we didn't know what it was or what the heck he was saying—so we just followed what his troops did. He seemed to get a chuckle out of that.

The training at Arisaig was more rigorous than at Camp X. We were taken through paramilitary exercises, such as trying to run in full kit across a boggy swamp with live rounds and explosions going off around you. But after going through such training, you began to build enormous confidence in your ability to handle any physical challenge.

From Arisaig, we were sent to parachute training near Manchester, England, which is what I'd always wanted to do, what I'd been waiting for, and which I loved. But unfortunately that course was only a week or so. Then the SOE started to separate us according to skills. Just like when

I first signed up at the CNE, my ham radio background was picked up on. I was sent to Bletchley Park near London for a month to get my Morse code speed up to about twenty words a minute.

During the war, Bletchley Park was the home of the British government code and cipher school. It was a manor house about twenty miles north of London, safely away from the constant air raid attacks. Given the code name of Station X, it masqueraded as "Captain Ridley's shooting party," which I guess was supposed to be a fictitious country retreat of a drunken British aristocrat.

Top-secret German codes were broken here, and needless to say, the instructors were top-notch. My assignment was RT [radio telephony], and so I did nothing else but get my Morse code up to twenty words a minute and memorize crystal set configurations and a variety of codes, especially one-time codes.

There were twenty or thirty of us of various nationalities, all taking wireless training. We had French-Canadians, Norwegians, Polish, Danish —you name it, they were there. I had a good Norwegian friend at Bletchley who I tried to find after the war, but couldn't. I also had a Polish friend there. He and I used to sneak into the storeroom and sneak apples for the day, which was our extra-curricular "spy school" activity. But I don't know if he survived jumping behind the lines into Warsaw. So many of the people I met during those years, because of the nature of what we were doing, I never saw or heard of again.

After a month at Bletchley, we were graduated and sent to SOE "finishing" school.

This was Beaulieu, which I learned was pronounced, with typical English logic, as "Bew-Lee." This was a group of manor houses southwest of London where you were grouped with other trainees according to your specialty. As a result, each house had its own personality and we didn't have a lot of interaction with the other houses. These beautiful manor homes had been commandeered by the SOE for the final stages of whatever assignments we were going to face. With that in mind, we were put under intense observation, testing, and review. Psychiatrists and psychologists were always checking us over, asking questions, and challenging us.

We started to hone our skills under expert instruction. All the instructors at Beaulieu were fabulous. We had an American who taught us what to expect behind enemy lines. He talked about the various political situations in occupied countries and provided some glimpses of what we might expect to happen if we were captured. He also gave us some practical tips about being behind enemy lines.

"Long hair is much easier to change than short hair; it can be cut and dyed. Your clothes can be rearranged to alter your appearance. A limp can be produced with a small stone in your shoe. Never draw attention to yourself by glancing behind. It would make even the Archbishop of Canterbury look suspicious. Avoid talking with strangers while drinking, and don't ever, ever get drunk. Finally, if you're stupid enough to date a girl in an occupied country, you're damn well on your own."

We'd been warned that Hitler was suspected of bearing a particular hatred for soe agents and had given standing orders to the Gestapo and the SS to extract information through any means possible from captured graduates of "England's gangster school." With this threat over our heads, we were shown techniques of surviving intense interrogation and torture without revealing key information. Failing that, we were given cyanide capsules, which were sewn into the lining of our jackets, to be used as needed.

In addition to the psychological testing and lectures, we refined our killing and self-defense skills, taught by some of the finest commando instructors in England, using the soe training manual. In the three weeks I was there, they taught us such skills as arson, blackmail, B&E, more extensive shooting from the hip techniques, forgery, invisible ink, sabotage, assassination, and even more ways of silent killing.

One night, out of a dead sleep, I found myself being dragged out of my room, thrown into a cell and aggressively interrogated by two SS officers. This nightmare went on unrelentingly for the better part of an hour. I couldn't tell if I was dreaming or not, but after a while it became obvious I wasn't. They screamed at you, threatened violence, even threatened your family. Emotionally, it felt like a remarkably realistic experience and to some degree prepared you for interrogation. But ultimately it was a pale comparison to the real thing. If, in the days that followed, you noticed any of your interrogators around Beaulieu in their day jobs as instructors, neither of you gave the slightest sign of recognition.

Training also included more mundane skills that would serve us well. For instance, we were shown how to break into a house or building without making a sound or leaving a trace. Our instructor was a professional burglar who went by the name of Blokey, and we became great friends.

He'd been in prison for safecracking and the authorities had let him out to instruct at Beaulieu. But he had a strict curfew and was locked up in his room by nine at night or something. Off the rest of us would go for an evening at the pub, leaving poor old Blokey buttoned up at the manor, and feeling a bit guilty about it.

The next thing you knew, you'd turn to order another pint and Blokey would be sitting next to you having one, too. He stayed for a while, and then slipped back to the Manor. No one ever caught him. He'd done a lot of plays at school, so in addition to knowing how to slip a lock, he did remarkable things with his appearance with a put-on voice and a touch of soot for make-up.

Blokey's experience was a great example for our practical espionage assignments and his common sense tips helped us a lot. We'd be sent to another town or city with somebody following us and we had to get rid of the tail, which was never any problem. I remember one such trip to Bournemouth. (I went with Rolly, an American oss [office of strategic services] lieutenant, and we decided to have some fun losing our "tail.") We ducked into a women's department store then slipped into dresses and stood around like mannequins. And it worked!

I refined my wireless skills, which had to be twenty words a minute minimum, and passed with honours. Then as a W/T operation, I was sent to two towns in Lancashire—Leicester and Northampton—with the equipment. In each town, I was assigned a billet—where there was always lots to eat and drink, and wonderful hospitality—and I had to make covert wireless transmissions from each house. Then I had to wander I wandered around town, making myself conspicuous by dropping suspicious remarks to try and get caught. The purpose was to learn how to handle being questioned. I was to try and talk my way out of a situation if I was picked up, but it didn't happen. Well, not at the first house.

In the second house in the second town, I managed to draw sufficient attention to myself to get arrested. I was put in jail and tried vainly to talk my way out of it using all the kinds of tricks we'd been taught, but the police were having none of the story I was feeding them. After a I while I started to get a little anxious, picturing myself being permanently locked up for espionage. I had no ID or papers to prove I was anything other than a suspicious character moving around making suspicious remarks with a wireless set slung over his shoulder.

Like a cyanide capsule, we'd been given a secret phone number to call in case of absolute and dire emergency, but had been discouraged from making use of it unless all was lost. I called.

Almost immediately, the police broke a smile. Somehow they must have been in on it all along, but they never let it show.

———

Once I finished at Beaulieu, we were sent into operations in early 1944. We flew out of Land's End with a bunch of generals and other high-ranking officers to Gibraltar for a brief two-day stop. I remember being swarmed by the legendary "Rock Apes" of Gibraltar—monkeys who swarmed the cars and tried to steal everything from our mirrors to my cap. Then on to Algiers for more trainging at a refresher school there. A few days later I was flown to Bari in Italy, and my real mission began.

———

The mission's code name was "Dibbler." Our objective was to enter Hungary through Yugoslavia to help the Partisans fight the Germans. I was assigned to cover it with Mike Turk, also of Hungarian descent. His SOE operative name was "Mike Thomas;" my cover name became "Joe Gordon." The similarity to our real names was meant to hide our ethnic background while providing a psychological link for remembering them under interrogation.

The first stage of the objective was to parachute into the mountains of Yugoslavia near Papuk. We had to find a way into Hungary via the Drava River to liaise with the resistance forces supporting Marshal Tito. One of our men, Gus Bertrand (real name, Bodo), had managed to do it, so we knew it was possible. Gus was a Hungarian who spoke perfect Magyar, but spoke English with a Hungarian accent. Gus, Mike, and I had agreed on a secret code. Gus sent a message back to us in Italy, which alerted us to unspecified problems. The colonel in charge didn't believe us, as Gus was under orders not to send any such message for anyone except the CO. So we went, not knowing what to expect.

Mike and I parachuted in to the Yugoslav mountains near Papuk with a planeload of supplies which were dropped by parachute after we'd landed. As soon as the supplies touched down, they just seemed to disappear into the forest. Although we hadn't seen them at first, the partisans had just swept the stuff into their hiding places. They then emerged and took Mike and me back to their camp. This camp was part of Tito's organization, but the British had a base there under the command of Captain Rollo Young. The building was a simple two-storey affair with storage below and offices and such on the second floor, including Rollo's wireless operations to keep in touch with HQ in Italy.

We had to stay there for several days. We were waiting for permission from Tito's people to cross the Drava River, which separated Yugoslavia and Hungary, and was some distance away. Yugoslavia was a mosaic of factions and forces. There were Tito's partisans, as well as the Chetniks, who were the anti-Tito loyalists of the King of Yugoslavia, the Germans, and various Allied operatives and pockets. That meant anywhere you moved or went, your movements had to be carefully co-ordinated and planned.

Joe Gelleny in Budapest, Hungary in 1944, disguised to blend in as a Hungarian civilian.

The British used to supply the Chetniks, but then they fell out of favour because they weren't attacking the Germans enough. So the British started to supply Tito's partisans with all sorts of ammunition and supplies, which was part of our mission. And I was to provide RT support where possible.

At the partisan base camp, we slept outside. It was great to be outdoors, but you always felt on guard. A few nights after we arrived, an enormously tall American Ranger, Captain Hamilton, ended up sleeping next to me. He warned us to make sure our guns were always close by—underneath our heads—just in case we were attacked. There was nothing secure about those camps.

Hamilton's mission was to contact and debrief American and Allied fliers who'd been shot down in the region and hidden by the Yugoslavs. I went on two missions with him in those mountains and we got to know each other pretty well.

He said his first love had always been ships and the sea, but that didn't pay much. Somebody put him on to acting, which he tried and liked because it made him enough money to support his love of boats. And after being spotted by a casting agent, he ended up with a with Paramount Pictures contract in 1940. But he hated the movie business and quit in 1942 to join the Marines. He passed basic training at Parris Island, got his commission and volunteered for the OSS, where he rose to his rank of captain in the Marines—and which brought him to Papuk as a Ranger.

The movie business? As he talked and I searched my memory, I recognized him as the film actor, Sterling Hayden. And sure enough, it was Sterling, operating under a phoney name like the rest of us.

Sterling had established a network of safe houses and routes through Yugoslavia for downed pilots to make their way back to Italy, for which service he was awarded the Silver Star. I still wondered what he was doing in the middle of nowhere. He shrugged and said, "The two things I despise are mindless militarism and fascism and I figure I'm fighting both. And it sure beats the hell out of sitting around in Hollywood."

He was a solitary quiet man with a good intellect and he showed me great friendship during those few weeks I knew him.

Mike and I eventually got our clearance from Tito's people and started on our way towards the Drava. We had a horse and cart and a Yugoslav-Canadian driver, also a Camp X graduate, as our interpreter.

While we were on our way to the Drava and Hungary, we were invited to a beautiful Yugoslav wedding in a nearby village. We rode through several villages in a cart to get there, but as you went through these isolated little communities up in the mountains, there'd be people hung from the telegraph poles, up and down the streets. These were Chetnicks who'd been killed by the partisans. The region we were in was an astonishing contradiction of a beautiful country wearing the scars of war and its victims.

Every town we passed, we'd see more people strung up by Tito, all from the infighting. If you weren't with Tito, you were against him. The partisans would shoot Germans, too, but the Germans and the partisans tended to stay out of each other's way.

We made it to the Drava. We could see Hungarian soldiers patrolling on the other side, but there was several hundred yards of unguarded riverbank and it looked safe enough to cross. This was late August, so we decided to try swimming across. The Drava was wide, but not impossible.

The problem was that no one had ever thought about the fact that the wireless equipment we had to carry was way too heavy, even for a good swimmer. The one unforeseen problem was that we couldn't swim across with our heavy load of equipment, so we'd have to carry it on our heads. In addition, the river was much too fast. The soldiers on the Hungarian side watched us with mild curiosity as we kept trying and trying, but as there were a lot of young girls swimming on their side as well, they didn't bother that much with us.

We tried crossing using a boat the partisans had given us, but halfway across it was half full of water and sinking, so we had to turn back. It was too dangerous to try to cross at night because of patrols.

Back at camp, we were told that a DC-3 filled with supplies was being sent over, and that HQ had sent word that we were to return to Italy. A few days later, the plane made a hurried landing in a clearing set up by

British paratroops preparing for a jump.

the partisans, unloaded the supplies and filled the plane with wounded returning to Italy. Then Mike and I got in. What I'd never expected was the overwhelming smell of the wounded; we could hardly stand it.

Back in Italy, I assumed the mission had been scrapped, but we were told it was as important as ever and we were going back. However, this time we'd be going in on a blind drop, just in case the partisans themselves had given away too much information and fouled up our first attempt somehow.

Mike and I were teamed with Captain John Coates, the leader of this new attempt, and this time we were taken directly into Hungary. We were flown to Hungary and parachuted in, but not into the area we were anticipating. So it was a blind drop in more ways than one. The pilots never seemed to find the right spot on those blind drop fights. They dropped us six miles off target.

This time the Germans' RADAR picked up our plane so they knew that Allied soldiers had likely parachuted into their territory. They were already looking for us when we landed. John and Mike were captured almost immediately. I saw the Honved [Hungarian home guard] capture them and take them in. Then they sent out a "posse" of about fifty soldiers with dogs searching for me.

In a situation like that, what I'd been trained to do to throw the dogs off was to pee someplace about a hundred yards away from where you were going to hide. I'd done this, then scrambled up a tree that overlooked the building where Mike and John were being held. I hid there for three days and my evasion worked with the dogs at first. But the Honved sent out their posses again and again and eventually one of the dogs sniffed me out and I surrendered.

These home guard men were very loyal to their country and considered anyone working against the pro-Nazi regime to be a traitor to the Hungarian cause. Better to be an Allied officer than a Hungarian traitor.

Generally speaking, if you were captured in civilian clothes, the Germans and Hungarians took this as a license to treat you as a spy and therefore outside the tenets of the Geneva Convention for treatment of P o Ws. That meant aggressive interrogation, severe torture, and the usual end of being executed. So I never let on that I was fluent in Hungarian, but I was able to understand everything they said.

"Should I shoot him?"

"No, the lieutenant wants to question him with the other two."

That meant John and Mike were still alive, which was a relief. The three of us were taken for interrogation to the train station at Abaliget, a village just inside the Hungarian/Yugoslav border. Our captors were very excited at having captured members of a secret operation, which meant they'd receive triple the usual bounty.

At Abaliget, I was questioned in Hungarian. But I simply shrugged my shoulders, indicating that I didn't understand. Then the same questions were repeated in English.

"Who are you? Who are you working for?"

I told them I was a lieutenant with the British army, which my uniform would have told them anyway. When they questioned me about this, I acknowledged that I was a Canadian serving with the British forces. It was critical that I convince them I was regular army, and better yet, Canadian, because that meant I would be accorded P o W status and, I hoped, be shipped off to a camp. If they thought I was a spy, however, I was in trouble. Local villagers were crowded around outside, anxious to string up the three Hungarian traitors.

The Honved officer kept the villagers at bay. We were eventually separated and transported to the city of Orfü and the headquarters of the Second Bureau, which was the Hungarian Secret Service. That's where our interrogations started to get rough.

First off, they didn't believe I was regular army; they accused me of being a British spy, which in fact I was. I wasn't beaten in the traditional sense. They hit the bottom of my feet with a rubber hose, which was very painful. But not as bad as it got. They had no luck getting useful information from us, which angered them.

They reported this to the Germans, who then wanted to have a go at us. We were taken to the town of Pécs and locked in a barracks. It was in an old military camp, and we each had our own cell. The interrogations there became very intense.

I was taken into a separate building, where I was put in front of a couple of bright lights for six hours, all alone. The same questions were asked over and over again, but I kept repeating my story. They'd come in unexpectedly, ask more questions and beat the bottom of your feet. The one advantage I had was that the Germans had to have their questions translated into Hungarian, then into English, to be able to ask me. In the meantime, I'd heard the original question and had a reasonable amount of time to plan my response.

The Germans were trying to loosen us up to do some very simple things for them. They wanted me to radio phoney information back to partisan headquarters in Papuk which they knew would be relayed onto HQ in Italy just as they'd had Gus send a message.

"I don't have a wireless set," I'd say.

They'd produce one.

"I don't have the right crystals."

They'd produce a variety of them.

"I don't have the codes."

They never believed me, but they also never got me to send anything. This motivated them to step up the intensity of the interrogations. Besides hitting the soles of my feet with a rubber truncheon, they also had a generator, which they'd attach to my toes with electrodes. They'd hand crank it and your legs would feel as though they were on fire. Eventually the generator leads were clipped to your genitals. When they cranked the generator, the pain was indescribable and I'd howl like mad.

At Beaulieu, we'd been taught about handling intense pain under interrogation. We'd been told to be prepared to give up some harmless information to appear as though we were co-operating. Also, that if you screamed like blue murder, it would help you survive. It would help you cope with the agony and also made the interrogators feel as though they were "getting" to you.

But the most important warning was never to mention the names of any other SOE member (most of which I didn't know anyway), or to even to acknowledge the existence of Beaulieu. To do so would be to invite weeks or months of relentless torture and a slow death.

The interrogation at Pécs went on for almost three weeks. One day we were dragged out of our cells and put on a train to Hadik prison in Budapest to meet with more experienced interview technicians.

Once again, their main purpose was trying to get me to acknowledge that I was a wireless operator and to send their message back to our HQ and to the partisans. To accomplish this, the Hungarians and the Germans again undertook intensive interrogations. Beatings, generator treatment, being woken and dragged out of your cell at all times of the day and night and assaulted with questions were all par for the course.

I was managing to survive, but didn't know how well the other two were faring. I was in charge of our SOE funds and had gold coins sewn into my jacket. By bribing some older, more kindhearted guards at the prison, I was able to buy some fruit and vegetables to keep us going, because the food was so terrible. Breakfast at Hadik consisted of a loaf of bread the size of a Kaiser roll, ersatz coffee, and a bowl of vegetables with a drop of oil in it. Dinner was whatever was left over. That was our lot for the day. I lost about seventy pounds, going down from 180 to 110 in the three months I was there. I'd been nothing but muscle to begin with, so I lost it all in my legs and my arms. Mike in particular was in need of attention.

There were signs that they were giving up on us. When we'd been captured, John and I were wearing British Army battle dress. After reaching dead ends with our interrogations, the Germans ultimately agreed to send us to a P o W transfer camp. Unfortunately, Mike was in civilian clothes when they captured him, and like Gus, Mike spoke English with a Hungarian accent. So the Hungarians gave Mike a rough time because they considered him to be a Hungarian traitor and said he was going to have to stand before a Hungarian tribunal as a spy.

During this time, in October 1944, the Hungarian general of the prison took me aside to his office. He told me that Hungarian Prime Minister (Admiral) Horthy was to make a speech stating his desire to get Hungary out of the war.

At the end of the First War, under the Versailles Treaty, Hungary had been stripped of all sorts of rights and properties and resources. Horthy came in as something of a white knight to rescue the country. He'd made a deal with Hitler, in which Hitler promised to restore the lands lost to Hungary in the First War, in exchange for essentially surrendering his country to the Germans. But then Hitler decided he wanted the troops from Hungary as well. So, in October 1944, Horthy had decided to make a speech declaring his desire to get Hungary out of the war.

The general said the Hungarian army were patriots and wanted to save the country from being completely ransacked by the Germans. Otherwise, when help came, there'd be nothing left but bleached bones. He felt it was imperative that I help convey the text of the speech to my contacts so that the Allies would know, from a trustworthy source (me), what was going on.

I felt this request was vital and agreed, under the condition that we be removed from the "care" of the Gestapo, and that Mike receive the medical attention he so badly needed. The general agreed, and before it had been broadcast publicly, I transmitted an abbreviated transcription of Horthy's speech message to Papuk, knowing my contacts there would relay it on to HQ in Bari. When Horthy made his speech, the Germans immediately removed him from power and things became increasingly difficult for the Jews as well as for us.

Hungarians looked after the first three floors of Hadik prison in Budapest and the Germans looked after the top floors. With our new-found liberties bought by my RT assistance, we were able to get out of our cells without any problem. But where were we going to go? There was wire mesh between each floor. We were still trapped under German guard in the prison and couldn't escape.

By this time, the Hungarian Second Bureau had become very nice to us, and we had free run of the prison. In the prison, I had met a Hungarian soldier named Captain Andras who was co-ordinating the effort of getting prisoners into safe areas in Hungary or wherever. The Russians were moving in from the east, so the Germans were starting to pull out.

The Second Bureau transferred us back to Zugliget prison camp, which had very loose security. We managed to get Mike into a hospital with the help of some Poles we'd met in there. He was in pretty rough shape. The Russian front was moving closer; you could hear the big guns in the distance. A few weeks after our arrival at Zugliget, the first captured Russian soldiers were brought in, gaunt and shivering with cold.

There we met up with Andrew Duravecz "Andy Daniels," also from Camp X, and he became part of our group even though he wasn't a part of our mission. A Lithuanian prisoner was put in a cell in with John and me. He wasn't anything more than a boy. His clothes weren't much more than the tattered remnants of a peasant's work clothes and for shoes he had straw wrapped around his feet.

Ironically, John and I had planned an escape from the camp that night. Word was spreading around the prison that the remaining German security forces, as a parting gesture, might have decided to eliminate Mike, John and me permanently. We felt it was imperative to find our way to the safe house before the Germans started getting trigger-happy.

Late in the evening, I left some money and food for the Lithuanian boy as he slept. John and I made our beds to look as though we were still in them and then slipped out of the camp. There was relatively lax security inside the Zugliget compound, but it was a harrowing experience getting out of it. The Germans were on the move on the main road; guards were patrolling the walls around the gardens. It was a three-hour game of ducking the guards, hiding in the shadows and behind pillars, and finally scrambling over the wall at one end of the compound and then disappearing into the streets of the city.

We were making our way to one of the safe houses we'd heard about from the Poles in Zugliget. We finally found it at about two or three in the morning, but as we approached the door, dogs started howling and a German soldier walked out.

We hid until he'd gone, then scrambled away, dogs barking and all, to find our way to another house. It was a narrow escape. The next address we went to was a house that belonged to a Hungarian lady named Karola. She didn't know who we were, but John explained it to her in German, which she partially understood. She let us in, but I still made a point of not speaking Hungarian.

Karola had a Jewish girl staying with her, so John and I decided that he'd move to another house in case either of us was caught. With his German, he'd have more success than me in communicating, if I were going to keep my Hungarian background secret.

I was hidden in that house for months, from December 1944 to February 1945. During that time, the house was subjected to five searches by the remaining German authorities. Each time they made a search, the Germans were looking for specified certain people, with increasing severity. At first they only took Jews and didn't bother with mixed married couples. Then they took the Jewish partner from the mixed marriages. Finally, they just took whoever they wanted. I was always hidden during these searches, but the threat hung over us continually.

I could leave the house at night, but only for briefs periods of time. It was too dangerous. When Andras considered it safe, we would walk through the streets, sometimes down by the Danube. There'd be dozens of dead bodies scattered on the riverbank. A lot of them had the Jewish star on their clothes, but not all. A great many were Hungarians, who presumably opposed the regime. Some were Gypsies and some—who knows? Workers would be rolling the bodies into the river and by the next morning, the bodies would be gone. It was extremely distressing, but there was nothing you could do.

Shortly before Christmas 1944, the Germans made an intensive sweep through Budapest looking for Jews. Our house was searched as well. Andras warned us whenever there was going to be a raid, and almost always came with them. The Jewish girl in the house with me hid under a feather duvet on the bed, while I hid in the closet right next to it. I was sure I'd be found.

On this search, there was a regular Hungarian soldier as well as some older ex-army home guard types. When they finally made their way up to this bedroom, the soldier thrust his bayonet into the bed, just missing the Jewish girl under the duvet. She jumped up and screamed and he grabbed her. She fought tooth and nail, but they eventually took her away. With all her fighting, Andras was able to divert them from looking any further and so I managed to escape by the skin of my teeth. I don't know what ever happened to the girl.

After that, I didn't feel too safe. I found a new hiding place in a venting shaft off the main bathroom. It was a nook about four by four feet set off to one side of the room and I was able to crawl in easily from the bathroom. The next time they came to search, the soldier looked right at me in the shaft—or at least I thought he did. I was tucked off to the side and I guess I disappeared into the shadows. The Germans rounded up a whole bunch of Jews and Hungarian dissidents that night.

During those months of hiding, Andras and a Polish captain I'd met in Zugliget came to help me find a way of getting out of Hungary. The Polish captain had a circle of informants and helpers who he relied on to help those of us in hiding. The captain invited a friend of his to provide some assistance getting forged identity papers. This gentleman was Swedish, a tall fellow, kind of ordinary looking, and one of the things he did was give was to give out Swedish citizenship papers (to Jews in particular) to provide them with safe passage. He introduced us to forgers who could create identity cards for John and me.

The Swedish man's name was Raoul Wallenberg, who I didn't know from Adam at that time. He had told us that the Gestapo, except at the highest levels, were corrupt, and money would almost always find a way. I gave several of my remaining SOE gold coins to Raoul to help support his work. As I learned after the war, he saved thousands of Jews with his forged identity papers. When I met him, he seemed to know he was a marked man, but it didn't trouble him. He worked his networks tirelessly

A Russian soldier with a submachine gun. It was a soldier
quite like this who Joe Gelleny
encountered in Budapest in 1945.

and fearlessly. The last time I saw him was Christmas Eve, 1944. He disappeared shortly afterwards.

As the Russians moved closer to Budapest, we were lucky in not getting hit by the continual bombardment from their artillery. In the last days of 1944, Russian paratroops started landing in waves in parts of the city. Something that I found very unusual was that the German troops wouldn't shoot at the Russians until they landed. It was as if they were giving them a chance, then once they'd landed, it became survival of the fittest. Not many survived, but they weren't being shot in mid-air, which is one of the biggest dangers to a paratrooper.

Street fighting became increasingly open, and it wasn't safe to venture out. Shells, machine gun fire, hand grenades were going off everywhere. Eventually the Russians took over the city, and in the middle of February 1945, they announced, "...the end of the fifty-day siege of Budapest and all German forces had unconditionally surrendered." As knowledge of some of the terrors of Stalin's regime began to filter through in comments overheard from the city's new conquerors, the fear became whether the Russians would now be worse than the Germans.

I felt bold enough to go looking for some of the people I'd known who had disappeared. But couldn't find anybody. I wandered around for about a week trying to find Andras and Raoul or any of their circle, but there was no sign of them. A rumour went around that Andras and Wallenberg had been seized, but neither of them was heard from again.

It was a terrifying period for the women in Budapest. After the

Russians had captured the city, the soldiers were granted a free-for-all for seven days. Their officers gave the soldiers license to do whatever the hell they liked. As a result, these wild army types were having a great time, going ruthlessly after women, loot, and booze. They'd even break into beauty salons to drink anything with alcohol in it. The soldiers were raping girls, regardless of age, and rather than be assaulted, all kinds of women were jumping from upper stories of buildings, often with a drunken soldier in pursuit.

One day I was walking down the street with my watch exposed. A Russian soldier with a Burp gun came up to me and pointed at the watch. I shook my head "no," told him I was British, and kept moving. He stopped me by poking me in the gut with the muzzle of his machine gun, and kept poking me until I handed over the watch.

After those seven dreadful days, the Russians restored order. I went to visit Andras's wife, Ilona, to see if she'd heard anything and there was a Russian colonel waiting there. It turned out the Russians had been looking for me. During the week of the rampage, I'd stayed at Ilona's flat a number of nights to protect some women who were hiding from the Russians. Now I was to be placed under arrest and become a prisoner of the Russians. The colonel gave me a half hour to say my goodbyes to Ilona, and then led me off to Russian HQ. I never saw her again.

At Russian HQ, they didn't believe anything I said and declared I was to remain a prisoner of war, which likely meant being shipped back to Siberia or something. I was moved to a P o W camp that was about a mile from the Russian-German front and they put me with a bunch of German and other prisoners. We were stripped naked and then doused with turpentine to get rid of lice. Our clothes were boiled and eventually returned to us.

After I got my things back, I managed to find the colonel who'd arrested me. Desperate, and through much trying and broken Russian, I was somehow able to talk him into believing my story. I have to assume he figured since I hadn't tried to escape, that I must be telling something like the truth.

He gave me a Russian soldier to accompany me to the area where the British and American delegations were. Over the next several weeks, I walked 142 miles to Debrecen with my Russian soldier, as well as several other fellows who were finding their way back. On our way to Budaörs, I spotted Andy Daniels, who had been taken into custody by the Russians.

He was standing behind a high barbed-wire fence. Through some fast talking to the major general in charge of the camp, I managed to get Andy released. He joined our motley crew. When we reached the American legation, we were welcomed with open arms. They asked us what the first thing we wanted was and we all said the same thing: "A shower."

Later that night, they took me to the British Embassy, where we were interviewed and where Andy and I wrote out a report of our experiences, then flown back to Italy and eventually travelled by boat to Southampton. I was debriefed back England, but in typical army FUBAR fashion, I hadn't been formally transferred to the British army (which is what the SOE was). So there was no official record of my rank. The Canadians decided that everyone who served in the SOE would be made a sergeant, so at the end of the war, that was the rank they gave me. By the time I travelled back to Canada, I was made a lieutenant, which was the rank I'd been when I went over two years before.

The war years are very meaningful to me. At twenty years of age, it was all a big adventure. The adventure was to get Hitler out of our lives. While I was in Hungary, the objectives were to help the partisans fight the Germans, and to get Hungary out of the war. But even after Horthy's speech, it was too late. Following an agreement with Churchill and Roosevelt, Stalin had decided that Hungary was going to be a part of the Soviet Union. Therefore, whatever we'd done for Hungary didn't have a lot of effect.

During the war, I was fortunate to have adventured further into dark unfriendly places than most and then return to tell my story. Helen, my wife of fifty-two years, continually encouraged me to tell the story properly. I went about reconstructing this exceptional period of my life over the next fifty years and discovered that all my original reports had become "unavailable." I was also never able to find any of those who offered their friendship and help when I was a prisoner and in hiding thereby making it possible that I might live. It's for them that I wrote my book, *Almost*.

I would advise my sons not to ever get involved in a war, because politicians control it. They don't decide what's good for you. In the long run, they may decide what they feel is good for the country. Certainly do everything you can to help the war effort, if such a thing is necessary. But do not get into the lines; there's no way that you're going to win.

Barney Danson

Birth Place: Toronto, Ontario
Residence: Toronto, Ontario
Regiment: Queen's Own Rifles of Canada
Theatre of War: NW Europe
Decorations: Order of Canada

I REMEMBER HEARING ABOUT KRISTALLNACHT IN NOVEMBER 1938, and there was a rally down at Maple Leaf Gardens. We didn't know what the consequences of all this would be, but we knew it was something that we had to be concerned about. There were German-Jewish families coming to Canada, getting out just in time. They felt something terrible was going to happen; at the very least that they had no future in Germany. They couldn't get proper jobs, couldn't get into proper schools if they were teachers.

I had a very close friend, Freddy Harris, whose father was our family doctor. We felt it would be best to get into the army before war broke out, to get trained and be ready. As we were both Jewish, we had a special motivation. We had no idea how bad it was going to be, but we were starting to get a sense of the evil that we might have to deal with. We joined the Queen's Own Rifles at the University Avenue Armouries in Toronto, and went off to Niagara-on-the-Lake to train with terrible equipment and uniforms.

Around June 1939, the king and queen came to Toronto, and the Queen's Own were to mount a Guard of Honour for them. We had full dress uniforms in storage, and thought we'd put the full kit on and look pretty smart for this visit. I don't think these uniforms had been used since 1911, and when we got them out of storage, they were full of moth holes and had turned from a dark rifle-green into a blue-grey, rather like the German uniforms. They were terrible! But we had an officer in the regiment whose family owned Parker's Dye Works, so they went to work on them. They sewed up holes and re-dyed them to more or less the original colour, then went around to find soldiers who would fit them. I was one of the lucky ones, so I duly became a member of the Guard of Honour.

Down at Union Station we came smartly to attention. We presented arms and did all the things that soldiers did—we thought we were very, very good. The king and queen didn't say anything—they may have seen better in their day. But as soon as they moved off, we rushed back into Union Station, put on our khakis and putties, and then whipped up University Avenue. As the king and queen drove by, we presented arms again.

I think they were going to the University and then on to Queen's Park. So off we went, all spic and span, and waited for them to arrive. The

Governor General's Horse Guards and the Royal Canadian Dragoons came on their horses and stood in front of us. Not only could we not be seen, but the horses did some awful naughty stuff on us which made it particularly uncomfortable. Nonetheless, when the king and queen arrived, we presented arms, then moved back down University Avenue and presented arms as they drove past on their way to Niagara. We presented arms a few times down there as well. Finally, the Royal Train crossed over the Rainbow Bridge on their way to Washington, so we presented arms there for the last time.

I've always felt that the king was so impressed with this huge army he had in Canada that he declared war three months later. I put a quarter on the railroad tracks so the Royal Train ran over it, and that became a lucky charm. I had it in my money belt all through the war—still have it.

Several Jewish members of the Queen's Own Rifles including Freddy Harris (front, left) at a private home during High Holidays in Debert, Nova Scotia.

When war was declared in September 1939, our regiment was not mobilized immediately, which was a great disappointment to us kids of eighteen. We wanted to get into the fighting before it was all over. I was getting impatient, so I tried to join the air force, but it wasn't easy to get into the RCAF in those days. I went down to London and tried to join the Royal Canadian Regiment, who had been mobilized, but they weren't recruiting. In June 1940 I got a call from the air force, saying they would take me, but that same day my regiment was mobilized, so I stayed with the Queen's Own. They had two divisions called up initially, and we were the third. There just weren't enough uniforms, weapons or training areas: Canada's military was minuscule when the war broke out.

Freddy and I became close friends with two other fellows: Gerry Rainer, an Englishman from his family's plantation in Trinidad, who had come up to join the army in Canada; and Earl Stoll, who was from New Toronto. We were all about the same age.

War is not all hell. The four of us had an awful lot of fun in it. We'd go to London together, up to Scotland together, be in the pubs together, chasing skirts together...I actually caught one. There was something special about being a Canadian in England during the war: walking down Whitehall or Haymarket, or through Trafalgar Square or Leicester Square. When you knew you had those Canadian badges on your shoulders, you threw your shoulders back and saluted a little more smartly when an officer passed by. It was a wonderful feeling.

On our dog tags, there was CE for Church of England, RC for Roman Catholic, UC for United, then OD for Other Denomination for all the rest of us. Very upsetting for the senior religion to be just another denomination! Freddy and I were Jewish, and on Sunday there were church parades in Aldershot. There weren't too many reform synagogues there, so we had our choice between the Anglican Church parade, the RC parade, or simply not going. But we never considered that an option: I guess we felt we had to get to God somehow. So we used to go and listen to the prayers, editing out the words we couldn't say and saying the ones we could. It was pretty difficult when you got to "Onward Christian Soldiers," because there was just so much enthusiasm you had to join in.

Now, when I go back to our Regimental Church Parade at St. Paul's in Toronto and read the Apostle's Creed, I have no idea how we got

Left to Right: Earl Stoll, Gerry Rainer, Freddy Harris, and Barney Danson, soldiers from the Queen's Own Rifles.

through that. Maybe that's just another one of the casualties of war.

I come from a religious family, particularly my mother. When anyone would say, "Why did Barney survive?" she'd say, "It was the will of God. God is looking after him." She had a very strong faith.

It's no surprise that in battle everyone is pretty religious. I went around to my platoon and asked if everyone had a Bible. They all did, tucked in their left-hand pocket over their heart. Soldiers spend a lot of time praying, and it comes in many different forms.

The four of us had become corporals and sergeants. Earl took his commission training in England, while Gerry and I came back to Canada for ours. Freddy was the only one who refused a commission: he didn't want to be away from the regiment when the invasion came.

I stayed in Canada for almost a year: my training took about three or four months, and then I became an instructor. I was working with a great, great man, Milton Gregg, who'd won a VC [Victoria Cross] in the First War. He took me out to Vernon, British Columbia, where we took over a sort of run-down school and turned it into a first class battle-training centre in the mountains in the Okanagan Valley. But we were afraid of missing the invasion.

A Canadian soldier guarding a German prisoner at the ruined Caen railway station, July 1944.

I left Vernon in May '44 to try and rejoin my regiment. I was a captain by that time, so I reverted to lieutenant, because I'd never get back to my regiment as a captain. When I was in Debert, Nova Scotia, our last stop before going overseas, we got word that D-Day had come. I also got word that Freddy had been killed on the beach. He hardly got out of the landing craft; I don't think he hit dry land.

———

When I finally rejoined the regiment it was August, and I heard that Gerry had been killed near Caen. So now there was just Earl and me left of our crew. Revenge was part of the deal in those days, and we were going to win the war all by ourselves. We had adjoining platoons, platoons that we'd been sergeants of, which was unusual, and we worked well together, which gave our troops a lot of confidence.

On August 19th we were moving up to Turin, a place just east of Falaise. We stopped to have lunch. The battle was changing: the Germans were evacuating, and Falaise had virtually fallen. All of a sudden, we started being mortared. I'd never been mortared by Moaning Minnies before. I thought we were being dive-bombed; they make a hell of a whistling noise when they come down on you. No one was hit, but to be safe, I put on my tin hat just as another barrage came in.

As well as I can figure, a bomb landed behind me on my left. Something hit the edge of my helmet, came down through my temple, across the back of my eye and stuck in the roof of my mouth. I thought I was losing my teeth, which upset me terribly because I'd always had good teeth! It was only a piece of shrapnel, but my eye has never been any good since. And that really ended my war.

Earl came over to say good-bye, and I guess we both cried a little bit. He went off to win the war by himself, and about a month later he was dead. I was in hospital when Earl was killed—my last friend from the foursome—and I remember going into the chapel. I sort of fell to my knees, which is not a Jewish practice, and mumbled prayers I'd forgotten even existed.

Those are the tragedies of war; and although there were some compensating things, nothing is worth it.

———

We knew what we were getting into when we enlisted. We knew our chances were pretty damned low. In the infantry you walked into the enemy and were more exposed than any other troops on a continuing basis. I didn't have the chance to do as much as I'd wanted; Freddy didn't have more than forty seconds. I'm not saying we expected it, but perhaps in some way we did, because we certainly talked about it. We were all bachelors when we enlisted, and would say, "Our parents will feel badly, but it's part of the job that has to be done." We were terribly young.

The greater tragedy from my point of view was the older soldiers who were married with young families, and were killed. That hits me very hard every time I go back to one of the cemeteries. On my last visit, I went down a line of gravestones and found Bob Sawyer, who had been my platoon commander at one time. He had two kids back home when he was killed.

I still have one more grave to visit in Holland. He was a young man I met when I was back at battle school in British Columbia. We were both instructors in Vernon, both captains, and both anxious to get back overseas. He was an only son, a fine, fine young man, just married, and he and his wife had just had their first baby. Our wives were good friends, and we were going to go into business together after the war. He went with the Irish Regiment up through Italy and finally up into northwest Europe. About ten days before the end of the war, he was killed.

———

After the war, life goes on. You get involved in your new life after the war—raising a family, new jobs, starting a business. But I always maintained my association with the regiment. You had too many friends who were too close, and you felt a great attachment in the infantry, particularly a regiment with a tradition like ours. It's more like a family: everybody knows each other, and your commanding officer is more like your uncle. You don't lose that easily.

Personally it was one of the richest experiences of my life, physically, mentally and emotionally. Working with people from all walks of life— people just out of jail, bums off the street from all parts of the country. You found that virtually everyone had good qualities. They wouldn't have lasted if they didn't.

Our liberties—freedom of speech, freedom of expression, freedom of the ballot box—all these things we take for granted were maintained at a very, very tragic cost. That is all part of our history. Some things are too precious, and without them life wouldn't be worth living: so you risk your life for them. If you do not have values that are that deep for you, I don't think life is worth living!

In the 1930s, we had a minuscule military, and yet this country of eleven million people put one million people in uniform, the third-largest army among the Western Allies. I think back to the immediate post-war years and remember feeling that this couldn't have been for nothing. The kids today know nothing about this history, and it's going to be lost unless it's nurtured.

I just hope we remember, when it comes to times of remembrance, that it's not just us guys with our medals, but the ones that did not live to wear them. That's what most veterans are concerned about.

For us, the greatest satisfaction is a personal thing: when everything, our way of life, was at risk and the chips were down, we were there. No one can take that away from us. When you come to the end of your life, it's a very comforting thought to know that you were able to do that.

Tom Gilday

BIRTH PLACE: MONTREAL, PQ
RESIDENCE: TORONTO, ONTARIO
REGIMENT: CANADIAN GRENADIER GUARDS, FSSF,
STAFF OFFICER TO GENERAL CRERAR
AND GENERAL SIMMONDS
THEATRE OF WAR: NW EUROPE, ITALY
DECORATIONS: DSO, MID, CD

In 1932, I joined the Canadian Grenadier Guards in Montreal as a second lieutenant. It was for a job as much as anything. My father and uncle had been in them [the Guards] in the First World War; it seemed to be a family affair. I wasn't really a military man at that time. I was more interested in sports and skiing and swimming and I was well known in the athletic world, especially as a skier.

In 1935 there were good jobs to be had in Sudbury, so I went up to paddle in the Canadian Championships and never came back. I stayed and got a job in the mines. At that time I was making good wages, thirty-five cents an hour, a ten-hour day, a six-day week, and you got time-and-a-half on Sundays. That was big money in those days and a good way to start life. After a year or so I had enough money from the mines to get out and start my own insurance business.

I think we all knew war was coming around 1937. Things started to flare up in Europe and people were becoming aware of the trouble brewing. The regimental units started to try and get people in, and then in 1938 and '39, when Germany really started moving, that was it. As my regiment became active, I rejoined the regiment [Grenadier Guards].

It was the phony war at first, of course. Then as things started to get more serious in 1940, the Canadian army decided to put everybody on skis and snow shoes in the winter of 1940–41. Because I was so well-known as a skier, I found myself designated as Chief Instructor for the First Canadian Army Winter Training School. I temporarily left the regiment and went off to run this thing.

At that time, the Grenadier Guards were infantry. In 1941–42 they became the 4th Armoured Brigade Division, which meant that all the boys had to change from infantry to armour. Now with these flat feet infantrymen suddenly being stuck in a tank with three or four other guys, some of them couldn't take the claustrophobia. So that took some adjusting. But the main point is that the regiment was getting ready to go overseas, which is what I wanted.

I had just come back from winter training school in May '42. The Guards were set to go overseas in three or four weeks, so everybody was wrapped up in preparations for that. But right after I returned, the colonel called me into his office.

"Tom, you're wanted in Ottawa."

I didn't like the sound of that. Another distraction.

"It's probably something to do with the winter training program. Maybe I did something wrong or they need some help. Whatever it is, I'm sure I can clean it up in two or three days, then I'll be back."

"No. You're being transferred to Ottawa indefinitely and are to take your stuff with you."

"But we're just shipping out! What's it all about?"

"I don't know, but here's the telegram: 'Gilday report to Ottawa immediately.'"

I was wondering what the heck was going on and was not pleased about having to leave the regiment again. At this point I was a captain and felt I was ready to take a command and see some action. But you didn't have any choice in these things. I packed my trunk and away I went, wondering what they had in store for me. In Ottawa, I reported to the colonel who'd sent for me.

"Gilday, we need you badly because you're an expert in winter conditions. We're bringing together a group of tough, hardy men—hunters, trappers, miners, fishermen—guys who are big and strong and who know how to live in the snow. We've asked for volunteers and they'll be arriving five days from now. We want you to decide which ones to take. Some are coming from England, some from the States, and they're coming from all over Canada. So it's up to you to decide how you want to go about it."

That's how I found myself in charge of a battalion with the FSSF [First Special Service Force], half-Canadian, half-American. The motivation for the creation of the FSSF was to use snow mobility to reach vital installations in occupied Europe during the depth of winter. The immediate objective was an operation code-named "Plough." Plough was going to go into Norway to assault heavy water plants and hydroelectric installations as a diversion for Operation Bolero, which was the cross-Channel invasion planned for 1943.

The FSSF was a secret force and nobody was supposed to know anything about it. To avoid attracting unwanted attention to us, our commander, Colonel Robert Frederick, named the force, "First Special Service Force," avoiding the more familiar terminology of "commando," "ranger," or "parachute infantry." Who knew what special services were? It could have been mobile kitchens, for all anybody knew.

We went to Helena, Montana, in July 1942 to train. I was a battalion commander with a half-American, half-Canadian group. It took us a little

1st Canadian Parachute Battalion troops training in the snow.

while, but we all fitted in together and became great friends and a terrific fighting unit. The boys were from all over both countries and were as mixed a group as you could imagine.

We got extensive training in demolitions, parachute jumps, hand-to-hand combat, rock climbing and winter warfare. My specialty was doing pretty much anything in snow, so I would show the boys some of my ski tricks. One of the things I had them do was jump off thirty- and forty-foot rock faces into deep banks of snow, with skis and without, just to get them used to manœuvring in heavy winter conditions.

We were pretty isolated out there and became a pretty close bunch as a result. There was a movie made about our bunch and one of the stories was about a big fight at a bar near the Canadian–US border. Some of it was true enough; some of the boys stood up for some of the others when they ran up against a bunch of locals who were looking for a fight. The Americans tended to have a little more of the renegade personality, while the Canadians were just plain tough and stubborn. Our boys all ganged up together to teach the locals that if they took one of us on, they were going to have to take us all on. The fight at the bar brought our boys pretty much together into a single group.

The training continued through the winter of 1943 into April, when we moved to Virginia and took amphibious training. Then we were off to Vermont for more rock climbing and sharpening up our raid tactics. Physical fitness was always a big part of whatever we were doing. The boys would challenge each other to keep up and help each other if somebody fell behind.

Personnel of the First Special Service Force boarding Douglas C-47 aircraft during parachute training at Fort William Henry Harrison.

We were expecting to ship out to Europe. Italy seemed like the obvious destination. But when we piled on the train in Vermont at the end of June, it went west. We were issued summer uniforms and so assumed we were headed for Italy by the Pacific route, which sometimes happened. We landed in 'Frisco and boarded a ship and headed out to sea. When we were almost at Hawaii, we were ordered to turn in all our summer uniforms and were issued a complete new winter outfit. Now we had no idea where we were going. They had us out in the middle of the Pacific and all locked up tight so we couldn't talk to anybody but ourselves, so that's when they told us our objective.

The whole exercise of travelling across the country with summer uniforms, getting on the boat in San Francisco, and then heading off to Hawaii and getting refitted with winter gear in eighty-degree weather was all a scheme to throw off anybody trying to follow us or figure out what we were all about.

Where we went was to Kiska, at the far end of the Aleutian Islands, about a thousand miles west of the Alaska mainland. The Japanese had occupied it since 1942 and the boys in charge decided they wanted it back.

My battalion was taken in on an American destroyer in the middle of August '43. We were supposed to paddle in to shore by rubber boat, but there was fog and I couldn't see anything. I wasn't going to take my battalion off that blinking destroyer until I could at least see land and know that I wasn't paddling into outer space. I stood on the bridge of the destroyer and made the captain keep moving in closer. We coaxed him in close enough that I felt it was okay to take off, and we landed about midnight and wandered around. But there wasn't anybody there. The Japanese stoves were still hot and food was still on the table. The last of them had just pulled out in the fog by submarine, right under the noses of the Americans, who were pretty upset about that.

We spent three days at Kiska, then were whisked back across the continent to Virginia to wait for our next assignment. The Norway scheme and the 1943 invasion had been scrapped, so we weren't sure where we'd be off to next. We sat in Virginia until November 1943, when we were loaded onto a ship and set out across the Atlantic. This time I was sure it was for the Mediterranean somewhere.

The Americans had gone into Italy by that time and were halfway up Italy's boot. They'd come up against the German winter line, which was well-prepared and heavily defended. There was a line of mountains that historically had always protected Rome from invasion from the south. The Germans had taken control of these mountains and fortified their position on Monte la Difensa very effectively. Judging by how high and how steep it was, my guess is the word "Difensa" must translate into something like "You gotta get past me before you can move north." The Germans were going to hold the whole thing as long as possible to keep us from getting too far north.

The British had tried to overtake this position and been thrown off. Then the Americans tried and they were thrown off. Allied command whistled us in because we'd been trained as mountain troops and were prepared for that type of fighting. Colonel Frederick had figured out a back route up and so it was our turn to try.

We were trucked forward to the base of the mountain and marched through the mud to a tree-covered area to begin our assault. The colonel's secret route was a 350-foot rock face, which went at about a sixty-five-degree slope up the back of the mountain. But that didn't bother my boys. They only seemed happy when they got to do something that nobody else had been able to do.

We couldn't possibly do the climb in daylight, because we would all be killed, so it had to be done in stages over two nights. The first night we moved up into the trees, as far up as we could go without being caught by the Germans, then slept all day. As soon as it got dark, we made our way up the rock face to get us into position behind the German line at the top.

Moving in single file, my battalion worked its way around the mountain to the base of the cliffs. On the way we passed the bloated, unrecovered bodies of some of the guys killed in the earlier assault attempts. Our artillery fire over our heads at the German position on the top of the mountain continued through the whole climb, and it was loud. But I don't remember it bothering me much. We had a long way to go and so we just kept moving.

We had to haul our equipment up with ropes and on our backs. It was steady climbing and cold, but the rain was the real problem, because it made things so slippery. It was our first time going into battle and everybody was pretty keyed up for it, I think.

We reached the top before dawn and were so close to the Germans that we could hear them talking and smell their food cooking. We literally slid in behind them, took them completely by surprise, and that's when the fight started up there.

There were four or five days of intense fighting. The Germans threw everything they had at us. They kept sending more troops in. We were about equal strength, but they could reinforce theirs much easier than we could. The weather was terrible: there was snow, ice, rain and clouds. The clouds hung so low over the mountains that they became our worst enemy. Everything was sort of ghostly.

The clouds would suddenly lift and you'd see five or six Germans moving blindly towards you. Both sides would be a little stunned. There'd be fireworks, then BOOM!, the clouds would drop down again. It kept you constantly tensed up. I kept asking myself, "Where were those guys going? Should we stay here, or move?" And if you moved, as often as not you just ran into them again.

We had sniper fire and some mortars and artillery shells hitting us over the next few days. We lost a few men in that first clash, but gained a solid foothold around the rim of the clifftop. We eventually took the mountain and moved on and cleaned up the other German positions on Monte la Remetanea so the British could move up.

That was our first time into battle and you learned in a hurry, seeing your friends get wounded and killed. Up to that point, it was all fun and games. The rule of thumb was that if you survived the first four or five hours of battle, you might be good for a long time. It's those first hours that make or break you. If you weren't there, you couldn't understand what that means or how it feels. But I think it's something everyone who has seen front-line combat knows.

Some are lucky, some aren't. You hear a machine gun bullet go this way, then that way. Somebody gets killed beside you; someone is hit over there. One of the tough things is that when somebody is wounded, you can't stop and help. The first aid people are moving in behind you, so you give the guy a shot of morphine or something if you have any. But if you're fighting a battle, you've just got to keep moving. So you pat him on the shoulder and say, "I'll see you back there. Lucky fella, you're probably going to have a nice holiday with some beautiful nurse in some hospital," when you know damn well that he's going to die. You have to learn to live with it; you learn quickly to live with it. That's war.

———

After the British forces came in and reinforced us and took over, we were pulled back. That meant we could get our wounded looked after, have a shower, and get cleaned up. Two weeks later they sent us to the Anzio beachhead.

Anzio was close to Rome. If the Allies had been able to make an end run, they'd have been able to cut off the German supply lines to Cassino. But there weren't enough resources or men to pour in, so they had to draw back and ended up forming a beachhead at Anzio. This beachhead was a big circle about fifteen miles across that our side could feed troops into. That's what gave us the strength to resist the German attacks.

We were stuck there for ninety-nine straight days of fighting, day and night. The Germans threw everything they had at us and we had nowhere to go except into the sea, so we just had to stand and fight. They'd push us and then we'd push them back again.

At the Mussolini Canal, I had two miles of front to hold with only three hundred men. Our artillery was what kept us there and forced the Germans back. There was no place that was safe and you couldn't move in the daytime because they had high ground and they could chase you all over the place with an 88 or a mortar every time you stuck your head out.

We couldn't move forward. But our boys wouldn't stand for the Germans breathing down their necks, so they took out after the enemy lines every night by patrol. That's when we did our best work. The Germans were frightened to death of us because they didn't know who we were. We'd come in as a secret force and had these special uniforms that they couldn't identify. Our outfits didn't look like Canadian or American uniforms. We had specially-made baggy pants that had originally been intended for the snow in Norway. They were very comfortable and had lots of pockets.

At first, the Germans used to call us "The Men in Baggy Pants." Then it became "The Black Devils," because we used to blacken our faces and move in on them at night. Colonel Frederick had little stickers made for our men. We'd move on the Germans at night and kill them silently. Then we'd put one of these stickers on their heads or helmets, which said, "The Worst is Yet to Come," or "The Little Black Devils Were Here Tonight." We had quite a reputation. At one time the Germans were offered something like a month's holiday if anybody could capture one of our boys and bring him in.

One of my best men was Tommy Prince, an Ojibwa from Manitoba. He won the MM [Military Medal] while we were at Anzio. Tom was a superb marksman with tracking skills that he'd picked up on the reserve. He trained as a member of the 1st Canadian Parachute Battalion and moved from there to the FSSF. No one could match him for some of the stuff he pulled.

Sergeant Tommy Prince (right) with his brother, Private Morris Prince, at an investiture at Buckingham Palace, 1945.

He'd slip away at night and get behind the German lines all by himself. The Germans thought he was a ghost or a devil because they could never figure out how he passed the sentries. He moved with absolutely quiet because of a pair of moccasins he'd wear. Sometimes, instead of killing the Germans, he'd steal something from them, like the shoes off their feet. Or he'd leave one of our stickers behind, just to let them know he'd been there. Other times he'd slit their throats and not make a sound. When the soldiers woke up and found one of their men lying next to them dead, that's when they got scared. They figured Tommy must have been an evil spirit or the devil. He was a lovely, quiet guy, one of the best Devils.

We broke out of Anzio at the beginning of June. The Germans had to draw back north of Rome to establish another line, and we were fighting the rearguard all the way back. We broke through and pushed the German rearguard through the streets of Rome. Our objective was to take the eight bridges across the Tiber before they were blown up and we managed to do that.

Again, we lost some good men in that final part of our war. We had to bring ourselves up to strength, get our wounded out, and have a rest while we waited for our next assignment, which was to move up through France from the south at the Italian border.

But I'd reached a point where I couldn't sleep anymore. My nerves were turning bad. In the summer of 1944, I'd turned thirty-four and I was too old. Most of the boys were nineteen or twenty. When we got to France, I discovered all kinds of battalion commanders and the like coming out from the front were in the same condition as me. A person can't command a battalion on the front lines for more than six months without something wearing down. The responsibility and non-stop pressure get to be too much.

My battalion needed a fresh guy in there, a fresh face to carry on. I'd been on the front lines for eight or nine months and knew I needed a rest. I asked to be relieved from the FSSF, then rejoined the Canadian army in Holland. The boys carried on and did great things, but the regiment was disbanded at the beginning of December because the need for that kind of special operations force had disappeared.

From that day to this, we've had a society of our own. We don't talk much about the war outside of our own, because talking about it brings back too many friends and too many bodies. When we talk with each other, we talk as a way of working through those experiences in our minds. The memories will never fade, so you're always dealing with them. But when you share them with the men who lived them with you, it helps you keep them in perspective.

To this day, if any one of the FSSF were ever in need, any one of us would do everything we could to help them out. That will never change. I would trust any one of those men with my life.

Joe Jamieson

BIRTH PLACE: NORTH RUSTICO, P.E.I.
RESIDENCE: GUYSBOROUGH, NOVA SCOTIA
REGIMENT: 86 ANTI-COAST BATTERY, FSSF
THEATRE OF WAR: NW EUROPE, ITALY
DECORATIONS: BRONZE STAR

My name is Joseph Thomas Jamieson, and I was born September 8th, 1916 in North Rustico, P.E.I. My dad was in the fisheries business. He was with the Maritime Fisheries, the National Fish Company, and went to P.E.I. every summer buying mackerel. He found me in one of the mackerel barrels, I think.

He wasn't a bad chap; always working. My mother was born in Scotland and was brought over to Canada by the Ministry of Fisheries to train the people in Canso in how to put up Scotch-cured herring and how to mend nets. There were twelve girls that came over, and two of them got married and stayed in Canso. One of them was my mother. She was born in Lossiemouth, Scotland, near the Moray of Forth.

I had one brother and one sister. My older brother Jimmy was shot down and killed over Malta with the RCAF in 1941. He was a navigator on a British Blenheim.

He was twenty the last time I saw him in 1940 in Mulgrave; we shook hands, and that was the last I ever saw of him.

My father's business was in Canso, so that's where I grew up. My mother and my brother and I went to Scotland in 1919, just after the war. My father was being transferred to Port Hawkesbury, and they were going to build a house for us. So my mother thought it would be nice to go home and visit her family, so we did, and stayed for five years. Trouble was, when I came back to Canada, I spoke nothing but Gaelic.

In 1929, the business my father worked for went bankrupt in the market crash, so he went out on his own. We moved back to Canso, and that's where I finished my grade eleven and twelve. Work was scarce there, but I picked up some work in the fish plant. You got your board paid, but the wage was ten cents an hour. Times weren't too bad. I bought myself a car for fifty cents. I stayed there until 1937, and then I went down to Chester Basin to work at the gold mines.

I was taking a miner's apprentice project: two years working underground for fifty cents a day, plus our board. But when we were finished this, we were being offered good pay up in the Northwest Territories for eight or ten dollars a day, so that was something to look forward to.

But just before we finished the two years, war broke out. I didn't know anything about what had been happening, so it was all news to me. What it meant to me was that if I joined up, I'd get a dollar-twenty a day, which was double our pay doing the mining apprenticeship. So we weren't long joining up!

The Antigonish battery was thirty miles from my home, so two other fellows and I went up to see what was going on. They said, "Gee, we got openings for just three more fellows. So you're it!" And that was that. My brother wanted me to join the air force, but I wanted my feet on the ground.

It was November 1939. I was sent to Halifax for five months to become a gunnery artificer. When I came back, they promoted me to lance bombardier. I eventually became an artillery sergeant. I was older than some of the guys—twenty-four at the time.

I stayed with the artillery until 1942. I wanted to get overseas, and was approached by a sergeant-major who had trained me in Halifax. He wanted me to go overseas with him, but my colonel said, "No deal. I need you here. You're not going." So that put the end to that.

One day a notice came out on the bulletin board.

"Volunteers for the 1st Canadian Parachute Battalion. If you qualify, you automatically transfer."

Joe Jamieson's brother, Jimmy.

My friend and I both applied and both got accepted. Of course I was in good shape then, just out of the gold mines.

We were transferred to Ottawa and stationed at Lansdowne Park, under the stadium seats. We stayed there for about three or four months, waiting to be shipped down to Fort Benning, Georgia for paratroop training. So we decided to take some time off and head home. On the way home, I stopped in Mulgrave to catch a boat to Canso. I stayed there for night at my old camp before heading off home. When I was there, they said, "There was a call for you. You're to meet the train in Mulgrave tomorrow at noon. There's a man there wants to see you."

So I took my kit and headed back into Mulgrave the next morning and met this guy. His name was Major Jack Secter.

"I understand you've taken your parachute training."

"I haven't jumped, but I've been all through the training."

"Well, I need you. Where's your buddy?"

Dodie had headed off home to Antigonish. I reached him and said we had to meet in Sydney the next day. There, we interviewed about fifteen or twenty fellows for the major; then we had to head over to Debert and Truro to interview more guys. It was a late night. We'd got about a hundred recruits to go to this First Special Service Troops.

These guys were just raw recruits who said they wanted to jump. We looked for guys who were kind of daredevils. You could tell if someone just wanted to go for the trip, or if someone was real serious about it, and that's how we made our choices.

When this was all done, I started to head off home at last. But the major said, "You're not going home. You're going off to Montana." So I always said I never joined the FSSF, I got shanghaied.

We were six or seven days on the train, and we arrived in Montana on a Sunday afternoon. They gave us a welcoming talk.

"First off, we don't care how good shape you are in. You're going to learn to jump. You're not a paratrooper; but you're going to become a paratrooper, but only as a means of transportation as far as we're concerned."

Monday morning we went out to the parachute shed where the instructor was waiting for us.

"This is your parachute. You put your main chute on your back and your emergency chute on the front." They showed us how to put it on, and that was it.

Next morning, Tuesday, they had a mock-up jump platform.

"You climb up there, you get your hook-up, and then you jump."

Wednesday morning, we went up in a plane and jumped. And that was our parachute training. If you didn't break your leg, you were okay and could stay in the outfit. If you broke your leg, you were no good to them and you were out.

We trained for a whole year. Our job was to go into Norway. Each group of five men were provided with what they called a "Weasel." It was built by the Chrysler Corporation, and it was one of the first snowmobiles. It was made so it could be dropped in by parachute. Our objective was to jump into Norway and destroy the heavy water plant they were building there, then try and get out to Switzerland.

That year, we had every kind of training. Mountain climbing, skiing—our instructor for that was Tom Gilday. We called him "the old coot." He was a great soldier, a great soldier. He was as tough as a nut, and died as he lived: no nonsense about him at all. When he passed (in June 2001), his orders were to be buried in a plain pine box with no funeral.

A combat exercise designed to develop aggression and self-confidence.

The training was unbelievable. Unbelievable. Fifteen, twenty hours a day sometimes. It never stopped. It was nothing for them to wake us up at three in the morning, throw us in the back of a truck, then take us off and drop us somewhere up in the mountains.

"If you get back by seven, you'll get breakfast. If you don't..."

Every day, there'd be a fifteen- or twenty-mile route march. But we liked it. You got in great shape. I weighed a hundred and forty-eight pounds, six foot one. At least twice a month, we did a fifty-five mile route march with full kit in the hot sun.

Demolition was one of our exercises. We had a fellow from DuPont, and he invented a special demolition for us. It was called a Rhine Special. It looked like a big sausage. You could twist it, pound it around, but it could only be detonated by a detonator. We used a lot of it, but they could never figure out why: we never blew up anything. The reason was that one of the guys tried an experiment. He cut a little chunk off and set light to it with a match. It was like a little acetylene torch. It was great for boiling a cup of coffee. So every fellow had a chunk of RS in his pocket all the time!

We trained on every kind of weapon. No special weapon. We even trained on German weapons. We knew their machines guns as well as a German soldier knew them. We knew their anti-tank weapons as well as them, their mortar systems as well as them.

The Weasels were beautiful things: big engine, track vehicle, but we never got to use them in combat. On our first assignment they took us across country to the Pacific. We didn't know where we were going, but we ended up in San Francisco. We met up with a bunch of marines there and they wanted these Weasels, because they were great in mud. So we made a dicker. They had what they called the Johnson submachine gun. It wasn't used by the general American army because it had a slight recoil and they couldn't put a bayonet on it. But the marines liked it because it was a good weapon. So we traded the marines our Weasels for a bunch of these "Johnny" guns. They were made of Swedish steel. You could fire seven hundred rounds through it, slip the barrel out, throw it in a barrel of water, put a new barrel in and keep on going. It was our favourite gun.

Our first job was being put on Angel Island, right next to Alcatraz. After about two or three days, they put us on some ships and we didn't know where we were going. Once we were at sea—it was a fourteen-day trip—they told us we were headed for the Aleutian Islands. A lot of the guys had never been on board a ship before. Two meals a day, and most of them couldn't keep much of it down.

We landed at Amchitka Island, where we did some training for a landing at Kiska, which is where the Japanese had dug in. We set our tents up on boggy ground; it was foggy and misty all the time. Doing guard duty, we had to have ropes to find our way around. Couldn't see anything. We tried route marches, and it took us about four days to do ten miles.

Then we loaded up to go to Kiska. Our company was to land on Kiska beach, haul our boats overland to an inland lake, and then row around behind the Japanese position, which was a 6-inch artillery piece up on a hill. We landed, got over to the lake and were halfway up the hill when we got word.

"Boys, don't worry. The Japs are gone. We don't know where they are. Their grub's still on the table; they must've just left."

We were quite happy about that. We only had one box of K-rations anyway. They didn't expect us to come back: it was going to be a wipe-out thing for us.

I've been asked, "Were you afraid?" We were never afraid of anything. Or more appropriately, we were never afraid to do something, but were hellish scared doing it.

Tom Gilday, as one of our officers, was terrific. Some officers say, "Okay boys, here's what I want you to do." With Tom and most of our other officers, it was always, "Okay boys. Here we go." And he'd be out in front of the rest of us, leading us in. Especially at Anzio, which is where Tom got beat up quite a bit.

We had three officers from Nova Scotia with us: Tucker, Mitchell, and Perry.

After Kiska, we were brought back to San Francisco. Then all of us from the east coast were sent back to Burlington, Vermont. Then it was on to Newport News, Virginia and then we went across and landed at Casablanca. But we didn't know where we were going.

Casablanca was dangerous in those days. Beautiful country. But I remember one incident. This fellow would come around camp every morning, shouting, "Lemon! Lemon! Lemon!" This fellow a couple of tents down from me said, "If that bastard wakes me up tomorrow morning, I'm going to shoot him." I never thought any more about it.

First thing next morning, I hear a shot and go out and look. Here's this lemon fellow outside this other guy's tent, lying there dead. This trooper pulled his wallet out, tossed it down beside the dead man's body, then called the military police and said, "I caught the little bastard trying to steal my wallet. I couldn't stop him, so I shot him."

He was sent to trial, and was found guilty. His sentence was that he had to pay the dead man's wife all the money that the dead man would have made for the rest of his life, and he was only a fellow in his twenties. He had to pay the widow forty-eight dollars. So, quite happily, she took the body and the forty-eight dollars and went off.

Then we shipped out and landed at Naples. Naples was still being bombed pretty badly in those days. We got ashore and went into a little town called Capua; it had been an army training base for the Italian army. We still didn't know at this point what our objective was.

One day, this General Keyes came in.

"I just came to see you bunch of Hollywood glamour boys. I hear you're tough. Well, we got a job for you. We've been trying to take this hill now several times and couldn't do it. So when you get there, you're going to see fifteen or sixteen hundred dead lying there, piled up against the wall. We can't get close enough to bury 'em. Those guys lying there couldn't take it. Colonel Frederick, says you can take it."

"Damn right we can take it!"

"If you can take it," he said, "I'll come back and apologize to you personally."

I should mention that Colonel Frederick was incredible. He knew every man in the outfit: his name, where he came from, what he could do. Everything. He was a good man, wounded nine times.

We loaded up with everything. Food, weapons, ammunition, stretchers, supplies, whatever. It was a little over a ten-mile march in miserable rainy weather to get to the base of the mountain. Monte la Difensa. We holed up there at the bottom; the Germans up top couldn't see us, because they were off looking the other way. We were the third regiment; the supply regiment. We were to be at the top of the hill immediately after the second and first regiments had gone up and hit the Germans.

We couldn't see what we had to do too clearly, so we didn't think that much about it. Years later, when I went back and looked at it, I thought, "That's impossible. Just impossible." But up we went.

The force planners had decided to try a new tactic to surprise the enemy, an approach up the steep, north-facing cliffs, which were probably thought to be unclimbable by the Germans. And where it was determined the Germans had not set up defensive positions.

The first slope was about three hundred and fifty or four hundred feet of wet slippery rock, at about a forty-five degree angle. The last bit was only about seventy or eighty feet, but it went straight up. We went up there that night, as soon as dark hit. We were at the base of the sheer face by morning, and lay there under cover all day. When dark came again, the assault went in up this steep face. We had fifteen hundred artillery guns hitting the German positions from the other side to keep them occupied. When those guns took off, we took off behind them.

It took seven or eight hours to get up that last face. When the first two regiments went into battle we were right behind them, with ammunition and stretcher-bearers. When the battle started, we had to go up and down, bringing up supplies and bringing down wounded. It was a thirteen-hour round trip to the base camp.

But the Germans didn't have a hope. We came in above them; they were down below us. We took the position in four hours. But it was heavy fighting; somebody being killed every few minutes. We had ninety-one killed up there that day. The first man killed was Lieutenant Tom Williams, from New Brunswick. Then, for three days, we were up and down that mountain.

When things settled down there, they pulled us back. Then, three days later, they shoved us up the mountain again, in the mountain range leading up to Monte Cassino. Christmas Eve, the Canadians were going to storm Ortona. There was a German company we figured were going to try and move in behind the Canadians. So we got orders to take that German company out on Christmas Eve.

We killed about thirty or forty of them; we lost about eight or ten men. Christmas Day, we got back to an olive orchard. I got a pint of beer and a cold turkey leg for Christmas dinner.

So we kept moving up the mountains. This one night, our platoon were on patrol. A beautiful night; minus twenty degrees Fahrenheit. They'd pinned us down behind these mountains. Every time you'd poke your head up, they'd take a whack at you. Come along midnight, there, some of the guys were getting antsy, because we couldn't move. I tried to

First Special Service Forces dug in on Anzio beachhead, 1944.

calm 'em down and keep 'em straightened out. This one guy jumped up and said, "I'm not staying," and he took off. He just made it to the top of the hill and they cut him in two.

Around about two o'clock in the morning, we were getting cold. I said to one fellow, "John D, I think my feet are frozen."

"Well, if you can get back down the mountain the way we came, there's a little first aid post there that's pretty good. If you can sneak back down the mountains and get back to it, you should get them looked at."

I made it down and into the tent. There was one guy there with most of the back of his head blown off. The doc said, "What's your trouble?"

"I think my feet are frozen."

"Take your shoes off."

I did, and he had a look at them.

"Yes, they're frozen. Not quite stiff, but they're frozen. Best thing you can do is get out of here."

He cut my shoes off, and bandaged up my feet, wrapped them up in blankets. Then they gave me eight prisoners and a wounded fellow to take out. We left about four in the morning, just before daybreak, heading down the mountain.

There was this German sergeant who was with me. He was Czechoslovakian and he spoke pretty good English. He carried my rifle for me. I was a little nervous, but he said, "Don't worry. If any of them try to go back, I'll shoot them myself."

So we walked all that afternoon and until two o'clock the next afternoon. Just blankets around my feet. I was directed to a MASH station a ways away, and all that night I had a nurse bathing them in cold water and hot water. The doctor came in and said, "You're lucky. The circulation's gone back to your feet."

The nurse came up with her hands up.

"Somebody light my cigarette." She had blood running down her arms, and she was crying.

"What's the matter?" I asked her.

"I just cut the feet off a young fellow over there, eighteen or nineteen. They were frozen."

They sent me back to Capua, and I was there four or five days. The doctor came in and said, "How's your feet?"

"Pretty good."

"Can you walk on 'em yet?"

"Yup."

"Good. Then you're going back up the mountain."

So I went back up and joined the boys, and we fought right up to Cassino. Then we got orders we were being pulled out. We figured the war was all over for us. The transports were waiting for us, but instead of taking us home, they took us to Anzio harbour. And we went right into Anzio.

The first night in Anzio, Frederick and a couple of captains and I went on patrol. A shell came in and one of the captains jumped into a hole, right on top of a mine. So that was the end of him. We didn't like the position there much, with a canal running through, so we nosed around for a better position. You couldn't move by daytime. You just stayed in your hole in the daytime.

When you went out on patrol, you never wore any kit on your back or a helmet. You'd have four or five hand grenades hung on your belt, a knife, and whatever gun you wanted. We'd go out on what we'd call a "shoot 'em up" patrol. We'd sneak across the canal and we'd hide and wait for a German patrol. Then we'd kill 'em all; or maybe leave one for them to tell them about it. We had little stickers to stick on the dead Germans' helmets. They read, "The Worst is Yet to Come."

They were petrified of us. They kept moving back, and we kept moving after them. We moved them back three miles that way. The biggest patrol was in the early morning—we called that the egg patrol. Because if you got there first, you could scoop up some eggs from the farms you moved through. Tommy Prince served with us there. He was a nice fellow, like the rest of the guys, but he liked to go out on patrols alone. He kept the Germans busy. He wouldn't tell anyone where he was going. He was real quiet, and wore moccasins all the time. Instead of sneaking in and killing them, he'd steal something, like a pair of shoes right off their feet. Once in a while he would kill one of them, slit their throat so as not to awaken anybody and leave the body there for the Germans to find in the morning.

Tommy won the MM at Anzio. He ran a telephone line about four or five hundred yards out to a farmhouse, real close to the German line. The phone line got broken during the shelling and Tom acted real angry, shaking his fist at both sides, then grabbed a hoe and worked his way back, looking for all the world like a farmhand, while looking for the break in the line. He bent over to tie his shoelaces—which he didn't have because of the moccasins—and repaired the break.

Ninety-two days we were at Anzio. Finally, they pulled us out; the British were coming in to relieve us. We moved up with some tanks on the 23rd of May; we never stopped after that. We went right on up through the Lira Valley. [US] General Mark Clark came up with a bunch of tanks, and said, "Let's go!"

On June the 3rd we drove right into Rome, which kind of disheartened the Germans. General Marshall tried to negotiate a retreat for them, but they weren't having any part of it. When he was leaving, they shot him, so all bets were off.

At four o'clock in the morning, me and my section were in the city of Rome by the Coliseum. Our objective was a bridge called St. Marguerite, which led into the Vatican City. We were to take that bridge and hold it until relieved. It was held by an artillery bunch, so we didn't figure that would be too hard. We moved up on them and cut a few throats, took 'em by surprise, and held it until June the 5th. That day we had an audience with the Pope. He told us he was going to give us his personal residence as a rest area.

June the 6th was D-Day. I was sitting under a great big cherry tree at the Pope's place, a big keg of wine out in front of me. We passed the glasses around, and toasted the boys over in Normandy.

"Go to it, boys. Have a good time going ashore!"

We'd lost about four hundred killed and another thousand wounded by this point. The regiment was pretty worn down. Meanwhile, this dame in England [Lady Nancy Astor] called us the "D-Day Dodgers," which didn't go down too well. But we were completely shattered, lousy, tired, and weary.

We were out of the line until late July, when we were sent down to Naples to try and fill the ranks. We recruited most of the fellows who were in the regiment now. We were told that we were going to lead the invasion into southern France. It was going to be just like Kiska: we were supposed to paddle ashore.

After we brought ourselves back up to strength, we loaded up on the *Prince Henry* and took off to Elba and went ashore there. We stayed there all day—we were about a day ahead of the convoy—and a day or two later we started the assault. Picked our boats out, inflated them, put them over the side, and moved towards shore in pitch darkness. There were five hundred men in these boats going in at once. Towboats took us in to about a mile off shore, then we paddled the rest of the way. Light crews had gone in ahead of us to mark the landing spots. The lights they used had no beam at all; you had to look directly at it to see it; all different colours, just a little glow. Our light was amber.

We were paddling in, and I said to John D, "There's our light."

"No no no! There's our light over there!"

"Okay." And we kept paddling. We hit the beach, and it was a bunch of German soldiers with a fire, making breakfast. But they never knew we were there. This was just east of Marseille. Then we moved up into the mountains. We walked across France, six hundred and some odd miles in thirty days, fighting a rearguard action all the way across. Every day there was something.

We got to the Maginot Line, and that's where the Germans decided they were going to make their stand. On the night of September 7th, 1944, we were sitting down underneath a bridge. John D said to me, "I got a job for you tomorrow," then handed me a bottle. He didn't drink, and I didn't much either.

"Tomorrow's my birthday."

"Well, maybe that'll work out good then. Over there's a pillbox on the Maginot Line. It's got to be taken by daybreak. There's a column moving up from the shore, and that's covering the road."

"Okay. What's the trouble?"

"Trouble is, between us and them, there's a minefield."

"When do we start?"

"Midnight."

"Go through the minefield at midnight?!"

"Any other way you know to do it? You want to put the lights on or something?"

I took off on my belly with the company behind me. At first I was using a bayonet. I came across a box; it was what we called a "shoe" mine; a little square box. You could lift the cover up and there was a pin in it. You had to step on it to set it off. They weren't too dangerous if you knew where they were. After a while, I put away my bayonet and just used my fingers to find these things.

Just before daybreak, we reached the pillbox. A fellow by the name of Sam McGee went over with a couple of fellows, threw a couple of hand grenades in, killed a couple of fellows, then thiry-five of them came out with their hands up.

That was September, and it went on and on and on like this to the middle of October. We were way up in the mountains, just below Switzerland, trying to stop the German army from escaping, coming up through Italy and getting out. Some mortar shells came in; I didn't think anything of it.

Next thing I knew I had blood coming out of my knee. McGee came along, had a look at it, and cleaned it out, put a couple of stitches in it. By the third day, it was starting to fester a bit. By the fourth day, it was getting pretty bad. I carried twelve shots of morphine with me all the time, but I never used it. But it kept getting worse.

An American unit was moving up nearby, so they rigged up a stretcher for me and took me to them. The Americans took me up to a hospital near Cannes. In the ambulance that took me there, there were a couple of Americans on either side of me. We were in hospital together till December. I got to be pretty good friends with one of the guys, Jim Minor, from Indiana.

The doctor came in to have a look at my knee. It wasn't too bad, but there were these little fragments, like pencil leads, stuck in there, so he was the one to operate on me. He looked me over.

"You're Canadian. Where're you from?"

"Little town in Nova Scotia. You wouldn't know it."

"What's its name?"

"Canso."

"I know it well," he said. "I'm from Sydney. My name's MacDonald."

I got out of hospital the 27th of December. When I was leaving, Jim Minor said, "Drop me a line when you get home." I said, "Okay."

When I got home, I dropped him a Christmas card. And up until two years ago when he died, we sent Christmas cards to each other.

By that time, the FSSF had been disbanded. There was no more use for a small unit like that. When I got out of the hospital, I was given an American uniform and really had nothing else to my name. Another fellow and I from the unit didn't know where to go, and no one seemed to know where our guys had gone. One of the Americans suggested going to a British outfit near where we were, that they might know something more. So we took off.

We ran into this British lieutenant, who we persuaded to give us some money. That took us down to Marseille, where we hoped to get picked up on a draft. But the Americans kept putting us in jail every night because we didn't have a pass. Then the British would pick us up because we were in these American uniforms looking out of place. And we were out of money.

We were falling on hard times. One day, we saw this sign: "Pint of blood: $10.00 and a shot of whisky."

"Boy, that's for us." So up we went, up went the sleeve, shot of whisky and away we went. That ten bucks lasted us till about eleven o'clock that morning. For the afternoon, we went back in again for another one. Great. But the next day when we tried it, the guy said, "Get out, you fellas, your dipstick's down on low as it is!"

We got word a ship was leaving for Taranto on the 14th of January, so we went off down there. Spent a couple of months in a convalescent hospital. End of February, they tried to get me to take officer training. I kept crossing swords with the guys who were training me; I was brought up on court martial twice. Finally, the CO asked me if I wanted to get back into battle.

"I wouldn't mind, sir."

So I went off to Belgium, which is where I ended off the war.

———

I made it back to Canada in October 1945, and spent a lot of time in hospital for the better part of a year after that. My leg was bad, my head was bad. Then finally I went back to school—business college here in Nova Scotia.

It was pretty tough settling back into ordinary life after all that we'd done. A lot of us hit the booze pretty bad. I don't know why. The monotony of nothing to do. Work was scarce. And when you did get a job—I got one with Customs in Canso—you'd go half crazy, stuck in an office all day.

———

I was pretty much grown up when I joined, and I was a rapscallion anyway. So the war didn't change me much. I was a scrappy bugger during the war; I didn't back down before anybody. But the FSSF guys—we were always close. You could rely on them for your life. Always. If I was going out on a patrol, I never looked behind me. I knew my guys were behind me. I never had to say, "Do this or do that." You just knew they were there.

Makes it hard, after the war, when you're dealing with men—educated fellows and all that—who hadn't seen battle, and had no idea of what it meant to work together in tough times.

———

I don't want anything in my obituary. Just predeceased by, and survived by. I don't want them to know I was in the army, I don't want them to know I was in the Legion, or in the Masonic Lodge, I don't want them to know anything. And I won't tell you why. That's just the way I want it.

Alex Colville

—

BIRTH PLACE: TORONTO, ONTARIO
RESIDENCE: WOLFVILLE, NOVA SCOTIA
REGIMENT: ROYAL CANADIAN ENGINEERS

MY FULL NAME IS DAVID ALEXANDER COLVILLE. I WAS BORN IN Toronto on the 24th of August, 1920.

My father was a Scotch immigrant, born in Fife in 1890. He emigrated to Canada at the age of twenty. My mother was born in Trenton, Ontario, in 1888, the daughter of a tailor, Alexander Gault, who'd been born in 1856 in Scotland and had emigrated as well.

My mother's mother died when Mother was fourteen, and she went to work as a milliner at age fourteen, working on women's hats.

All these people who emigrated had people who'd come over before, and so they had a whole network of people they could link up with when they came over.

My father had worked in the mines in Fife—coal mines—and I think this involved surveying. When he arrived in Montreal, he met up with his sister and her husband, a man by the name of Stark, who'd been trained as a stonemason in Scotland. This Stark had come to realize that there were stonemasons everywhere in Canada, so he got a job with the Dominion Bridge Company, which at the time was a big steel fabricating operation in Montreal.

Through Alex Stark, my father got a job through one of the railways as a surveyor in the west. Then he came back to Lachine and got a better job—again, through the intervention of Alex Stark. He went to company night school to upgrade his skills; I later figured out that he worked something like seventy or eighty hours a week. He'd become involved in inspecting bridges—whether for the railroad or for Dominion Bridge, who'd built them, I don't know—he travelled. Then he met my mother and married, and he settled down. He didn't want to travel as much.

When I was born in Toronto, he was working in a structural steel company, MacGregor-MacIntyre. They were a small-scale Dominion Bridge and made structural steel for buildings and so on.

In 1927, my father was offered a job as a riveting gang boss on a job building the new steel gates for the new Welland canal, running between Lake Ontario and Lake Erie. For this kind of job, Dominion Bridge— who oversaw the job—formed a number of small companies. These smaller companies would execute the work and Dominion Bridge would disclaim any responsibility for anything that would happen. It was very risky work: high steel stuff.

The second year we were there, there was a major accident with one of these gates, when three of these riveting gangs—sixteen men—were on one of these gates being moved into place, ninety feet in the air. The crane moving it swung out too far, and the whole thing fell. All the guys on the gate were killed. My father, by sheer luck, was standing on the edge of the canal and not the gate. Then, of course, Dominion Bridge would say, "This is not our problem." There was no workmen's compensation; you were killed and that was it.

We lived in St. Catharines all through that for two years. Then we moved to Amherst, Nova Scotia, to a company that Dominion Bridge had taken over. This was the first time since his marriage that my father had what you might call a white-collar job.

My dad was a small, slight man. Sometime after my father died, I was in Amherst, New York and met a fellow who knew my dad. The steel company was on strike at the time, and this fellow had said, "If Dave Colville had been here, this wouldn't have happened." It's lovely stuff to hear years later.

When I was growing up, I had a little contact with the military, mostly through coincidence, through an English family who were casual friends—and contemporaries—of my parents. The father worked at a firm in a similar field to my father's. They had three sons and my parents had two, so we had a casual friendship with the Caldwells. Their youngest son was a friend and contemporary of mine. But their older two boys had gone to RMC, gone into the navy, and served all through the war—and both survived, which is remarkable, in a way.

So I had this kind of contact, through these two older brothers of my friend, with the military. My brother, although he was five years older than I, had become a mechanical engineer, and worked in essential services during the war.

I started out pretty seriously when I was fourteen working on my art, and by the time I finished grade eleven, I knew what I wanted to do. I'd been going to evening classes from grade nine on, conducted by the extension department of the nearby university, Mount Allison. It was one of only two universities which offered fine arts degrees.

Through that, the English painter, a Mr. Royle, who was the head of the fine arts school, would come and visit the young people and see what they were doing. He told me, at the end of grade eleven, that he thought I was doing some really good things.

I had won a scholarship to Dalhousie, through what I remember as mostly a series of morning-long essay writings on various topics. I did it partly to get out of doing something else, never with any serious intention of doing anything. So I had that option of going to Dalhousie, where I thought I might like to study law. But that also brought my whole situation to kind of a head. I had to either take this scholarship, or decline it.

In the end, I declined it. I'd spoken to Mr. Royle and told him that I'd won this scholarship, but that I felt I'd rather be an artist.

"If I become an artist, will I be poor?"

Mr. Royle, who was a very quiet, understated person, said, "No, I don't think you'll be really poor. I'm not really poor, although I'm not rich."

So I thought, "Well, that's enough for me." If he'd said, "Yes, you'll be poor," I would have said, "Okay, I don't want to be poor. I won't be an artist." If I'd been the son of a millionaire, and Mr. Royle had said I'd be poor, I would just have likely said, "Oh, I don't mind being poor!"

I had a Fine Arts degree when I graduated in 1942, but there was nothing else to do. I didn't have a degree in Physics or anything, so I wasn't in any particular demand. I expect, in time, I would have been conscripted, and everyone was joining, so that's what I did as well.

Lord Beaverbrook, in the First War, I believe, persuaded the Canadian government or, at the very least, played a part in determining that the Canadian government had official war art done in the First War.

At some point it must have been decided that the appropriate place for such work was within the historical section of the military. Professional military people, for reasons I understand and approve of, are interested in history from the vantage point of a career soldier wanting an historical record of their service. Within each division, which was around fifteen thousand men, there would be a little historical section and in it was an historian, someone who'd have at least an M.A. in History, and then a corporal clerk, a driver and a Jeep, and a war artist and his driver and another Jeep.

All the stuff went back to London through divisional headquarters every month, and then back to corps headquarters, and from corps on to army headquarters, to the best of my knowledge.

The historical component first and foremost kept track of orders, operational plans—both in their conceived form and their executed form—and the two never resembled one another that much. When you look at most North American museums, you realize that a lot of early paintings had been done by army officers, or in more rare cases, naval or marine officers. This was part of their engineers' topical watercolour drawings and maps. Someone undoubtedly made a drawing of Waterloo and other major battles to record what had happened. So it's probably reasonable to say that the tradition of war art came out of a long history of officers recording a particular perspective of a particular event or moment.

———

I had been a good Fine Arts student, and had been, in effect, commissioned to do a poster for a propaganda thing. I was asked to do a poster to go in the shipyards that built corvettes, so that the people who were building the boats felt that they were doing something important. Someone arranged for me to visit a shipyard in Halifax; I made drawings, talked to some of the people, then made a drawing looking back over the stern of a corvette as it dropped and was exploding a depth charge.

———

I took this drawing up to Ottawa, to the Wartime Information Board, I believe it was called, which was at the then-new supreme court buildings. It was actually used (although I think it was modified by one of the artists there to make it a little bit more spectacular). Then, coinciding with that same trip, I was asked to go and see a Colonel Duguid, who was a veteran of the First War and the head of the historical section of the Canadian army. (And it's important to remember that a man who'd been, say, twenty at the end of the First War, would only be about forty-four at this time in the Second War—not that much time had passed between the wars).

He was a very nice guy, as professional service people are. I find they tend to be more courteous, actually, than most people. Far from the crass picture most people have of the military.

"Universities are jungles compared to life in the service," I've said on more than one occasion. All kinds of back-stabbing and intrigues going on.

This Colonel Duguid was very kind to me.

"I think your work is very good, and we'd be interested in having you as a war artist."

I was in love at the time and wanted to get married (to my present wife!), so this seemed to be a fortuitous opportunity.

"If you enlist in the army and get your commission, we'll make you a war artist."

So I enlisted in the tank corps. I was always fond of cars—I still am—and that kind of thing appealed to me. The tank corps were the inheritors of the old cavalry regiments; I'd hoped to go into reconnaissance in an armoured car unit.

I was sent to Brockville for officer's training, and while I didn't do anything obviously wrong, after two months there I was called on the mat of the company commander. I was told that it had been recommended that I be returned to unit, which meant I would effectively be expelled as an officer candidate. I have to admit I was shocked and not a little astonished at this.

I didn't have the usual background and was certainly more unusual than most of the trainee officers. As a boy, I'd joined the Boy Scouts, and after a few weeks of it, thought, "I'm not getting anything out of this," and so I quit.

I played football for a short time in school, and once got knocked out by a great big guy. Again, I thought, "I don't like this much." I was of an independent mind. So for whatever reason, I must have rubbed people the wrong way at Brockville. I wasn't out of the army, but I was out of the officer's training stream.

I was sent back to corps headquarters. I'd enlisted in April, and we'd planned to be married in August, and to my great relief, after I was excused from Brockville, my wife didn't change her mind. I became a corporal in the army, which isn't the very bottom, but it isn't very far up the ladder. I made a dollar-seventy a day.

The main thing was that I knew my hopes of becoming a war artist were now over. I didn't have a low opinion of myself, but it was clear that the people at Brockville did.

Now I was a corporal and worked in the manning depot in New Brunswick, doing parade ground drill and that kind of stuff. There was a notice looking for people who wanted to become paratroops. You had to go see an army examiner for evaluation. There was an "M" test, which

Before an Attack, **Alex Colville.**

everybody who entered the army took. It was a form of aptitude or intelligence testing, which must have had some good qualities of prediction. Everyone who was in the army did this.

I went to see this army examiner, who probably had some sort of background in this kind of testing, and told him I wanted to volunteer for the paratroops.

"We'll have to look into your records," he said. I went back the next day to see him again.

"There's a problem here. You can't get in the paratroopers because you're underweight. You'll never make it through the first medical." I had been undergoing pretty strenuous training.

"So that's out. But I've been thinking about you. You have this degree in Fine Arts, and there's some relevance with this to the Royal Canadian Engineers. They're involved in camouflage stuff, so I'm going to recommend that you be transferred to them."

I felt that was fine, and was sent to Petawawa—still a corporal—for officer's training. My wife followed me and lived in Pembroke. I was sent to this section of the RCE which were involved in camouflage of defense emplacements. This unit was headed by a veteran of the First War, a company sergeant major, a very nice guy who was very good to me. We got on very well together. I was instructing people as they came through, and since I could talk in front of groups, I did very well for several months.

Then again, quite mysteriously, I was called in by another colonel and told that I'd been recommended for a commission in the infantry, and that I was to go to a place in Trois-Rivières. I was to go to a place that was called the Officer's Appraisal Course, which was a six-week thing. And off I went.

In that course, there was a mixed bag of people. People just out of university, ex-NCOs like myself who various officers had recommended for a commission. This course at Trois-Rivières was a pretty strenuous thing, with a pretty high drop-out rate. But I was accepted, then went on to infantry training for another three months. At the end of that, I was commissioned as an infantry lieutenant.

I ended up as a basic training officer in Yarmouth, taking raw recruits through their eight-week initial training course. What most people don't realize—the Germans realized it very well—is that an NCO was basically a teacher. You're teaching people to read maps, drills, how to handle weapons, gas mask routines, marches. It's a very interesting thing: you have a company of thirty-five guys, three corporals, a sergeant and a junior officer that work pretty well as a training group. In effect, you had five students for every teacher. It worked very well.

I was there from October 1943 to May 1944. During the late autumn of 1943, I remember a notice coming through saying that any junior officer who wished to could transfer to the British army under a thing called the CANLOAN scheme. D-Day was in the works, and the Brits figured they didn't have enough lieutenants. This is where the highest casualties occurred: in infantry and in tanks. But particularly infantry.

A number of guys who'd gone through Trois-Rivières with me became CANLOAN officers. Some of them were killed, some won MCs [Military Crosses]. There was quite a high casualty rate. Some would suggest to you that the Brits thought, "Well, we'll send this guy out. He's just a kind of rube from Canada—and perhaps a kind of red Indian who'll be good at going through the woods."

Whether they said that or not, every Canadian officer who was CANLOAN was a volunteer. I'd been pretty well through the mill at this point, and was no longer the volunteering type. I was married; I was in love with my wife, who was pregnant with our first child. I didn't even consider volunteering. Looking back on it, I'm surprised I even volunteered for the paratroops, although that's not quite the same thing.

I carried on working away in Yarmouth. I had Number One platoon in Company A, which I guess meant the company commander thought I was doing a good job. He was a veteran of the First War as well. I had a good sergeant and good corporals; it makes all the difference when you do.

One night, I had gone home downtown. My wife and I were going out for dinner, when a junior officer at the colonel's office came up in a Jeep and said that the colonel wanted to see me. Right now. I was thinking, "What have I done now?"

The colonel was a guy who seemed to like me well enough. About a month before, I'd been out for a ride on an RCAF Canso, an amphibious flying boat, on coastal patrol. That night I was on duty as orderly officer, where you have to stay up for twenty-four hours. Just to pass the time during the night, I wrote my brother the mechanical engineer an account of this flight and a lengthy description of what this plane was like.

About a week later, I was called into the colonel's office.

"Colville, you're in bad trouble."

"What's wrong?"

"You've written a letter to your brother in which you've given a very extended and exact description of the characteristics of a particular aircraft. The letter has been opened by censors, and you're being charged with a breach of security. You'll have to go to Halifax and appear before the brigadier." Then, he said, "I'll go with you."

This was an overnight trip, which meant serious stuff. We got on the train and were seated in a little compartment. Then the CO got down to it.

"Now Colville I want to talk to you about this."

I spoke up. "But sir, you know this airplane was first produced in 1933 or '34, and was used as a commercial aircraft. Everybody knows the plane; there's no secret about it."

He took this in, then said, "When you appear before the brigadier, don't say any of the things you've just said to me. Just say, 'I very much regret this incident and I apologize,' and that's it."

That's what I did, and the brigadier warned me to not do so again, and we went back to Halifax. That was the end of it, and I always appreciated my CO's lesson on discretion.

Now I'd been called for at home and driven to the colonel's office in the early evening. I went in to speak to the colonel not knowing what to expect this time, thinking, "What the hell can *this* be?"

I went in and saluted.

"Well, Colville," he said, "Churchill has decided they can't win the war without you. You're being flown in a Canso at three A.M. this morning to Halifax, then onto Montreal, and then to London, where you'll report to an officer."

So at three A.M., I went out to the field and climbed into one of the little gun bubbles on the side of this Canso—the same plane I'd been brought up on charges for talking about—and flew into Halifax and then on to Montreal.

I flew out on a Liberator, which flew about a hundred and fifty miles an hour. First, we went to Bermuda, and then we went to the Azores, just to refuel, then finally up to Glasgow, where I caught a train back to London. I was told in Glasgow that I was to report to a Colonel Stacey at Military HQ in London.

I went there and reported to Stacey and he said, "Colville, you're a war artist." And that's all there was to it; that's how I became a war artist.

It happened, that of all the war artists, I was the one who spent virtually all my time in various theatres of war—from May 1944 through to 1945.

We worked with a field kit in a canvas bag. In this was a little Winsor & Newton china mixing dish—I still use it every day I'm working, which is most days, and that's sixty years later. There was also plywood drawing board, which was exactly the size of a half sheet of watercolour paper. There were watercolours, pen, ink, pencils, all tucked into this bag.

We were given complete freedom. Many people find this hard to believe, but I was given complete *carte blanche*. No one said, "You've got to make us look good and the Germans look bad," or anything like that, which you might have expected.

There are two things that came from the experience of that year in the field. The first was an accelerated sense of maturation. For instance, the business of thinking about dying, which you might start doing in civilian life when you're about sixty. Not that I was ever in great physical danger, although there were a few times in which—through no deliberate act on my part, trying to find my way into the heart of the action—in which I was somewhat in danger. But I was never wounded or anything.

You see dead bodies and the rubble of war, so there's that effect on you as a human being—that sense of accelerated maturation.

The other side of it, that's perhaps equivalent in my case, is that it was a wonderful opportunity for me to mature as an artist, as a technician. I worked fast and virtually every day. Of course I liked what I was doing. People have asked me, "What did you think when you were made a war artist?"

"Look," I'll say, "I was an art student; I wanted to be an artist. The thing I wanted to do was draw and paint. Then I became an infantry officer. Do you know what you do as an infantry officer? Essentially, run across a field while people shoot at you. If I had to choose between running across a field while people shot at me, or drawing and painting, what do you think I'd prefer?"

In addition, I had this unbelievable liberty to do whatever I wanted.

I also had another, more significant task. Surely there was something important in all that was going on, and I had to decide what it was.

"What is it that's important? Of the things that are happening, what should I be zeroing in on now? What is the war all about? What is human existence all about? What's important and what isn't important?"

In the end, it certainly had a profound philosophical effect on me. I remember reading someone from the nineteenth century who said, "A poet should be in love and in war before he's twenty-five."

Well, of course, I was turning twenty-five in the fall of that final year of the war. I don't mean to either trivialize the experience or to sound in any way flippant. What that person meant was, of course, that you have to have experience to find expression that speaks to all people. You have to have it at the right time—or at least it's an advantage to have it at the right time.

I produced a lot of work during that year. I did something virtually every day. I kept a diary during the work and a progress report of my work for each day, accounting for the hours and using six-figure map references to site my location at any given time. That would bring you down to something like ten yards of accuracy.

Most of the finished canvases were painted after the war from drawings that were done sketchily in the field during the war.

The sketch of the bridge at Nijmegan was inspired by my father's work as a bridge person. I've been fascinated and done a lot of things with bridges over the years.

The Nijmegan Salient, **Alex Colville, December 1944.**

When I returned to Canada in the fall, I'd only been away a year and a half. But one thing surprised me. I'd never considered myself much of a patriot, and as a kid, I'd moved around some—Toronto, St. Catharines, Amherst—I'd never felt I had any deep attachment to places.

And yet, I remember as we sailed into Halifax harbour on a beautiful October morning on the *Île de France,* with thousands and thousands of people waiting—I found it to be a most moving experience. This surprised me. I hadn't expected to have such an emotional response. My eyes filled with tears, and you couldn't help but be caught up by everyone else's emotion.

I was with my family again. We had a child that I'd never seen; he was fifteen months old when I first saw him.

I'd thought—like most people who'd been overseas—that, "When I get home, I'll have a place to live." That would be the least of our concerns. But in fact, getting a place to live was extremely difficult; we didn't find a place until the fall of 1946. In a sense, it felt like I was starting all over again. My wife and I hadn't lived as a civilian couple, with kids and everything. It was a whole new sort of thing.

I'd got a job teaching Visual Art with the university where I'd been a student. Among the students at that time were returned veterans. One of the most wonderful things that someone in the federal government had the brains to think up was that if a veteran wanted to have an education, there it was.

A surprising number of people did go to university as a result. Perhaps as many as a fifth of my students were vets. This was an enormously valuable thing to have done for them.

I went to a school graduation where the president of Dalhousie University spoke to graduating high school students. Now he was a generation younger than me. He said that the main thing on his mind when he went to university was, "What do the girls think of me?" Which of course is very natural for any eighteen-year-old. And of course, that kind of thing can make it very difficult to concentrate on what you're actually supposed to be doing.

But the veterans were, for the most part, beyond that, out of that. I don't mean they were sexually inactive, but they were no longer in the mindset that an average eighteen-year-old would be in now. They were hungry to learn. And there were certainly examples of guys who'd had very bad times overseas and wiped out at university, in most cases from drink or nerves or both. It was the only way they could handle what they'd been through.

But by and large, what you had were people who had had this early maturation experience, and here was a situation that they were ready to handle, and they grabbed it with both hands. Anybody who taught university or college, or even high school, in the late forties would talk about that wonderful couple of years when there were these wonderful veteran students who were more matured and more concentrated on what they were doing. They had this appetite for learning, and I enjoyed teaching them tremendously.

They were wonderful years.

Frank Cauley

———

BIRTH PLACE: OTTAWA, ONTARIO
RESIDENCE: OTTAWA, ONTARIO
SQUADRON: 106, 422 SQUADRONS RCAF
THEATRE OF WAR: NW EUROPE, COASTAL COMMAND

In '38, the Germans were occupying the Sudetenland and everybody in the country was getting keyed up. Mackenzie King was premier and told the country to relax, saying that if Britain went to war, it didn't necessarily mean we would. I think he was trying to gradually get us out of the Commonwealth.

When war was declared a year later, I was eighteen and had just started working as a clerk in Veterans Affairs. All around me my friends were enlisting. Which was great for me, because my social life picked up; girls were calling me! But I had an Irish mother and she made short work of most of them: girls didn't call boys in those days. But I felt left out working in an office. I also had friends who were in the reserves and had gone in right away. So there was a bit of peer pressure.

I decided the army wasn't for me, because I'd seen some of the pictures from World War I, slogging in the ditches and the mud. I can't swim, so the navy was out. Which left the air force.

When I did enlist, in September 1940, some of my family was proud because I was going into the air force and going to be a flyer. But my dad was devastated. He cried for two weeks.

Once you enlist, you come through Eglinton to the ITS: they look at your background, your physical condition and your marks from school and with me, it was, "You're okay in maths: navigator."

I'd never flown before. I'd never travelled beyond Smith's Falls before! So it was quite an adventure. There was a lineup of guys waiting to enlist for aircrew; everyone wanted to be a flyer. We all wanted to have the white scarf and the goggles.

The reality was a little different. First off, I did six weeks' guard duty in Trenton. Four hours on, eight hours off. I certainly learned how to guard a building, but more importantly, I learned how to fall asleep standing up. Which isn't easy!

I was at Manning Depot for about six weeks, which is where you were posted until formal training started. There were about a thousand of us, all in double-deck bunk beds. It was at the CNE cow palace in Toronto. At that time, the Big Bands were booked in to play at the Ex. Almost every week they'd have a different band: they had Benny Goodman, Ida Ray Hutton—all kinds of acts.

Each flight—there were about twenty-five of us in a flight—would be invited backstage to meet the bands, which was great. Our flight had been picked to go backstage and meet the Tommy Dorsey Band. I asked a friend of mine, who'd seen them the previous week, "What are they like? I'm a Glenn Miller fan."

He said, "They're not too bad. But they got this new vocalist—a skinny guy. No hell to look at and his voice is a little weak." So I said, "Forget it," and headed over to Adelaide Street for a beer and missed meeting Frank Sinatra.

When I graduated and got my wing, my family came down. All along, my dad thought I'd been training to be a ground observer. I never told him I was flying and my family never told him. It was easier than having him cry for a year. He was just flabbergasted when he found out, but was also proud that I'd made it as a flyer and had earned my wing.

In May 1942, we shipped down to Halifax on our way overseas. Our ship was a "pre-war Polish Luxury Liner." Oh man! The S.S. *Batory*: rough as hell. Of course we were down at the bottom of the ship: we called it "Torpedo Junction." It took us eight days to get across at the height of the U-boat attacks, and we lost six ships on the convoy; it was a terrible trip.

Once we landed, we were shipped down to Bournemouth and lived in Bath Hill Courts, right up on the bluffs. It was a beautiful holiday spot. But there were surprises. Guys would be walking through the park with their girls and German Focke-Wulfs would come blazing across the Channel and strafe the whole seafront. That was my first taste of the realities of war.

When I moved into advanced training, I had the misfortune to fly two-engine Whitleys. "Flying Coffins" were one of the better things said about them. The problem was that there just weren't enough modern aircraft to train on. I picked up a crew and we were shipped down to St. Eval in Cornwall. In the eyes of the RAF, we were still "technically" training. We'd go out over the Bay of Biscay and back, just to get used to the feel of the aircraft and the routine.

It was on the fourth such trip that we lost an engine and had to ditch.

When we went down, I was seated in the centre of the aircraft at my navigator's desk. On impact, the plane broke in half and a dinghy automatically popped out and inflated. Because I was right there, I could get right in, which was fortunate, because I couldn't swim.

The plane went down fast. Our wireless operator, Dick Jackson, was the guy who was supposed to rescue me. It was always, "Okay Dick: you rescue Cauley, 'cause he's going down like a rock," and Dick would roll his eyes. Tragically, he was the last guy I saw, trapped in the plane as it sank. A five-man crew, and I was the only one who made it.

I spent two days in the Bay of Biscay, drifting alone in that dinghy. I had a flare pistol, three cartridges, blocks of chocolate and water. I fired two cartridges trying to signal an aircraft, but it was a waste of time because at three thousand feet, they couldn't spot something as small as me against the ocean.

Going into my third day, I saw a ship off the horizon and used my last cartridge. It was a British destroyer and they picked me up. Once on board, my big concern was to let them know what base I was from, because after three days the telegram goes out to your family. "We regret to inform you that Warrant Officer Frank Cauley is missing in action."

The four guys I lost were like family. I got a month's survivor's leave, so I went up to see Dick's family. I'd been there before when we were training up at Kinloss and had a weekend off. Dick and I had hit it off pretty well and he used to invite me down to meet his family, so I knew them pretty well. This was kind of a judgment call, to tell them what had happened in person, instead of them just getting a telegram.

They were polite and everything, but you could see them thinking, "Why is this guy walking around while Dick is at the bottom of the Atlantic?"

It was the right thing to do. But I don't feel any better about it sixty years later than I did then.

———

I had a month's leave, then joined 106 Squadron and picked up a crew there. Our pilot was nineteen, the tail gunner was twenty-three and I was twenty-two. We were all about the same age. This was Guy Gibson's Squadron before he formed the Dam Busters. I flew thirty missions to Germany and France, and one raid on Turin in Italy. The casualty rate on these trips was pretty high—about sixty percent of the aircraft got hit. We were chased by a Junker 88 one night, but turned into the attack and managed to get away. But you never know who's going to make it and who's not. I was one of the lucky ones.

Frank Cauley's Sunderland coastal patrol aircraft. Sunderlands were deadly foe against U-boats and most surface vessels because of its heavy armaments.

I finished that tour and was slated to go home in 1943. But before I could get away, a smooth-tongued RCAF wing commander talked me into staying in England.

"Cauley," he said, "We need navigators on Coastal Command. I'll make you a deal. We give you a month's course at Squire's Gate outside Blackpool (which was like Coney Island). After that, you'll pick up a crew on a Canadian squadron. It's a piece of cake."

"Why me? I spent two days in the drink trying to navigate."

"You're just what we want. Twenty-two and experienced." So I agreed.

I did the course, went to Blackpool every night and had a great time. In March 1944, I was assigned to 422 Squadron in Northern Ireland, where we flew Sunderlands for Coastal Command.

Our first trip out, we're doing anti-sub patrols about four hundred miles offshore: it's all visual spotting, just staring at the water. We're out about three hours, on the third leg of the search and we turn and see this

Frank Cauley with his crew from 422 Squadron RCAF at the hatch of his "Chewing Gum" Sunderland.

sub out on the surface. There are guys swimming and sunbathing. It was a beautiful day. The pilot said to the screen pilot, Sid Butler, "You'd better slide in here and take over; you're more experienced."

Sid slid into the pilot's seat and we broke W/T silence and gave our position and said we were going in to attack. The Germans hated the Sunderlands because we had eight guns, with a front turret and a back turret. They used to call us the "Flying Porcupines." We also had four depth charges. The sub only had a .5 gun on the conning tower and they were fighting back as we swooped in. It was the only thing left for them to do. We dropped the depth charges and hit them, then circled around and got beautiful photographs of the attack, the sub going down and the dinghies with the German survivors.

What we didn't realize at first was that the Germans had blasted a hole underneath our waterline—a big hole and dozens of other little shrapnel holes. Our engineer said, "We can patch the big hole with the emergency 'leak stoppers,' but I dunno what we can do about all these other little holes. When we land, we're going straight to the bottom of the lake." There was a tense silence among all eleven of us.

The engineer thinks for a bit and then says, "I know. What about some gum?"

So eleven men started chewing, five sticks each and as fast as we chewed it, Ted Higgins came around and patched the holes. We went up to about three thousand feet so the gum froze, then we went back to base. Now of course, we've radioed ahead about our problem and they're all waiting at the base with all kinds of rescue boats. We went in with our fingers crossed, because it doesn't take long to go to the bottom of the lake.

The plane just "sat down" as though nothing were wrong; a dinghy took us back to shore and the pilot got the DFC [Distinguished Flying Cross]. I was "Mentioned in Dispatches" and I got my commission. The Belfast and the London papers picked up the story—especially the part about the gum. A lady contacted her son in Ottawa with the Belfast paper, he contacted my parents and the Ottawa papers picked it up: it was all over the place: "Local Hero Chews Gum to Save His Life."

Right after it first happened, Wrigley's in Chicago got hold of the story and sent each one of the crew twenty-four packs of gum, air mailed from head office to Great Britain. That was my first trip out on Coastal Command.

We covered the Channel on D-Day. That was something you'd never forget. You could see seven or eight thousand ships up the Channel and I have to admit I'm glad I wasn't landing on the beach. After a mission, we'd get to go home and I used to think, "Those poor buggers on the ground—they're going to be sweating it for the next couple of days and here I am, safe and sound under clean sheets." After that, we flew another eight hundred hours and never saw another bloody thing.

When the war ended on the 8th, I was in London celebrating. It was wild in there: God, it was great: everyone was delirious. I'd already been booked on the *Île de France*—a beautiful ship, especially considering what we'd gone over on. I'd finished my second tour, so I was back in Ottawa long before a lot of guys.

When I think back on those years, I think a lot about the crew I lost. And the good times we had, too; you tend to gloss over the bad times. You lose your youth, because of the war. You go over at twenty and back at twenty-three as an officer with two tours of operations and seven medals. Suddenly you're grown up. You miss your early twenties. Death didn't strike me as much later on; you'd seen so much of it. I'm proud of what I did. I did what I think the country expected of me and I think I did a fair job.

When I was in that dinghy floating around the Atlantic—you learn how to pray. I prayed to everybody: I prayed to the Pope, I prayed to the King, I prayed to Mackenzie King, Frank Sinatra—I prayed to everybody I could think of, because it kept my mind going. One of the vows I made was that if I survived, I would help my fellow man. I came back to Ottawa and made my contribution to public life after the war: I've been doing volunteer work for the past fifty-five years.

In the same circumstances, would I like to see my son enlist? I would expect he would. That's the way I felt about the country. Do your duty by your country and your fellow man: that would be a legacy I'd like to leave.

Bob Grant

———

BIRTH PLACE: HAMILTON, ONTARIO
RESIDENCE: TORONTO, ONTARIO
REGIMENT: FORT GARRY HORSE (ARMOURED CORPS)
THEATRE OF WAR: NW EUROPE

IN 1935, I TURNED TWENTY AND WENT ON A STUDENT'S TOUR TO Europe. I think there were twelve of us on the trip. Among other places, our tour went to Berlin. At that time, everyone was aware that Germany was becoming very aggressive, and my dad wouldn't let me go on that leg of the trip. He thought the political situation was to the point where I might get into some kind of trouble in Germany. Of course, the others all went off to Berlin and didn't have any kind of trouble of all, but I stayed in London.

We were all conscious of what was happening, but we still couldn't believe it was going to develop into a war. The first time anything really disturbed me was in 1938. We had a German salesman visiting us who was a friend of a friend of my dad's. Dad asked this guy out for a day's sail on our boat and I went along. The German was blowing off a lot of hot air about what a great man Hitler was, what he was doing for Germany, and how he was no threat to anybody. My old man was so mad I thought he was going to shove him in the lake. Dad was looking at the situation through First World War eyes, but this kind of fanaticism was new to me, and that was the first time it really hit home.

As far as joining up was concerned, it was taken for granted. I wanted to. I remember my dad saying, "Why don't you wait a little while?" He really didn't want me to go, but I said, "After all the advantages I've had in life, if I don't go, why should anybody?"

Labour Day weekend in 1939 we were having a big party over at RCYC on the island [in Toronto Harbour]. We all knew we were going then. As far as the navy was concerned, anybody who'd sailed at the yacht club would be given a commission right off the bat. So early in the war, they practically handed out commissions. It was a great opportunity.

Tuesday morning a group of us went over to the naval barracks, but I failed the medical because they said I was colour blind. I'd sailed all my life and I was busting to get in the navy. But it was not to be. (Towards the end of the war, I was involved in exercises for the invasion, all of which were signalled by coloured lights. They gave me no trouble whatsoever, so the navy's tests had been wrong all along).

Instead, I joined a militia regiment, the Queen's York Rangers. We were training down in Niagara-on-the-Lake and we had the exciting experience of firing a World War One machine gun. When your turn came, you'd press the button and it'd go "brrrzzzzzttt!" for about three

Bob Grant (back row, far right) with the Fort Garry Horse officers a few days before D-Day.

seconds, and that was it: you didn't aim or anything. So I knew we weren't going anywhere with that bunch.

The father of a girl I was taking out at that time was a friend of Brigadier Worthington up at Camp Borden, who ran the Armoured Corps. This girl's father said, "How'd you like to join up with us?" I said, "Great, I won't have to walk!" So I ended up at Camp Borden in the Tank Corps. I didn't know whether I was going as an officer or not, but I'd been an officer in the militia regiment. I wore my officer's uniform and it stuck.

About two weeks after I got to Borden, the CO of the Fort Garry Horse interviewed me and took me in. I didn't know anything about one regiment from another; I didn't know anything about anything. But I joined the Fort Garrys around February 1941 and was with them for the next five years.

They were mostly a bunch of small-town Prairie boys who'd grown up hating easterners. I didn't even know this kind of prejudice existed. There was a senior officer in the regiment who literally wouldn't speak to me for the first six months except in an official capacity. The others made it pretty plain that they didn't like the east very much either. Having said that, though, they were great guys and became great friends.

We didn't really have any training equipment, certainly no tanks. In early 1941, they got hold of a few old French World War One tanks that seated two people, but the engines didn't work. We'd have parades and stand in front of these goddam French tanks and pretend we were an armoured regiment. We never did have any equipment in Canada.

Our regiment was to go overseas in November 1941. When we finally got on the ship in Halifax, we officers lived in first-class civilian quarters. There were stewards, waiters, we even had peacetime meals and open bars. It was like being on a cruise. I think we were one of the last convoys to go over with that treatment. It was one of the advantages of going over a little early. Meanwhile, the poor troops were stuck down in the bilge, but they got their own back.

The ship's men were loading beer onto the ship; the stevedores would carry a case up the gangplank, and one of the crew would take it away to store it. However, as it got dark, there was a little gap between the stevedore bringing the next case and the guy from the ship coming back for it. So one of the Fort Garry troopers would step into line, take the case, and hustle it right down to their quarters at the bottom of the ship.

The next morning, we were tipped off that the ship's captain was going to search the ship to find the missing beer. So we warned our guys that they'd better get rid of it somehow. They got rid of it all right—they drank it. The captain never found a bottle of beer, but if he'd looked over the side of the ship, he would have seen the harbour bobbing with empties.

In England, we were shipped down to Camp Borden, south of London. The barracks were all broken down; God, they must have been from Cromwell's time, but it got us started.

We were the 5th Canadian Armoured Division at that point, but still we didn't have any tanks. Finally we got a Jeep—one Jeep—and that was the biggest event in the regiment. All the guys wanted to drive this strange Jeep. We had a few motorcycles, but never any offensive equipment. So we did route marches and lectures, which were pretty much a waste of time.

We were moved into a small town just outside of Aldershot. Still no equipment. We did exercises such as charging up a hill to attack a German position at the top. Theoretically, we were using assault vehicles for the attack, but we didn't have any, so we had to do the attack on foot. It was pretty pathetic.

We finally got some Rams, which were Canadian tanks—not good enough to go into action, but good enough to train on—and yet we still weren't firing any guns. I don't think we fired a shot until late '42. By then we were getting more active training and better equipment. It wasn't our invasion equipment, but it was better than what we'd been using.

We moved down to Brighton and went out on the South Downs for a week at a time, training at night. That was a good conditioner, because you'd wake up in the morning with snow all over your sleeping bags. If you were going to make it, you'd have to get a little tougher.

In early '43, we were moved into a new independent armoured brigade with the 1st Hussars from London and the Sherbrooke Fusiliers from Quebec. Four squadrons were chosen for special training in new amphibious tanks: two squadrons from the Fort Garrys, and two from the Hussars. This was a great morale builder, because these tanks were highly secret equipment. We were under screens, and nobody could get in or out of the base.

The trick was to make a tank amphibious: if you just made it float, that meant there was not enough armour on it. They came up with an idea to put a platform around the tanks, fixing to it an inflatable canvas skirt. The skirt was inflated with compressed air, which pushed the screen up high enough that I could just see over it when I was standing on top

A damaged DD tank and an anti-aircraft gun deserted on Normandy beachhead, June 7, 1944.

in the turret. And in this way it displaced enough water to float a thirty-ton tank—ingenious.

The first thing we had to learn was how to use submarine escape equipment in case the tank sank and we got caught under water. Using this equipment, they made us go down into a long narrow pool, walk along the bottom, and then walk out the other side. It didn't bother ninety percent of us, but it weeded out a few. The next thing they did was to cut the ends off a Sherman tank, sticking the tank in an empty concrete pool. Our five-man crew would get in, and then huge taps were turned on. Water rushed in and flooded the pool, not to mention the tank you were sitting in. We sat there until the instructor banged the outside of the tank, which was our signal to put on our escape gear. It was a little unnerving at first, but you got used to it. We sat down there until the instructor banged again, then we could open the hatch and float to the surface. The real morale booster was that we now saw ourselves as a top-notch secret squadron that was going to be involved in the main event.

Back down on the south coast, our invasion equipment was issued to us, with screens all around our top-secret equipment and guarded by British troops. Our DD tanks were so secret that nobody knew anything about them until long after the war was over. We joined up with the Sappers, the early-assault engineers, and the Queen's Own Rifles. We were to land at H-Hour minus 5 minutes, the Sappers at H-Hour minus 10 minutes, and the Queen's Own at H-Hour. Again and again, we practiced our landings on the beaches at night on the south coast.

That was our final exercise.

———

Field Marshal Montgomery came and spoke to us a couple of days before the big day. He was a pompous man. My squadron put on a demonstration for him on the Isle of Wight. He hopped up on the back of one of the tanks and started to harangue us about how we were going to go into the invasion, and we had to "KILL THEM ALL!"

"There's no such thing as a good German! Kill every one that you come across in France!"

My friends in the Fort Garrys, a lot of them prairie farmers, weren't very impressed, and neither was I. Everybody was prepared to do what they had to do, and we'd been warned that casualties were going to be high, a lot higher than they eventually were. Everybody was anxious to get on with the job, but Montgomery didn't do us any good with that speech. About a week later we got the order to load onto the landing craft for the invasion.

That last week was great fun. Everybody was keyed up and anxious to get going. Nobody could get in to see us, and nobody could get out. We had good meals and were well looked after. Crap games started. We'd been issued these phony French francs, so we started gambling night and day because nobody had anything else to do while we waited.

I guess I was involved pretty heavily in this crap game. An order came in about three A.M. to load the tanks onto the landing craft, and two of us were left in the game. I'll bet we had fifty percent of the French money

A map of the advance of the Fort Garry Horse, from the D-Day landing to the end of World War II.

issued to the officers between us. We looked at each other and said, "One more game." Well, I won and now I had a huge stack of francs. When I went outside it was just starting to get light. There were a bunch of trucks with us in the compound that were going over a month after we were. I went over to two drivers I knew very well and gave each of them a third of my winnings.

"When you come to France, one month from today, I'll meet you, and give you a chunk of this, but I want most of it back."

They agreed and I stashed the last third in my own tank. Well, my tank burned up in Normandy a couple of days later, and four weeks later was July 4th, the day I was wounded. This meant I was on my way back to England when those guys were on their way over to France. By the

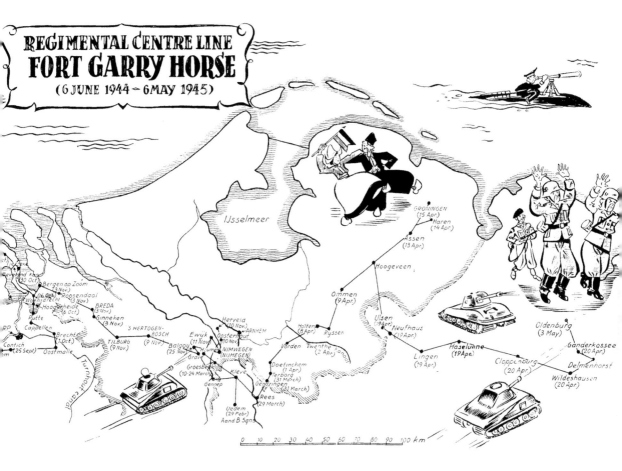

REGIMENTAL CENTRE LINE FORT GARRY HORSE (6 JUNE 1944 – 6 MAY 1945)

time I got back to France and tracked them down, they said both trucks had been hit in an air raid and that all the money had been lost. Whether it was true or not, I still don't know! So much for ill-gotten gains.

We loaded onto the landing craft at dawn on June 5th. At the last moment, they postponed our departure for twenty-four hours because of the weather, so we had to stay on the landing craft overnight. We weren't very happy; the guys had to sleep on the deck, and it was raining. We just wanted to get underway, which we finally did at about four o'clock the afternoon of the 5th.

The landing craft were very slow, so it was about a twelve-hour trip to France. We were in a huge line-up of them, and it was quite rough. The crew of the landing craft was no more seaworthy than our soldiers. Our captain was an old tough-as-nails Royal Naval Reserve man. He had a young midshipman with him who I don't think had ever been off dry land, and who was sick as soon as we left the Isle of Wight and didn't surface again until we off-loaded at Juno.

We towed guide boats to help us find our way onto the beach. But in the rough water, the towlines started to chafe. The old RNR skipper said, "Goddam it, none of these people are well enough to do anything about it." I said that I could probably handle it for him, and he agreed. So I got some of the men who were okay and sorted it out. I don't know what would have happened if we hadn't been able to, since we would have eventually ground to a halt.

The night passed without any great excitement. There was a lot of fire in the sky. Aircraft were making their sweeps and we thought, "Okay: this is it. Here we go." But you still couldn't see anything; just flashes of artillery and cannon fire up in the clouds.

Just before dawn on the 6th, the senior British naval officer came alongside in a fast little boat and asked our squadron commander if the DD tanks were good enough to go into the sea three thousand yards offshore. I thought he was very smart; most big shots would likely have said, "Put 'em in and get on the shore and get on with it." But he took my major's advice.

"You'll have to take us in closer, or we'll lose a lot of tanks on the way in." The 1st Hussars beside us did go in at three thousand yards and they lost a lot of tanks on the way to the beach.

I think we might have been a couple of hundred yards offshore when we finally went into the water; it was light by then. The Germans had these hedgehogs in the water with mines on them. We had to weave around between them, which made us a little bit late. Instead of being five minutes ahead of the Queen's Own to help clear the beach for them, we were still trying to manœuvre around those damned hedgehogs when the Queen's Own landed. Had we been able to hit the beach on time, we could have taken out all the machine guns that were firing at them. We would have saved dozens and dozens of lives. But we were late and those poor guys in the Queen's Own were beat to hell.

From our point of view, we saw a few Queen's Own landing craft on the beach and not much more. But our landing was very easy. We didn't lose a tank from my B Squadron of the Fort Garrys. My boss was wounded when we got into Beny-sur-Mer, and one of the other officers was killed after we started inland. I guess everybody was kind of confused.

I remember Eddie Goodman's squadron was supposed to go inland ahead of us, but they were stopped. The infantry was stopped, and everything was jammed up.

Eddie's tanks were lined up and right in front of the tanks were signs with skull and crossbones on them, "*Gefahr: Minen.*" "Danger: Mines." Some big shot came up and said, "Get those tanks moving—get on your way." Eddie said, "Okay," and went off into the minefield. After a couple of minutes, he had the tracks blown off of several tanks and didn't get anywhere.

The brass finally got smart: tanks don't have to stick to roads. So they ordered our B squadron cross-country through the wheat fields to head for the day's objective, which was a hill at Anguerny. On the way up, we were tackled by a bunch of high-angle guns and one of our officers was killed with a lucky shot. The rest of us went on for nearly two hours before the infantry got there.

We didn't have a lot of trouble at first. But the Germans were starting to wake up. German soldiers who'd been partying and whatnot were now dashing to get inland. At the bottom of the hill below us, these Germans were escaping in half-tracks. It was just like shooting pigeons.

The resistance we were meeting was minimal. There was enemy infantry up the main road bothering our infantry, but nobody was bothering us. I climbed out of my tank to confer with Captain Jim Hall, who'd taken over as my boss, and suddenly there was a lot of machine gun fire that was very close. Whether they were firing at us or not, I didn't know but didn't wait to find out either. We hustled back into our tanks.

During the night of D-Day, we had the first counter-attack from Kurt Meyer's famous Panzer division. After a pretty tough night, the infantry was able to stop them. We couldn't do much in the tanks at night. You could sleep under a tank or in it, but in the dark, you were ineffective as a fighting machine. The next morning, there were dead Germans all over the place; one of them was about twenty feet off the nose of my tank, which was a little disturbing, to say the least.

D-Day plus two, the squadron took off on a raid into Vieux Cairon, which was occupied by the Germans. We didn't know what they had there. Fortunately, Vieux Cairon was occupied by nothing but enemy infantry, a lot of whom we took prisoner. We shot the place up a bit, and then started moving these Germans back to our lines. We were about a mile in front of the line when someone started firing on us. I looked to see where the shots were coming from, and saw it was from tanks which were obviously Canadian. They just as obviously couldn't tell who we were: a case of mistaken identity. But there's no way of signalling the other tanks to let them know you're on their side.

As soon as the shelling started, the German infantry prisoners saw we were in trouble. Still armed, they dropped down into the wheat fields and started firing at us.

Our CO could see what was going on, so he fired a smoke shell to give us cover. Unfortunately, it was the type of smoke we used to signal aircraft to enemy targets. They'd fired the wrong smoke! We were lucky that there weren't any aircraft around, but one of the shells from this confused Canadian squadron hit my tank. It only knocked the tread off and nobody was killed, but we had to abandon it. There we were, surrounded by German infantry, trying to get back to our lines on foot. But we made it.

Being fired on—by anyone—was terrifying. And anyone who says it wasn't, well, they're a different type than I am. Those big rounds made so much noise you could hear them coming, and you'd just reflexively cower at the sound.

During the day of the 9th, we moved on into Villons les Buissons, which was a very small wooded area occupied by a very small town and a few farmhouses. Things were very hot there and the infantry were taking quite a beating. We only had six or seven operational tanks of the original nineteen we'd landed with. My friend Captain Jim Hall, who was my immediate superior, was out of his tank checking a position and was killed by mortar fire, leaving me in charge of the depleted squadron.

We were in an orchard, and our very competent CO, Lieutenant Colonel Ronnie Morton, came up to take stock of the situation. He told me that the infantry had taken a terrible beating in this little orchard and it was essential that we do something to take the pressure off.

"What would you like me to do?"

"How many tanks do you have left?"

I told him I had three here and four down at the end of the orchard, but one of those was no good because the turret was broken. So he said to take the three I had, go out and circle around the end of the wheat field in front of the infantry to draw some fire off the infantry.

I thought "Great, I'm drawing it off them, but who's gonna draw it off me?" I looked at him like he was out of his mind, but off we went. We'd been out about twenty minutes and were working our way around the front of the orchard and the wheat fields, which were full of Germans. All of a sudden, an 88 round blew through the side of my tank and went out the front, passing between my driver and co-driver. Our tanks were just like butter to those things. We all got out, although my driver had been slightly wounded. The other two tanks were knocked out, too. Now we had three men who were pretty badly wounded and had to be moved back to our lines.

We started back through the wheat field. I was nervous because I knew there were Germans hiding in this damned field as well. To make things worse, when we were getting close to our lines, it suddenly occurred to me, "How the hell do I let our guys know it's us, and not Germans?" I held my tin hat up on a pistol, and put it up over the top of the wheat. Then I heard this Canadian voice say, "Come on in, soldier," so we made it back. That was a bad day.

We hadn't had much sleep or much to eat in the three days since we'd been in France. I remember my driver, who hadn't washed since we landed, cracking open a can of bully beef, dumping it into his hands, and handing it up to me, saying, "Here's your dinner, boss." I took it and bit off a huge chunk without hesitation.

After that battle, the CO interviewed me. He'd lost his tank and driver when he'd tried to come out and help us, and was looking for my thoughts about the experience. But as we were talking, I was so exhausted I fell sound asleep in the middle of our talk. We finally got a bit of a break over the next couple of days

We then headed up to Carpiquet Airport. That was a bad show. We went in with the Royal Winnipeg Rifles, behind the lead troops. But as we went in, I pulled an awful dumb stunt. There were German tanks—Panthers—up at the far end of the runway. We could see them about a mile away and fired at them, but the round just bounced off. I bet we lost ten tanks to every one of theirs. They made mincemeat of us. So we stayed put, buttoned up inside our tanks, because their artillery were firing a lot of airburst fragmentation shells which were exploding all around us. That meant we had to run things through a periscope, but you could never get a clear picture that way.

I opened up half the tank's hatch and poked my head up just as a round exploded between the next tank and mine; we weren't too far apart. The shrapnel sliced through my helmet, and cut me down my neck

A Fort Garry Horse Sherman tank on the occupied portion of the Carpiquet Airport, July 6, 1944.

and arm. I was stunned at first. I thought I'd lost my hand, cause I couldn't feel it through my glove. But there it was. The other guy in the tank next to me had also poked his head up at the same time, but the shrapnel from the shell was closer to him and it took his head right off. One of his crew jumped up to try and help him, but it was obviously too late. He took one look in the tank and a look of revulsion came over him, then he just ran.

Something made me lose control of myself at that point, and I jumped out of the tank, which was the worst thing I could have done. God bless those tough westerners from the Fort Garrys, because they dropped the plate out of the bottom of the tank, crawled out and dragged me back in with them. I just lost my head—and God knows I'm not proud to say that, by any means. But I was lucky. They were tough, great guys, those fellows. Saved my life.

I was bleeding pretty heavily; so they took me to the first aid station, and wouldn't let me go back to the squadron. I was shipped off to England, and was gone for a while.

After I got back to the squadron, we went up through Holland towards Groningen. We entered a little town behind the fighting troops with the supply trucks and took over a house to live in for a day or two. That night there was a knock on the door and this good-looking young lady introduced herself. She was a schoolteacher and had her class with her. She wondered if they could come in and meet us. We said sure, come on in. They were a great bunch of kids, all dressed to the nines. The teacher lined them up and they sang, "O Canada." The Germans had occupied the town that morning and she'd taught these kids our national anthem while the Germans were still there. Pretty wonderful people.

The night the war ended, I was in Oldenburg. The troops were just north on the way to the big naval base at Wilhelmshaven. The MO [medical officer], the LADO [light aid detachment officer] and I were sitting in the doc's Jeep when the announcement about the war's end came through on the radio and the whole world went crazy. We were sitting there, and thought, "Gee, this is great," and had a couple of drinks. And not fifteen minutes later, our conversation had drifted back to exactly what it was before the announcement. There was just no excitement about it at all.

Civilians greeting the Fort Garry Horse (and the Régiment de Maisonneuve) as they enter Rijssen, Netherlands, April 9, 1945.

I've heard a lot of people who were up in the front lines say they felt exactly the same way. There was no elation.

The next morning, the three of us were driving in the doc's Jeep. Our troops were lounging around by the side of the road kidding the girls. There was a stretch of unoccupied road. A hundred yards further on, the Germans were lounging around by the side of the road kidding the girls. It made me feel that the whole war had been utterly useless, which of course it wasn't. I just think that the average soldier just did his job and wasn't mad at anybody.

———

At the end of the war, there weren't too many of us left who'd landed on D-Day. You think of my generation—we were all over there. All the Canadian kids, the English kids, the Yankee kids: it was just something that was done.

It wasn't all bad; we sure had a lot of fun, too. On the whole, it was ninety percent fun or boredom, and ten percent sheer terror.

But I came back a changed man. I learned responsibility that might not have otherwise come my way. I remember, back in the thirties, hearing an uncle of mine talking about the First War, about standing beside an officer who suddenly got a bullet through his shoulder. I couldn't conceive of what he was talking about. It's hard to understand if you haven't been there. But once you have, you can never forget. Many times I've said that I don't know anybody who went to war, was shot at, and—as long as he came out with his health—wasn't a better man for it.

David Arksey

BIRTH PLACE: TORONTO, ONTARIO
RESIDENCE: ANGUS, ONTARIO
REGIMENT: QUEEN'S OWN RIFLES OF CANADA
THEATRE OF WAR: NW EUROPE
DECORATIONS: CD

THE FIRST LANDING CRAFT WE TRAINED ON DIDN'T HAVE RAMPS. When you were landing, you jumped up on the deck and then out. The problem was that might put you four and half feet or more above the water when you jumped, and you didn't know how deep the water was. We were getting guys with sprained and broken ankles, so they recommended having ramps installed.

The ramps served two purposes, because they were all metal. They gave quite a bit of protection from small arms fire, in addition to the outer doors, which swung open like gates and were also metal. All the rest of the boat was wood, you see, maybe an inch or two thick. So you'd hear guns popping as you approached the beach and you'd be watching the sides more than anything. I never forgot that!

I never got seasick, even on D-Day, which was one of the worst days for rough water. We had our ground sheets over top of our weapons, because the spray from the water kept coming over the top. But we all had throw-up bags and quite a few of the guys were using them.

I had a pal, Harold Cook, who never got seasick either. We were waiting to make the run in for the landing and we hadn't eaten for a while. Most of the guys didn't want to. But Harold cracked open a can of rations and yelled, "Anybody want some sardines?" Poor guy, he got killed. I can still remember his serial number. We were real pals and he could play the piano every bit as good as Eddie Duchin. He and I would go into a pub in England and he'd sit down and play that piano and before you knew it, the whole top of the piano was full of beer and we were drinking it. He and I were great pals. He was killed on the 11th of June; the same day I was taken prisoner by Kurt Meyer's 12th SS Panzer Division.

The landing craft held thirty guys, three rows of ten. A naval officer was in charge and a naval rating was his assistant. The naval officer had complete power; whatever he told us to do, we did. We got on the mother ship the 1st of June and got ready to go on the 5th. Our major got on the PA system and said, "D-Day is tomorrow," which is the first we knew of the specific day. Sometime during the night, we moved out from Plymouth and grouped up. Reveille was at three-fifteen in the morning and we had bacon and eggs and white bread toasted, which was the first time I'd had white bread since I left Canada. Even some canned peaches.

"Holy geez, it looks like they're giving us our last meal!" some of the guys said. And, of course, for some of us it was true.

About five-thirty, they lowered us and we were quite a ways from shore. We had to go in on the assault craft. Our company was in the second wave; A and B company went first. We'd been told, "You don't stop for anything."

We knew very well that we'd have probably fifty yards of water and if it was ideal, it would be knee-deep, then about a hundred and seventy-five yards of sand until we got to the wall. There again, we were very fortunate, because the first guys out of the boat carried a bamboo ladder and the next guy carried a Bangalore torpedo in a rubber case.

But we were lucky. Directly ahead of where we landed, the wall had been breached and there was a hole in it wide enough for a guy to get through. We all went in that way.

They had told us if we do happen to get hit and can move at all, get off the beach. The beaches would be wired by mortar fire, because the Germans had been there four years and would know exactly how far it was to the beach and you'd be blown to bits.

As you've probably seen in films, there were the hedgehogs all through the water and you had to dodge them, even when you were running. They were mined and if you'd hit your foot on one—which did happen—you would've gone up. That's one thing I don't remember, is going around those things. But I had to have done, because you couldn't go straight.

We got everyone out of our boat, with no casualties on the beach. We moved through the wall and headed into the town. One section moved down one side of the street and the other section moved down the other, to watch each other's flank.

I was going by this house and a door opened. I turned and almost fired automatically. It was a woman! We had been told that there would be nobody in the town but Germans, but there she was with a little kid in her arms. The first thing she said to me was, "Tommy," which is what they called the Brits. I just smiled and kept on moving.

We got out on the far side of town and then dug in. We were there about two hours, when the Chaudières came in behind us and their first objective was to move just beyond us to two or three 88 mm guns, mounted on 360° travellers, which were very dangerous and had to be

A map of the D-Day objectives for a platoon of the Queen's Own Rifles.

taken out. We passed through their ranks once they'd knocked the guns out and by the end of the day, we were about seven miles inland at our objective. The Canadians were the only ones to reach their objective on D-Day. And Juno had the second strongest German defense to overcome of all five beaches. Omaha was the worst, of course, which was just rotten luck, running into a German division on training exercises.

The colonel sent a message round about six-thirty on D-Day night and saying we'd done a good job. We'd been told to expect fifty percent casualties on the day and we actually wound up with only one-third.

We were there three days with just a little mortar fire back and forth. We came across a German officer who'd been killed, so my sergeant, Jack Mitchell, and I buried him.

Jack said, "Gee, this is the first person I ever buried!"

I looked at him and said, "Me too. Whaddya think I was? An undertaker?"

Jack was killed on the 11th, too. He was a little older than me—twenty-four, I think. A nicer guy you'd never want to meet.

On the 10th, we were moved back down to the coast, so we could get cleaned up, pick up any mail and have a bit of a break. The morning of the 11th, we were told that there'd been a slight change of plans. They just had one little thing for us to do. They came and picked us up in trucks and took us out about five or six miles back inland and dropped us off in an area where there were fifty tanks mustered.

I thought, "This can't be some little job with all these tanks." They told us to get on the tanks and we'd get a ride in to where we were going. There was an apple orchard down by the end of this great big field and that was our objective, to reach that orchard.

I thought our major (Neil Gordon) had to know what was about to happen, because the colonel at an O group meeting definitely would have told him. Our real objective was to be sent in as a sacrifice to try and stop the advance of the 12th SS Panzer Division. We didn't know that until afterwards.

But Gordon was right out in front of us, knowing full well what to expect, when they really started to open fire on us. We jumped off the tanks and kept on moving. Then they started to knock out tanks. I saw the major reach up to his face and then he kept on moving for a few minutes and then he went down. A bullet went through the side of his face, took all his teeth out and went out the other side.

This was only five minutes into the battle. The fellow with me had only joined us the day before as a replacement; I didn't know him. Lou Bridges, from British Columbia; a big man, about six foot two. He asked me if he could stick with me, since he'd never been in action before.

"Lou, I'm in the same boat as you. I was there on D-Day, but I didn't see much action. But sure, come on."

So he stayed right with me all the way as we moved forward through this field, until finally there was only the two of us alone. The grass was high enough that, crawling on hands and knees, we couldn't see the Germans or where they'd dug in, but we could still hear fire. They could see us, though. I remember saying to Lou, "Take off your pack; it's sticking up above the grass." He did this and stayed behind me.

"I think there's some of our fellows out to the left," I said. "I don't know if we can get out to them, but we'll try to crawl that way a little bit."

A platoon of the Queen's Own Rifles in Normandy, 1944, being briefed alongside their scout cars and carriers.

We took as much time as we could, feeling our way to wherever we thought we should be going. All of a sudden, I heard a shot close behind. I turned around and Lou had been shot in the head. There was a German standing right behind me.

"*Raus.*"

So I got up and he took me out to the left, where there was a German officer. He had four other of our guys with him. Our sergeant major was there, but had been hit in both legs and couldn't walk. The officer said, "I have two wounded and they need to be carried to first aid." He pointed to me and the other guys. "You carry the wounded and we'll take care of your sergeant." Well, of course they never looked after him at all. And the only reason I was taken prisoner was to carry out German wounded.

We got back to the first aid post with the two wounded guys, and then they took us to the German headquarters. One of the first things one of them asked me was, "Got any candy?" This was a kid about eighteen, but he was already a hard-nosed SS trooper, the whole Nazi thing completely hammered into him. There was a vehicle with a desk in the back and a major we were paraded in front of. He could speak English quite well.

"I don't know why you were taken prisoner," he said. "I have a letter here, signed by a captain in the Winnipeg Rifles, saying that Canadian troops take no prisoners."

"That's not right," I said. "We took over sixty prisoners ourselves last Tuesday. Where's the letter?"

"You don't have to see it! I'm telling you!" he snapped back. Then he said, "Stand up."

Well, we were standing up.

"Stand up! I'm an officer!"

"Oh! You mean stand to attention."

"Yes!!"

He asked the first fellow what unit he was with and the guy said, "All I can give you is my name, rank and serial number."

"That's fine," the major said. He called over his lieutenant and led that guy away into the woods. Then he asked the next guy in line the same question and he said the same thing. And I said the same thing, and the last guy, too.

A few minutes later, the guy who'd been led into the woods re-appeared. The major called over two privates with Schmeissers—submachine guns—and they took us over by an embankment and stood us in front of it.

They raised their guns and I was so scared I couldn't have talked if I'd wanted to. Then I thought, in my own mind, "I won't hear the guns anyway. It'll be over fast." And that was the only thing I could think of.

Three minutes or so, we're still standing there. I started thinking, "Maybe they're not going to shoot," and after another five minutes or so, the major came out and said, "Sit down!"

I had no problem sitting down; my legs were just like rubber. They kept us there for another hour, when a German captain came along. This guy had a real American accent.

He said, "I'm taking you to my bosses. Any questions they ask you, tell 'em. You'll probably get a good job working on a farm, or somethin' like that. But if you don't co-operate, it'll get a lot worse."

SS General Kurt Meyer in Normandy, 1944.

"Where'd you get that American accent?" I asked him.

"I lived in Boston," he said.

"When?"

"For twenty-five years," he said. "I came back to Germany in 1937 because we were told we should come back to our country. Now I'm an interpreter."

I didn't think much of him when he told us that, anyway. There was one of the fellows from a tank crew already there being questioned. He was burnt terribly; he'd been caught in a tank that went up and his hands, neck and face were all burned and he couldn't see. I remember hearing this German captain through the door, talking to this poor guy, "If I get salt and put it on that face and hands of yours, you'll probably want to talk!" But the guy never said a word; he died two days later.

The four of us were taken in all at once. The guard shouted, "Sit down!" I was looking around for a chair and he shouted, "On the floor!" He tried to question us, but never got anywhere.

A while later, we were all picked up in a truck and moved to Paris by the next day. I remember being moved through the Gare du Nord and being put in boxcars. The sign on the car said, "*Quarante Hommes ou Huit Chevaux.*" So forty of us were put in and we were given a big milk container to use as a latrine. We also got half a loaf of bread and a chunk of meat, but they never opened those goddam doors for three days.

We were machine-gunned twice by our own planes. During an attack, the Germans would stop the train and all the Germans would hop off and take cover, leaving us out in the open. There wasn't any red cross or anything on top of these boxcars to warn the planes away. We had a couple of guys hit, but nobody killed that I know of. Then we got to our first camp, Stalag 12A, right near the Belgian-German border.

They asked two Americans and me if we would help the Red Cross by registering prisoners. Since this would help our guys as well, we volunteered and stayed there about a month or so. Then we were moved to Poland.

About three weeks after arriving at that camp, I was taken to work in a coal mine near the border. I'd never been in a mine before in my life! We were down about six hundred metres and it was all Russian prisoners down there with us. At that time, I think I was the only Canadian. The three guys I'd been questioned with back in Normandy I didn't see again until I got back to England after we were liberated.

We worked from August through into December, when twenty of us—including me—got diphtheria. Our doctor was South African and sixteen of the guys, including the doctor, died from it. About two weeks later, we got notification that we were going to be evacuated because the Russians were breaking through.

We started moving west away from their line of approach. Besides us, there were Jews, political prisoners, everyone and anyone you can think of. All told, there were five million people being moved on that march away from the Russians. It started for us on the 14th of January, 1945, and we marched until the 18th of April. We covered about eight hundred miles during one of the worst winters they'd ever had in Europe. There were 429 of us when we left our camp and 219 survived the march.

You couldn't go twenty-five feet where there wasn't a body alongside the road. Near the end of April, we started to see American planes flying overhead. They seemed to know who we were, since they'd wag their wings to acknowledge us. But two weeks prior to this, all the Jews had been taken out and shot. Some SS troops came in, took them all out in a field next to us on the right and machine-gunned them all. This was in Bavaria, only about fifty miles from the Danube.

The guards who were looking after us had no way of feeding us anymore, so the only food we could get was what we scrounged. About that time, the Germans decided to move out again, but our interpreter—a young Jewish man from London—told us he thought we should stay put, so we did.

The Germans said, "You won't be safe. If we leave you here, other German forces might come along and shoot you. You're safer with us."

This Jewish fellow said, "If the Americans come along, you're going to be a lot safer staying with us." The officers thought about it for a couple of minutes and stayed.

Two days later, the American tanks started rolling in. I remember hearing them come, when I was up at the village trying to find some food. As soon as I saw the big star on the side of their tanks, I came running down the hill to the town and up to one of these tanks. I got along with them well, because I was a Canadian.

"Do you have anything to eat?" was all I wanted to know.

"Geez, I think we gave away everything we had." He ducked out of sight for a moment and then came up again. "This is all we got left." It was two rolls of toilet paper.

"Are you staying here overnight?"

"Yeah, then we're heading towards the Danube tomorrow." These guys were a part of Patton's Division.

"Could a couple of other Canadians and I come over and help make breakfast and maybe get something to eat?"

"Oh, yeah. No problem at all."

"When will they pick us up?"

"Oh, it'll probably be two or three weeks anyway."

"You must have supply trucks going back and forth," I said. "Couldn't we hitchhike?"

"You can," he said, "But you have to be awful careful. Every place we go through, they have a sort of makeshift government set up. And if they don't know you and you have nothing to show who you are, you'll get locked up until they find out definitely who you are. So if you're going through a town, stay in the vehicle."

We made it all the way down to the Rhine River, where there was an American headquarters. They deloused us, gave us American uniforms and seven day's rations in a box. We thought we had the world by the tail. But one of the fellows with us, Leo Roy, was awfully, awfully ill. He'd eaten the snow on the march, which I told him not to do. "There's millions of people tramping through here, you can't eat it." We didn't have water and he was desperate. But it made him real sick.

We were making our way to Belgium on a freight train. We stopped at a town and the Americans were already there and were settled in pretty good. I went over, got some food, and brought it back to Leo.

We ended up in Luxembourg City, where Leo got some medical attention and we got all we wanted to eat. A lieutenant questioned me about where I was taken prisoner and any other details I wanted to report.

"Did you have anything taken from you that you'd like to put in a claim for?"

"Sure," I said. "I was stripped of my watch, my pen and pencil set, my school ring, 850 dollars in French francs and thirty dollars in invasion money."

"Did you get a receipt?" he asked.

I looked at him like he was a nut. "Who would get a receipt from a German soldier pointing a machine gun at you and who didn't speak English? Not to mention the fact that, to put it mildly, you would irritate him by asking in the first place. Of course I didn't get a receipt!"

"Sorry. Can't do anything about it then."

The 850 dollars I had I'd won in a poker game a week before the invasion. I kept it with my phony invasion money, which was on top. When I was captured and the German soldier took it off me, he flipped through a couple of bills, and then threw the whole bundle away. He'd had probably three or four years pay in French francs in his hands, but I sure as hell wasn't going to tell him about it. He wouldn't have understood me anyway.

The next day they flew us back to England, where an ambulance and some medical guys met us and took Leo away. I didn't see him again. I was 175 pounds when I made the landing on D-Day and was 119 pounds when I got back to England.

That was early May and I stayed there until just before Christmas. I didn't want to go home, because I was still feeling so bad. I did odd jobs, guard duty and other stuff that didn't take too much out of you. Gradually I started feeling like myself again and started putting on weight. I came back to Canada on a ship over New Year's 1945 and was treated like a king on the way home from Halifax to Toronto, where my whole family met me. I'd been gone a long time—1941 to 1946. It felt pretty good being back and to have survived.

———

Years later, there was a meeting at the Royal York Hotel of ex-P o Ws. I wasn't going to go, and then at the last minute, I figured I might as well. I went down to the Royal York and there were hundreds of guys there. I got off the elevator and Leo Roy was standing right in front of me. I hadn't seen him since they'd taken him away in the ambulance in England. He said, "Dave, I knew you lived in Toronto and was sure you'd be here, so I came down from Sault Ste. Marie." He grabbed me and said, "You saved my life." And we both cried.

You formed an unbreakable bond with the guys you served with. We were like brothers; we all trusted each other. I still remember my pal Harold's serial number as well as I remember my own. That bond was a way of life.

I don't think I did anything outstanding. We all served because we felt it was something we had to do. We knew, before we ever went over, what a horrible time people were going through. But we felt it was the right thing to do, to get the war over with as soon as possible and get the world back the way it should be.

Ed Haddon

BIRTH PLACE: MANSONVILLE, PQ
RESIDENCE: TORONTO, ONTARIO
REGIMENT: SHERBROOKE FUSILIERS (ARMOURED CORPS)

MY NAME IS ALBERT WALTER HADDON, BUT MY FRIENDS GENERALLY know me as "Eddie." That's because during the war, you're usually called by your last name. So I was "Haddie," and that gradually became "Eddie." I'm first generation Canadian; my mother and father were from England, and I'm the youngest—born in 1922.

We were living in a rural part of Canada, because my dad had taken a Soldier's Settlement farm as part of his gratuities from the First World War. But he wasn't by any stretch of the imagination a qualified farmer, and he didn't do well, so he eventually lost it. Then he was killed in an automobile accident, so we had no cash flow. I was seven, and we had a very rough time. That was in Mansonville, Quebec. This seemed to persist through the 1920s, so in the 1930s I went out to Saskatchewan. But it wasn't much better there, so I came back to Quebec and went to Sherbrooke. There was little or no work there either, so I did a number of things: drove a taxi, worked in a garage. I also joined the NPAM—the Non-Permanent Active Militia—in 1938. We did two nights a week and summer camp. At the end of the summer of 1939, I just switched over to active service, on the 8th of September, 1939. I jacked up my age, otherwise they would never have let me in.

The regiment was called the Number One General Base Depot—it was part of the Sherbrooke Regiment, and they were due to be shipped overseas in December 1939. They discovered I wasn't old enough; that's because by that time, they'd jacked the enlistment age up to nineteen, and I'd said I was eighteen (even though I was still only seventeen). There were five of us like that, and we were all shipped to Montreal in a depot until we came of age.

We ended up staying in derelict hotels until we were old enough to join. The first place they put us in was so bad even the army finally condemned it, so we were moved to another place. None of them were very good.

Because I was a lance corporal, I had a number of duties. One of them was enlistment; there was a continual line of people on the street waiting to sign up. We'd get an order for fifty people from some regiment; we'd open the door, count in fifty guys, then shut it again.

But I wanted to go overseas, 'cause all my buddies had gone. I kept agitating and agitating, and finally I found an officer who was sympathetic to my cause. They were looking for truck drivers overseas—for some reason they didn't have any—so a call had gone out. We were amassed together in the regiment in Ottawa. We lived under Lansdowne Park in Ottawa, underneath the stadium; the ceiling was the bottom of the seats of the stadium above. We were there about a month; the unit was called the MTVRD—the Motor Transport Vehicle Reception Depot. Everybody was supposed to be a driver.

We were shipped out to England in March 1940, and landed at Liverpool.

———

We went into Emmerick in Germany, and my crew were given the afternoon shift. All you're given when you're given a shift is a map reference, and you relieve so-and-so at this map reference at a particular time. That represents a position on your map; you use your Slidex Code, find that position, and look after your shift.

This particular point this day was some spot in Emmerick. And just like in any city, you don't necessarily take the same route to get to the same place. What happened on this shift is that I met the person I was to relieve head on in his tank, and he damned near shot me. It was startling to find two of your own tanks coming at each other like that. He said, "You came from a place that wasn't even cleared!" I don't know how that happened.

Anyway, I relieved him and we finished clearing the city the next day. We were back and forth across the border there between Germany and Holland. That particular part of Holland had a lot of small towns in it, and generally speaking, I didn't allow my guys to destroy anything unless there was a reason for doing it. In Germany, you'd destroy anything and everything. You'd put a shell in just to see what happens; if it was a barn, you'd usually burn it. But in Holland, you generally didn't destroy things unless you had to—if there was fire coming from a house.

In action, we always got a new issue of maps every morning. Those maps had a defense overprint on them, which was the result of amassing all the information they could get in the previous twenty-four hours, from every source. Everything they knew about the enemy was on that map in purple.

This particular morning, I was to relieve the commander at a particular point, which I did. My orders were then to move on to a new map reference. On this map, there was an enemy gun marked at a spot where there was a crossroads: a fork in the road with an orchard. We had a telephone on the back of the tank, which is your communication with the infantry so they don't have to climb up on the top of your tank. All they had to do was pick up the phone and talk to you.

We started down this road, houses on both sides, towards this fork in the road. I'd told my gunner not to shoot the houses, but shoot down the street to keep the Dutch from coming out of their houses. They were supposed to be down in their basements. So he kept up a steady chatter of

Ed Haddon's graduation from Sandhurst in England. The soldiers were reviewed by General Dwight Eisenhower. Ed Haddon (front row, third from left).

the gun as we went, and we didn't have any civilian problems. I got down to a point that was as far as I thought I could go, because of this gun placement. So I told the infantry guy, "Go get that gun. It's your target, not mine." A tank gun is an infantry target, whereas a machine gun is a tank target. Tanks are basically for machine guns and rifles, but not big guns, because they aren't armed for it.

If you use your equipment intelligently, you don't waste it. I figured I was doing everything right, as I had been taught 'cause that was his target, not mine. We went slowly down this street with our clanking tracks on the pavement, moving at the same pace the infantry were walking. I stopped and talked to this guy, and immediately I was hit. A hell of a bang. There's tracks flying up past my field of vision. I didn't know if they were my tracks, or the tracks I'd welded onto the side of my tank. I had a new driver, I hadn't had much training with him. But he was a smart guy and he immediately shifted into reverse, which is the right move when you get hit. No time wasted having to give the order.

But right again we were hit, we were hit four times. And we went up. My gunner, who sits just below me, after the second hit shouted, "Get out of here! We're on fire!" I looked down and all I could see was fire below me. Now a turret's not that big, but he got out of there before me. And to this day I don't know how he did it. But he was on fire, which is why he moved so fast. He'd also been hit three times. He hit the deck. Then I jumped out of the turret, and hit the ground too. I still had my headset on, which was strange because you can't just unplug those; normally you'd have to cut them.

We were hit four times when I was in or on the tank. The two of us scrambled behind a brick building to take cover, then a fifth shot hit the building and bricks came down on top of us. I thought, "These guys are following us. They can see us." But I'd never seen him so he must have fired blind. I've been back a couple of times to that spot, been to where the German was firing from, and tried to figure it out.

The only thing I can figure is that he heard me. He would have known that I knew he was there, and what I'd do. So he fired through a blind corner. He had a very fast firing gun, five rounds, clip-fed 75 mm, and they're loaded HE/AP/HE/AP/HE, and that's exactly how they hit us.

The APs [Armour Piercing] went into my tank; the HEs [High Explosives] didn't. The AP went into my turret. After the first HE hit, we'd

A Sherman Tank of the Sherbrooke Fusiliers advancing through Caen, July 1944.

no sooner got out of that bloody turret when the second round, the AP, went through our side of the turret—it would have hit the two of us. It got the other guy, spun him right around on my back. The other two guys were killed by high explosive—it "dished" the front of the tank. All the bolts and hardware blew off into them as shrapnel, like a Gatling gun: cut them up.

Only the two of us made it out. The gunner was badly wounded—he had a piece in his head, a piece in his arm and a piece in his leg. Our gun had been hit, and shrapnel from that hit the gunner. When the German round came in, it was pretty much white hot. It was low velocity, so it came in, then bounced around inside, which was worse. It set the tank on fire. I had a full load of HE shells—I hadn't fired one—ninety-seven rounds of HE shells inside this tank, and of course it blew. Blew the turret right off.

I patched up the gunner with his shell dressings, my shell dressings, and the shell dressings from another guy, to stop the bleeding, then sent him off with a corporal back down the line. I watched this tank burn, but nobody else got out. On the back corners of the tank there're fire extinguishers, and if a tank catches fire and there's nobody in it, you bang the tops—they had a compression release—then drop them down the turret and they'll put the fire out. But I didn't do this; I don't know what to say. I kept staring at the ground and all these ball bearings rolling around and dropping down the storm sewers. For the life of me, I couldn't figure out where they'd come from.

I finally figured out that the turret sat on these ball bearings, about an inch in diameter, and when it blew up, the bearings went off all over the street.

My whole life, I kept thinking about that day. I had to go back and figure out all that happened. I went back forty-five years later, and was a guest of a Resistance fighter in Holland. I was the only Canadian there—with my blue blazer, beret and ribbons—at a reception that my host, who was a VIP, was having. There was a young man there, about twenty years old or so, who wanted to know who I was. So my host introduced us, said I'd been here in the Second World War, and the young man said, "Tell me all about it. What it was like."

"What do you want to know?"

"Everything. I don't know anything about it. The only thing I've ever learned is that there was this small town in Holland, and at six o'clock in the morning one day, a Canadian tank came in, was hit by a Panzerfaust [henuygun], burnt, and everybody was killed. And that's all I know about the war."

So I put this all together, and said, "Would the name of that town be Whel?"

"Yes. How'd you know that?"

"That was my tank."

"Couldn't be. Everybody was killed."

"Not me. I'm still alive."

They were flabbergasted. "That's not right. That's not what we were told."

"Who to believe?" They were still shaking their heads.

"I'll tell you what I'm going to do. I'll ask my host if he'll drive me to Whel. If you want to come along, I'll take you to the spot."

So we made an arrangement for the next Wednesday. I asked them if they knew anybody who was still alive from the war. This young man said his father had a friend in Whel, and he was wounded during the war, so

Ed Haddon's tank in Holland, which had been hit by a shell from a German Panzer.
Ed Haddon was given this photograph fifty years after the attack when he returned
to visit the Dutch village.

if anybody would remember, he would. So we were a guest of his father's
friend in Whel.

On that Wednesday, the whole bloody town was waiting for me, and
we marched down the street. Nobody believed me. Somebody even had
a picture of my tank, and said, "Is that yours?"

"Yes. That's mine."

"Prove it."

I looked at the picture. "See that house in the background? I can take
you to that house if you put me in the near vicinity. Will that convince
you that's my tank?"

"Yeah. You show me the house and I'll believe you"

So down the street we march with all these people. I said, "There used
to be a gas pump right there on the sidewalk. No gas station—they used
to serve gas from the house. The infantry had set it on fire, but I'd told

them to put it out 'cause it would set the houses on fire."

"That's right," he said. "But there's a gas station there now." A lot of things had changed. But the house that was in the background of the picture was still there. They couldn't believe it. We had a good day; there was an interpreter, and I spoke to all kinds of people.

At one point we were sitting in someone's house, and there was this banging on the window. I asked what was going on.

"That lady says you broke all the windows in her house. And she wants to talk to you about it." It had been the ball bearings when the turret blew.

I went over to her—she was about ninety, and had been there at the time. She had her kids in the basement when we were coming through. But she wasn't mad—it was just the thing that she'd remembered.

———

My dad was a military person. He spent fifteen years in the British navy, and five years in the Canadian army. I always admired him for that, and it was always in the back of my mind that he was a great man for that reason. It wasn't difficult for me to join the service. I guess I did it for a little bit of patriotism, but it wasn't difficult for me.

I hate to confess this, but my dad died a pauper: he was buried by the town. He had no money at all. My dad, having served so much time, and my mother had a terrible time trying to make a living, feed all her kids. So I had it in the back of my mind that somebody owed somebody something for something! And one way to get it was for me to get right in there. I thought if I joined the army, maybe I could get her a pension or something. She'd been turned down for a widow's pension, because my dad hadn't been killed in the service. I could get some leverage, anyway.

Ed Haddon's father in WW I.

I'd been supporting her to the extent I could before I joined the army, which wasn't much, but it was okay. So when I joined the army, at the first opportunity I said, "Who's going to look after my mother if I join the Services? I'm looking after her now, but who's going to if I'm overseas?"

The army had a policy that if you assigned half your salary to your mother, she could get a mother's pension. So all during the war, half my wages went to my mother, and she got a pension.

When I came out of the service, I took my gratuities in education, and took Engineering at McGill.

So that was one of the main reasons I joined up in the first place. The other reason was there was no bloody work. I used to get laid off at Christmastime. In the army, at least you'd get your food and clothing and a place to live. And a dollar thirty a day. Which was all right.

———

I was glad I did it. The older I get, the more I appreciate the guys I fought with. God, they were great guys. They never asked for anything from you. They weren't professionals; guys off the street, basically. We met the *best* they could throw at us. They were professionals; they were all prepared, they had the best equipment, they were better soldiers, some of them were so tough that rather than be taken prisoner they'd commit suicide. You've got to be pretty dedicated to do that. And we beat 'em. That's got to make you feel good.

The guys I fought with just went out and did the job. You can criticize the way we fought the war—and the Germans do criticize us—we still won. We liked life. We had a good life, and there was no way we were going to give it up easily. We were a bit more gun shy than they were; we used to take precautions. If there was gunfire, we used to hit the ground. They'd laugh at us. They'd be retreating and drop down a round on us, and we'd all hit the ground. Then they'd take off again. Just like some game.

I don't think of the bad things. I was young when I got in. I could tell you so many good things, happy things that happened during the war. I met my wife—she was a war bride—and we've been married fifty-seven years. You can't do better than that.

Laurie Wilmot

BIRTH PLACE: MINITONAS, MANITOBA
RESIDENCE: WINNIPEG, MANITOBA
REGIMENT: CANADIAN CHAPLAIN CORPS,
WEST NOVA SCOTIA REGIMENT
THEATRE OF WAR: NW EUROPE, ITALY
DECORATIONS: MC

I'd been a pastor in drought-stricken southern Manitoba for four years, when in 1935 my bishop moved me to Swan River in Manitoba, a beautiful agricultural community. I had a large parish there, with several congregations. One of them was in Renwer, where we held services in a schoolhouse. Being moved up there put me in touch with all kinds of things that were happening in the outlying regions of the country at that time. My congregation was composed of Lutherans, Anglicans, and United Church people. Our bishop had an agreement with the churches that wherever we had a congregation and they didn't, their people would come to us for pastoral care.

Whenever I moved into a new area, I made a point of visiting anybody who had any contact with the church. That way I could see them in their homes and get to know them and they'd get to know me. By 1938, all the tremendous social and political movements in Europe were taking place. There were a great many German families in that area and one was a farmer who'd come to Canada with his parents as a boy in 1903. Sandy was very prosperous, and an all-round good citizen. He'd become a friend and during a visit to his farm one day in 1938, he suddenly opened up to me. Emotion just poured out of him. He was terribly concerned that people were treating Hitler so badly.

"Hitler's one of the greatest men that's ever held power in Europe! He's doing tremendous things."

"Yes," I said, "But where's it going, Sandy?"

Sandy had a powerful short-wave radio that he tuned into Germany every day and would listen to either Hitler or one of his enclave.

"He's remaking Germany and is a great man who's misunderstood," he told me.

"We could spend a long time discussing that, but before we do, would you do me a favour?"

Sandy nodded yes.

"For the next week, tune in to the BBC overseas station. They're reading *Mein Kampf* back to the Germans in German and interpreting it for them, pointing out where it's leading."

"I'll give it a try," he said.

I came back a week later and Sandy was most apologetic. He said he now realized what was going on and had developed a totally different view.

"I had no idea. No idea!"

Sandy had three teenagers, each of them in a separate pro-Nazi German Bund in the Swan River Valley. In these Bunds, the children were being given the great leader's thoughts. After hearing the BBC's broadcast, Sandy took his children out of the Bunds and kept himself thoroughly tuned into the larger world picture. His oldest son eventually joined the Canadian army and served with distinction through the war.

This was only one case. There were many more situations like this through the valley. I served a congregation in the town of Minitonas, and there were seven Baptist churches in that community. When the Sudetenland was annexed to Czechoslovakia, there were terrible conflicts in Minitonas. Mounted police had to come in and settle it. When Hitler marched into Poland, the Polish and German Baptists were at pitchforks with one another. It was a terribly tense situation with a tremendous social upheaval in those rural Canadian communities. All kinds of people in this country had a very difficult time sorting out their allegiances because of the Nazi sweep through Europe.

———

When war was declared, I knew that I would have to become involved. I said to my wife, "Every man, woman and child in the free world is involved in this." I carried on with my preaching, but by April 1940, I felt it was just so much crying in the dark until Hitler's juggernaut was stopped. I contacted my bishop and said inevitably it was going to be a long war and I felt I had to be with the young men who were going, if I could.

He was extremely critical of me.

"You're doing fine work where you are, important work for the country. Forget about the war. Let the other people do it. The other pastors who have given up their parishes and gone into the service have become disillusioned because the army isn't really interested in their services. They don't need us over there."

I said I was sorry, but felt I must do something. I wrote to the principal chaplain at Ottawa and after taking a physical examination in Winnipeg, was approved for service. I was told to hold myself ready and would soon be called up.

I carried on with my work for another eighteen months while other younger, less experienced men were being pulled in as chaplains, but no one was contacting me! Finally I wrote to the chaplain general in January 1942 and asked what was going on.

He wrote back, most apologetic, saying there was nothing he could do.

"We have a list for each diocese and your name goes at the bottom of that list and is gradually moved up. But your Bishop keeps putting names above yours. And there's nothing I can do unless you can get him to stop."

I went directly and spoke to my bishop and suggested he'd better change his methods or I wouldn't continue my work in that diocese. With that, he finally agreed and I was called up June 2nd, 1942, two years after I'd first applied. By Christmas 1943, I was in Italy.

In February of 1944, I joined the rear echelon of the West Nova Scotia regiment near Ortona. The regiment had been without a chaplain for over a month. This was significant, because many of these men had been overseas since 1939 and their families at home were breaking up. It was a very difficult time for them on all fronts, but the poor fellows couldn't do anything about it.

The colonel who had led the regiment from the invasion of Sicily, July 10, 1943, was wounded in the battle for Ortona in late December 1943 and was replaced by the 2IC. He did a good job and was confirmed as commanding officer with rank of lieutenant colonel. He had the difficult task of establishing his own type of leadership in a tiresome holding position when the men in the line occupied caves. I also came to realize that the colonel had a low opinion of chaplains and he declared that he wished me to remain at rear battalion. When I finally managed to get in to see him, he gave me a lecture, announcing he would not lay on a church parade, which I'd had no intention of requesting.

I felt my place was in the line with the men. I spent my first week with the unit working with other units and medical people with whom I would be working in my new position as padre of the WNSR. Then when my truck arrived, I moved out to visit the men who were in reserve positions in the forward area.

A company in the line couldn't move around at all in the daytime because they were under observation. It was a difficult period, because the men were going out on night patrols and they'd be wounded and sent away before I saw them. Finally I got a pipeline going through the men and was able to find my way to visit the wounded before they were shipped out to one of the field dressing stations or a hospital from a central casualty collection post.

Our regiment was moved south to engage the enemy at the Hitler line. Throughout the winter we'd been holding a line north and west of Ortona, but this time it meant a real squaring off with them. I decided I would stay at the RAP [regimental aid post] until I was needed or there was something I felt I could do.

We had a squadron of British tanks accompanying us into the offensive. Unbeknownst to us, the Germans had taken turrets from Panther tanks and embedded them on steel-reinforced concrete pillboxes. They were concealed extremely well, so as our squadron of tanks moved out into the open the Germans just knocked our tanks out. Inside of three or four minutes, a whole squadron was flaming up. The whole attack was held up and we had to go to ground.

We were in reserve and could not move until the regiment in action had completed their assignment, and the attack could not be resumed until a squadron of Canadian tanks came up to replace those that had been knocked out. We had our RAP combined with the RAP of our sister regiment, the Carleton & Yorks. Just as I was thinking that I was going to have a few idle moments, a Jeep rolled up to the RAP loaded with injured tank men.

A young wounded officer refused to get out of the Jeep to be treated until someone agreed to help him rescue his wounded tank crew from the battlefield. I scouted around and rounded up half-a-dozen kids and three stretchers. The officer pointed in a general direction at the front and off we headed, and eventually found our way to the injured crew after much searching.

When a tank was hit, the shell "drilled" a hole through the tank and released a whole shower of shrapnel that would ricochet around inside the tank. As a result, there were some dreadful injuries to contend with. We managed to help those three men from the tank crew, but once you get doing this kind of thing, there's no end to it, because there's always somebody else in need. And so my small rescue party found ourselves with more casualties than we could keep up with.

We were making one of the countless trips back and forth from the line to the RAP when one of the kids kept hearing something buzzing past his head.

"Padre, what's that hissing noise? It's not shells, is it?"

"I'm afraid it is. It's some fool up in a tree trying to scare us."

I'd learned that when the Germans retreated from a position, they'd leave a sniper in a tree or some elevated spot to pick off our advance. Now he had us pinned down.

"But we can't leave those men lying in the ditches down there, because they've already been out all night," I said. I went forward to see if there was a way around this obstacle, but there wasn't and so I prayed.

"God, if you want me to get these men out, tell that young sniper to hold his fire."

Then I was given a brainwave. I took the Red Cross band off my arm, broke off a stiff stalk from some undergrowth and fashioned a little flag. I went back to the carrying party and they looked at me like I was out of my mind with this little makeshift flag on the end of a raggedy stick. But they also saw I wasn't being fired on any more, so they got up, lifted up their casualties, and we proceeded on our way and didn't have any more trouble from him.

We passed through a stone enclosure where there was a company of our men in position for a counter-attack. The officer said, "How in the world did you get through here? I've just had a man shot right out in front of us when he went out to bury his comrade."

"It must be my flag," I said. I had been fired on countless times wearing the armband. I had to bury too many of our stretcher-bearers because of that. But with the flag, the Germans held their fire. I eventually wrote command and urged that our stretcher-bearers be allowed to carry a Red Cross flag with them when they went into battle, because the armband was insufficient. It may have done the job in 1860, but it wasn't respected any longer.

The Generals sent word back that the Geneva Convention said "the stretcher-bearers need only wear a white armband with a red cross on the left arm," and they felt that was enough. Which was fine for the generals back at HQ, but no good for those of us down on the line. I ignored their advice and had the RAP corporal make small square red cross flags, each with two safety pins attached, to be carried by the padre and all stretcher bearers in the thigh pocket of their battle dress for emergency use in any future battles we went into.

From May 17–22, we were involved in chasing the enemy back from

Pignataro to their main defensive position at the Hitler Line. They put up a tough battle and our officer commanding C Company and a number of his men were wounded. I went up to see what I could do and was kept busy. Three men had been killed and had to be buried before we left the area. I buried them where they fell, securely marked the graves, and returned to the RAP, where I made three crosses to mark their graves.

Before I could go out and place them at the head of the three graves, word came of our projected move. However, three men were returning to C Company and kindly took the three crosses to mark their comrades' graves before leaving the area. All went well.

Several years later, I was attending a mess dinner as chaplain of a Winnipeg militia unit. The speaker for the evening was an ex-tank officer and he commenced his address with the following story.

"In Italy, I was returning in my tank from the forward area in preparation for the move, when I met three soldiers going up to the front, each carrying a cross strapped to his back.

" 'What are you fellows doing?'

"They held up their crosses.

" 'We're going back to our company and this is our padre's idea of efficiency. He figured if we carried our own crosses with us, then they wouldn't have any problem identifying us when they bury us.' "

After the Hitler Line battle, we were pulled out of the line for rest, regrouping, and to receive and train reinforcements. But these days came to an end as we headed north in August 1944. The enemy was given the impression we were attacking in the area of Florence. We moved up to the south bank of the Arno, but were then moved back and over the mountains to the Adriatic coast, where the 1st Canadian Division attacked and drove the enemy back to the main Gothic Line defenses. Our regiment had been in reserve during this phase of the operation, but we were now warned that we would be going into the attack at the Foglia River.

Both the brigadier and the colonel felt I had become involved in activities that were not in my line. They felt there were others who could have been doing it and there was only one chaplain. If anything happened to me, who was going to deal with the situations that would arise? Burials, letters to parents and wives, counselling the men, were all my responsibility.

I agreed that my place was at the RAP, but there had been no plan laid on for the evacuation of men during the battle in infantry tank operations. I only became involved because there was a vacuum and I just responded to the need.

This led to one of the most tragic events of the war for me.

On August 30, a strange silence fell over the front. There was no shelling and no evidence of enemy troop movements. We didn't know what was happening. Were they withdrawing, or were they preparing for a counter-attack? The colonel was instructed to send out a one-company reconnaissance to discover the strength and disposition of the enemy. The brigadier and the Colonel had, in separate conversations with me, impressed upon me that my place during future action should be with the RAP. And I agreed that under normal circumstances, that was where I should plan to be.

However, I happened to arrive at TAC [tactical attack] headquarters just as Captain Jones, the officer who had carried out the reconnaissance, was reporting to the CO over the field radio.

"The enemy is present in strength, securely dug in, and with strong machine gun, tank, artillery, and mortar support."

The tank liaison officer present said, "We can take out the machine gun posts on both flanks that the captain described, and since the attack isn't going in until the morning, we can have that road cleared of mines by then and accompany the infantry right in."

The artillery liaison officer pointed out how they could take out the strong points as the infantry went in and clear the way for them. But the CO, for some unfathomable reason, vehemently disagreed.

"We don't need the tanks, we don't need the artillery. This is an infantry show. It's our day! We're going to show you how wars should be fought and won."

I thought the colonel had lost his mind. I'd been through enough battles by this time that I was convinced this was going to be the big disaster that had been waiting to happen.

"Where is the brigadier?" I asked myself. Through all the battles, the brigadier was always on the scene to help make major decisions. But he wasn't anywhere to be found.

"Why isn't somebody countermanding these ridiculous orders?" I kept wondering.

The colonel picked up his phone and ordered the rifle companies to prepare to descend into the Foglia River valley, cross the river, and dig in for the night, prepared to go into attack at first light.

"Where's the brigadier?" I asked, but got no answer. What could I do? It was a dreadful situation, but I knew once the colonel had made a decision like that, he wouldn't change it unless somebody senior to him countermanded it and there was nobody there to do so.

I made my way back to the RAP and by the time I got back, I knew what I had to do. I told the corporal that I was going in with them and asked him to fill my small pack with bandages and equipment for first aid. Then I went out and joined them as they made their way down the face of the cliff, across the shallow river, and dug in for the night.

Around two o'clock in the morning there was a meeting of the officers, called by the two company commanders who had been ordered to lead the attack. They'd attended an OGp [orders group] at midnight called by the colonel. At that meeting the captain in charge of the company that was holding the line reported that the enemy had been out all

Laurie Wilmot and his aide in Italy, 1944.

evening laying anti-personnel mines right across the attack front. But the CO didn't even appear to hear him and nothing was done to clear paths through the mines.

Major Nicholson had called the two A.M. meeting. He said he disagreed with the way the attack was laid on and didn't like anything about it at all.

"But if I don't take it, that just means some other officer who has less information about it than I do will have to. So I'm going in on the attack and I ask you to give me your support."

We all went back to our slit trenches and tried to get some rest. I didn't sleep at all, but just lay there and wondered what help I was going to be. I felt, however, that I was where I was needed, whatever the outcome.

Around four-thirty or five we were awakened and started our way up to this great anti-tank ditch where Captain Jones had his men. As we reached this start line, Major Nicholson said, "I think the padre and the stretcher bearers should stay here in the anti-tank ditch and come forward when you're called." And that was that.

The two companies lined up in this ditch, one behind the other. They'd been given orders by the CO to fire a complete clip of ammunition at the enemy with their rifles, which did nothing more than say, "Hey, boys! We're coming!" They then reloaded and B Company climbed up and went on their way, with C Company about a minute behind them.

There was no enemy reaction at all until they reached the minefield. As soon as the mines started going off, then the German machine guns opened up from both flanks as well as mortars and artillery shells. All hell broke loose. There were cries from every element of the front. Men calling for help from stretcher-bearers and from the padre. It was a dreadful, impossible situation. I felt futile, totally futile. What could I possibly have done? What can you do in that kind of a tragedy?

Three young men approached me. They were stretcher-bearers for the two companies that had made the attack and the stretcher-bearer for B Company, which was holding the line, who was their spokesman.

"Padre, our company commander won't let us go out in the field and our wounded are calling for us. We don't carry arms; we don't take part in the fighting. We're trained to help men on the battlefield and to come when we're called. Now they're calling for us, but our captain won't let us go."

"But how can you get the wounded out? Do you have carrying parties?"

"Yes, we each have our carrying party."

So I went with them to his company commander, who repeated to me exactly what he'd said to them

"It would just be suicide to go out there at all. You'd be cut down in no time. Besides, I'd have to send an officer and I'm not prepared to do that."

"I'm an officer," I said. "I can lead them, if they'll follow me."

"I'm not willing to let the men go. It's suicidal."

"You don't need to do that either. Phone the CO to make the decision. He sent the men into the hell they're trapped in now. See if he'll let the stretcher bearers go in to bring them out."

When he was reached by phone, the CO said, "I think the padre's a fool to go out…" He used some other colourful language as well. "But I can't stop him. And if the men want to go, it's up to each one of them. No one will be asked to go out into that situation."

I turned to the stretcher-bearers.

"Are we all here?"

The stretcher-bearers and carrying party all said, as one man, "We're here, and ready to go."

"All right," I said, "We'll go single file to make a smaller target. Let's go." We climbed over the embankment and off we went into the minefield.

We'd just got nicely out into the open when they mortared us. There's only one thing you can do when you're mortared and that's get down. While we were on the ground, I had time to look around. I found a willow sapling, cut it down, pulled the Red Cross flag out of my pocket and pinned it into place. The stretcher-bearers each had one as well. Once the mortars had gone off, I climbed up again and said, "Let's go."

The Germans held their fire.

But then we came to the minefield. I'd never had any instruction about mines because I was never expected to encounter them. But as a kid, I made the only spending money we ever made trapping weasels, mink, and coyotes in rural Manitoba, and so I knew how to set traps, and more importantly, how to recognize them.

The first mine we came to, I stopped the boys, pointed to the ground and said, "Forget about the enemy. Look at that: that's a mine. You can't see it, but the dust has been disturbed, so you can see where it is. Take your mind off the enemy and focus on every step you take, otherwise you'll become one of the casualties we'll be carrying out of here."

On we went and found our way to the men. It was desolation, with men lying in every direction. Some dead, some wounded, some simply in agony of pain. The stretcher-bearers went to work and soon we were carrying them out.

It was a scorching hot day, and a long kilometre carry back to the river where the ambulance Jeep met us and took them back to the RAP start line. After several hours of watching us moving to and fro, two men from B Company, thinking there was nothing going on, climbed out of the ditch to see what was happening. Almost immediately a shell came in and wounded one of them before they could get back into the ditch again. The enemy had been watching the whole operation, but was holding their fire until we got our men out.

For the first few hours, we were the only people allowed to move at all.

Every one of the officers was either dead or wounded, and fifty percent of the troops were as well.

This tragedy went on most of the day.

By mid-morning, the men who had not been wounded were being recalled under cover of smoke. As they reached a cut-bank at a crossroads near the river, the enemy laid on a "killing barrage." They had the whole area mapped and knew the exact location and distance to every point. The only thing that saved us was a bamboo forest in front of us, which caught the shells and exploded them as they came in towards us. It destroyed the forest, but saved our lives.

It was an absolutely incredible day. I never dreamed we'd live through it and I really couldn't believe I was alive at the end of it all. When I got back to the RAP, the doc gave me a pill to give me a chance to get some rest, because I couldn't sleep.

The brigadier came to see me several days later to explain and apologize. He had ordered the reconnaissance in-depth to determine the strength of the enemy and once this was obtained, the CO should have responded to the situation. But he chose to ignore it and lost his command.

The day before the attack, the brigadier had chosen to fly over the area in a reconnaissance plane, which had developed trouble and crash landed. He'd broken his jaw, so when all those life and death decisions were being made, the brigadier was in hospital having his jaw wired.

A West Nova Scotia Regiment cemetery in Italy.

In battle, you know men are going to be wounded and killed. But not wasted. To send men into a minefield when there was ample time and resources to have tracks swept through the field was madness. Minefields destroy everything. Over twenty lost men their lives. Forty men lost a foot through mines and many more were severely wounded through machine gun fire, shells, mortars and mines.

But we had to keep going. I scarcely had the letters to the families written and information prepared for the War Graves Commission, when we were immersed in battle again.

After that experience, I felt destroyed. Everything seemed so futile, totally futile. I had no more stomach for the war at all: I was ready to quit. But I wouldn't, nor did I ask to be relieved. If I could have had even a day to go away and weep and get it out of my system! The dreadful waste of human lives was overwhelming. But there was fighting to be done and we had to go on. I had to measure up and do my job, just as the men did.

I withdrew into myself and drew closer to God. My faith was the only thing that kept me going. Without that, I wouldn't have survived at all. Many men didn't; many men broke.

———

In 1945, I was in England. Before embarking for Italy two years earlier, I hadn't received any leave, so I found myself in the week following Easter with ten days off to have a much-needed rest. After the end of the war in Europe, the command sent around a questionnaire looking for volunteers for the war in the Far East.

I said I felt I must get back to my family. My children needed me, my wife needed me, and I urgently wanted to get back to Canada. I was thirty-seven when I went overseas, and it was time for me to be home.

A meeting was called of all the chaplains, at which we were told by the senior chaplain of the corps that we were needed for the army of occupation and for the CAPF—the Canadian Army Pacific Force for Japan.

"We have to have men who've seen battle experience."

Laurie Wilmot sitting in the ruins of the Coliseum, reflecting on his faith and on the faithful.

Then he looked at me and said, "If we don't get the people we want, we're going to have to detail you. I'll ask some of you to go home and rethink your position."

What was I going to do? I went back to my room and wrote a letter saying that I had volunteered for the duration of the war. When the war was over in Europe, I felt the war was over. I realized there was still more fighting to be done, but I badly wanted to get home to my family, because they needed me. However, if he needed me, I would be willing.

The next message I received was that I was the 2IC of the CAPF Protestant Chaplain Force and I had ten days' leave before shipping out for the Far East. Several days later, we sailed for Canada and landed in Halifax. I took the train home to Manitoba for a few brief days before going to the Pacific. My wife, Hope, and I rented a car and drove out to the family farm to visit my mother and spend the weekend with her.

My little daughter, Hope, five years old, sat on my knee all afternoon—it was the only place she'd sit. My wife and mother were getting supper ready and I said, "Let's get the news," and turned on the radio.

The war was over; Japan had just surrendered. So now I was actually home, months before I would ever have gotten home otherwise. A tremendous moment. Absolutely unbelievable, to be back and to be safe. It would have been unbearable to have to leave them again.

———

War is a ghastly situation. It's organized chaos, with men ordered to seek and destroy one another, but with nothing ever working out as planned. I felt I did the job I had to do. The men—the boys—needed support, and it was the right thing to be there with them.

I would want future generations to know that their fathers and grandfathers went to a war that wasn't a lark. It had to be fought. I'll tell that to anybody who asks me. My experience in Swan River made that clear to me. Those Nazi Bunds were active right across our country, and I don't believe most people were even aware of them. Hitler had to be stopped and it's been a different world ever since he was. For Canada to be the tremendous place it is today, we owe an enormous debt to those men and women who died in that war. They were the ones who made what we have today possible.

But those years were very hard on the family. I'd ask my children to forgive me for being away so much, because I missed a whole period of their lives. And the war changes you. You're a different person when you come back; you can't help but be! I came out of the war with a deeper faith than I'd ever had before. I found myself able to do things after the war that I would have never been able to do before, because of what I'd been through.

Now we're in a brand new century. It's been wonderful to be alive for so many years, and to have watched the twentieth century pass with all that it held. Life has been a tremendous experience.

CHRONOLOGY OF
CANADA AT WAR

———

3 Sept 1939	Britain declares war.
10 Sept 1939	Canada declares war.
6 Oct 1939	Hitler proposes peace with Britain and France in return for recognition of status quo. Both countries reject this.
8 Apr 1940	British Commonwealth Air Training Plan opens No. 1 ITS at the Eglinton Hunt Club, Toronto.
9 Apr 1940	Hitler invades Norway and Denmark.
10 May 1940	Hitler invades the Low Countries and France.
15 May 1940	Netherlands surrenders.
23 May 1940	Canadian 1st Division ordered to France to secure Dunkirk perimeter. Canadian 1st Division reaches France.
24 May 1940	*Bismarck* sinks HMS *Hood.*
25 May 1940	Operation Dynamo: the evacuation of the BEF at Dunkirk begins.
26 May 1940	*Bismarck* sunk.
8 Jun 1940	Canadian 1st Division moves into France as a Second British Expeditionary Force.
10 Jun 1940	Italy enters war.
13 Jun 1940	Canadian 1st Division evacuated from Brittany.
14 Jun 1940	Paris falls to the Germans.
10 Jul 1940	Luftwaffe bombing of Welsh ports inaugurates the Battle of Britain.
26 Aug 1940	First engagement, over S England, between an RCAF squadron and the Luftwaffe.
31 Aug 1940	Operation Sea Lion in planning: German successes against the RAF incite Hitler to schedule a land invasion of Britain for 21st September.
7 Sept 1940	The Blitz begins.
17 Sept 1940	Hitler postpones Sea Lion indefinitely.
27 Sept 1940	Germany, Italy, and Japan sign tripartite pact in Berlin.

14 Nov 1940 Luftwaffe firebombing of Coventry.

13 Apr 1941 Germany invades Russia.

10 May 1941 Last night of the London Blitz and the Luftwaffe's heaviest attack on a British city.

1 Aug 1941 Camp X, SOE, goes into operation in Ontario to train special agents for secret overseas operations.

7 Nov 1941 Canadians land in Hong Kong to reinforce British.

7 Dec 1941 Japanese bomb Pearl Harbor.

11 Dec 1941 Winnipeg Grenadiers reinforce Gin Drinkers' Line on Chinese Mainland.

18 Dec 1941 Japanese land on island of Hong Kong.

25 Dec 1941 Hong Kong falls to Japanese.

1 Feb 1942 German U-boats adopt Enigma code machine.

11 May 1942 Canadian Parliament passes bill for the introduction of full conscription.

19 Aug 1942 Operation Jubilee: Assault on Dieppe by a predominantly Canadian force.

10 Jul 1943 Canadians land at Pacino Beach, Sicily.

15 Aug 1943 First Special Service Force, including 5,300 Canadians, lands on Kiska in the Aleutians.

3 Sept 1943 1st Canadian division lands on Italian mainland and captures Reggio di Calabria.

28 Dec 1943 Canadians capture Ortona.

24 Mar 1944 "The Great Escape" from Stalag Luft III.

11 May 1944 Canadian armour supports allied Attacks on the Gustav line and Monte Cassino.

23 May 1944 1st Canadian Corps breaks the Hitler Line; advances up Liri Valley.

4 Jun 1944 Rome liberated.

6 Jun 1944 Operation Overlord: Allies land in Normandy on D-Day, 1st Canadian Parachute Battalion dropped after midnight, 3rd Canadian Infantry lands at Juno Beach.

10 Jul 1944 Canadians capture Caen.

25 Jul 1944 Canadians capture Verrieres Ridge in Normandy. Black Watch suffers heavy casualties.

7 Aug 1944 Operation Totalize: Canadians mount an operation to close the Falaise Gap.

21 Aug 1944	Falaise Gap successfully closed, but 30,000 Germans escape.
25 Aug 1944	Paris liberated.
30 Aug 1944	Two Canadian brigades break the Gothic Line.
1 Sept 1944	2nd Canadian Infantry Division captures Dieppe.
17 Sept 1944	In the Netherlands Operation Market Garden begins.
21 Sept 1944	Gothic Line completely collapses; Canadians enter Rimini.
30 Sept 1944	Canadian 3rd Division captures Calais.
1 Oct 1944	Canadian 2nd Division begin Scheldt offensive to open port of Antwerp.
14 Oct 1944	Canadian ships land Greek and British troops at Piraeus, Greece.
31 Oct 1944	South Beveland peninsula falls to Canadians.
28 Nov 1944	First Allied convoy disembarks at port of Antwerp.
16 Dec 1944	Battle of the Bulge, the last German offensive in the west, begins.
8 Feb 1945	Operation Veritable launched towards Rhine.
21 Feb 1945	Canadian and British "water rats" break Siegfried Line.
23 Mar 1945	Operation Plunder: Canadians cross the Rhine near Wesel.
15 Apr 1945	Canadians take Arnhem.
16 Apr 1945	Canadians liberate Groningen.
5 May 1945	German troops in Netherlands surrender to General Foulkes.
8 May 1945	V-E Day.
31 May 1945	Camp X closes.
6 Aug 1945	Americans drop atom bomb on Hiroshima; Nagasaki targeted on 9 August.
14 Aug 1945	V-J Day.

ACKNOWLEDGEMENTS

My first debt of gratitude is to all those who have consented to be interviewed for the *Testaments of Honour* project, including those who are patiently waiting for me to meet with them.

The project has taken a number of years to come this far, largely based on the support and enthusiasm of George Weston Limited, Alliance Atlantis/History Television, Industry Canada's Digital Collection, the Richard Ivey Foundation, the Donner Canadian Foundation, The Norman and Margaret Jewison Charitable Foundation, the Charles H. Ivey Foundation, Manulife Financial, Hydro One, the McLean foundation, the J.P. Bickell Foundation, Hollinger, the Royal Bank Financial Group, Caldwell Securities, Apple Canada, Henry's Camera, DayMen Photo, JVC Canada, BeachTek Audio, Macromedia, FileMaker Inc., Palm Inc., Leon's, and Sorenson Media.

I have received boundless encouragement from everyone at Doubleday Canada and Random House of Canada. I am most indebted for the friendship and support of Suzanne Brandreth, Lisa Charters, Martha Kanya-Forstner, Christine Innes, Susan James, Maya Mavjee, Scott Richardson, and Carla Kean.

Numerous individuals, in addition to the veterans themselves, have also been instrumental in facilitating the work and the interviews I've conducted over the past three years. They include Ken Bell, Barney Danson, Norbert Luth, Charles Scot-Brown, John Dix, Andy Anderson, Brian Lawrie, Bob Hawkes, Colin Bernard, Michelle Braun, Steve Edgar, Amy Buskirk, Sherida Caldwell, Bob Cathers, Cliff Chadderton, Terry Copp, Fraser McKee, John Harbron, Brian Coatsworth, Alfred Young, Danylo Dzwonyk, Stu Eagles, C. R. Ivey, Jim Jamieson, Norman Jewison, Ralph Kamuf, Colin Bernard, Walter Levitt, Commander George G. Borgal, Patty Lewis, Major General Lewis MacKenzie, Ken MacLeod, Jim Knowles, Michael MacMillan, G. Kingsley Ward, Peter Silverman, Neil Stephenson, Brian Tobin, Al van Meer, Ed Pearson, Alf Hebbes, Charles and Alice Sharpe, Pat Ryan, Peter Worthington, Rolph Jackson, St. Clair Balfour, Nora Cook, John Acheson, R.W.D. Hanbidge, Wally Loucks, John B. Wilkes, Farley Mowat, Gordon Hogarth, Henry Jackson, and Bonnie Joan Graham, Tara Guild and Michelle Scott.

I am grateful to all those who have helped with *Testaments of Honour*, and hope that anybody who has inadvertently been omitted from this note will forgive me.

In particular, I owe a great deal to a number of exceptional people. Garfield Mitchell, for being enthusiastic and supportive from the very start; Elward Burnside and Bert Coles, two very dedicated archivists in their own right; Captain Beth Wakulczyk, a tireless cheerleader; Adrienne McLennan for her great kindness and advice; Yasmin Miller for her help refining the project proposal; Dr. Serge Durflinger and Dr. Dean Oliver of the Canadian War Museum for their friendship and constant willingness to provide advice and counsel; Mark Laurie for his fine research work; Donal Foley for his dedication and objectivity; my father, E. B. Heathcote, himself a veteran, for being such as a tremendous sounding board and font of historical information; and my mother, Barbara, for her transcription work, patience, and abiding motherliness. Finally, I owe most to my wife Ellen and our children, Elisabeth and Maggie, for their resolute faith and unbridled love. This book is for you.

NAME INDEX

VETERANS CONTACTED FOR
TESTAMENTS OF HONOUR

Jack Abbott
John Acheson
Bill Adams
Bob Adams
Allan Adlington
David Adlington
Percy Adlington
Joel Aldred
Andy Anderson
Harold Anderson
Tom Anstey
David Arksey
James Arnett
L. Arsenault
Larry Arsenault
Hilda E. Ashwell
Herbert Baldwin
St. Clair Balfour
Jack Banks
Russell Bannock
Allan Barker
R. E. Bartlett
Ron Beal
Gerhard Beck
William Betteridge
Stanley C. Biggs
Bill Bigras
Leonard Birchall
W. Arthur Bishop
Blackie Blackburn
George Blackburn
John Blakelock

Doug Blakely
Herbert Boake
David Bockus
George Borgal
Guy Boudaud
Roland Boutot
Madeleine (Bouzanne)
  Lannon
Elizabeth
  Breckenridge
John Breckenridge
Betty Brown
H.E. Brown
John Brychka
Elward Burnside
Hudson Byers
Jack Cahan
Jack Campbell
John Campbell
Willie Carey
Bob Catlow
John Caton
Frank Cauley
Cliff Chadderton
G. Chambers
William Charlton
Ron Charman
Bob Charters
Don Cheney
Eileen Church
Vince Clair
Gavin Clark

Roy Clark
A. F. Coffin
Bert Coles
Alex Colville
Nora Cook
Jack Cooper
Dick Corbett
Donald Cornell
Lawrence Cosby
Roger Coulombe
Mervyn Couse
W. A. Cowan
Don Cowling
Walter Cox
Stan Croft
Joseph D'Angelo
Robert Dale
Fenton Daley
Bart Dalton
C.O. Dalton
B.J. Danson
Gerald A. Davies
Taff Davies
Bill Davis
Joan de Bustin
Jan de Vries
Harry Dekker
Rod Deon
Richard Dillon
John Dix
Alec Dixon
Bob Dixon

Horace (Monty)
  Dobbs
Jim Dowell
Hunter Dunn
George Duthie
Derek Eckersely
H.C.F. Elliot
Bruce Evans
Hedley Everard
Peter Fairclough
Philip Favel
Dick Field
Bob Firlotte
John Fisher
William Fisher
Jim Floyd
Bob Foster
Harry Fox
Donald Francis
F. C. Frewer
Bob Furneaux
Doug Gage
Strome Galloway
Jim Gellatly
Joseph Gelleny
Jack Genge
Andrew B. German
Tom Gilday
Hugh C. Godefroy
Steven Gough
Jack Gouinlock
Bonnie Joan Graham
Bob Grant
Alec Gray
Bill Gray
Bill Grierson
Palmer Griffiths

Ed Haddon
Margaret Haliburton
H. Donald Hamilton
John Harbron
Reg Harrison
E.T.B. Heathcote
Fred Heather
Alf Hebbes
Art Henderson
Jean Henderson
Ralph Hennessey
Ike Hewitt
Bob Higgs
Dick Hilborne
Ken E. Hill
Werner Hirschmann
Gordon Hogarth
Steve Horan
Don Horne
Bill Hunter
Tom Ingham
Andy Irwin
Henry Jackson
Rolph Jackson
R. Jager
Joe Jamieson
Bill Jenkins
Arthur Johnston
Gwilym Jones
Jim Jones
William Joyce
Reinhold Kaudel
Wilma Kaudel
David Kearney
G. Keeler
Jim Kelly
Bill Kilgour

John Kilpatrick
Mac King
David Kingston
Jim Knowles
Michael Laffin
Stan Lancaster
W. Landymore
Tom Lane
Roger LaRocque
Remi LaRue
C. E. Law
Bruce Legge
John O. Leprich
Bill Lewin
R. T. (Bob) Lloyd
Wally Loucks
William Loucks
Alf Luck
Bill Lumsdon
Norbert Luth
Andrew Edison
  MacAskill
William MacAskill
Wally Mace
Alex MacInnis
Donald MacIntyre
Bob Mackett
C. Roger MacLellan
John Marin
Bill Marshall
Jack Martin
Martin Maxwell
Red McCormick
Peg McCullough
Donald E. McGregor
Norm McHolm
Don "Tiger" McKim

Mark McKinney
Elwood McLaughlin
John McQuiston
Grant McRae
Bruce Medd
Russ Melanson
Ben Misener
J. P. Moore
Farley Mowat
Bob Murray
William Needles
Bert Newman
Howard O'Connor
Ted O'Halloran
Ronald O'Reilly
Frances Oakes
Joe Oggy
Elizabeth Orford
Ian C. Ormston
Blake Oulton
Frances Owen
Lou Pantaleo
Clement Pearce
Florence Pennington
Herb Peppard
C.D. Phelan
Ian Pirrie
Art Plumb
Dr. and Mrs. Pow
Mil Prescott
J.K Reynolds

Howard Ripstein
Gordon Roberts
Major General
 Richard Rohmer
Walt Romanow
Larry W. Rowe
James Russel
Justice R.C
 Rutherford
E. Saunders
Jim Saunders
Father Harry
 Schmuck
Rayne (Joe) Schultz
Charles Scot-Brown
Ethelwn Scott
George Shearman
Brian Shelley
Raymond Sherk
Lorne Shetler
Chick Sills
Jack Simpson
Tommy Simpson
Sam Sinclair
Beryl Smith
Ernest "Smokey"
 Smith
Wally Smythe
Jack Staley
Bill Stern
Fred Stevens

Fred Stokes
John Stroud
Bob Symington
W. G. (Bill) Talbot
Diana Taschereau
Peggy Taylor
Alex Thorpe
William Waddell
Al Wallace
Bill Ward
Owen Watt
Reg Watt
Garth Webb
John Weir
Fred Wheat
W. Denis Whitaker
J. J. Whyte
Bill Wickens
Bob Wight
Frank Wilcox
John B. Wilkes
Owen Williams
Vernon Williams
Harvey Willis
Laurie Wilmot
Ralph Wilson
Norm Wilton
Frank Woods
Peter Worthington
Stuart Wright
Cyril Yarnell

339

Alex MacInnis

Andy Anderson

Charles Scot-Brown

George Borgal

John Stroud

Dick Corbett

Dick Bartlett

Tom Lane

John Weir

Clement Pearce

Nora Cook

Don Cheney

Jack Gouinlock

Hilda Ashwell

Joe Gelleny

Barney Danson

Tom Gilday

Joe Jamieson

Alex Colville

Frank Cauley

Bob Grant

David Arksey

Ed Haddon

Laurie Wilmot

PHOTO CREDITS